Empty Open Hands
A Survivor's Story

A Guide to Breaking the Cycle
of Family Abuse and Trauma

The Life and Legacy of Martial Arts Master
Willy Johannes Cristoffel Wetzel

By Wim H. Wetzel

First Edition

Copyright © 2016 Wim H. Wetzel

Printed in the United States of America

ISBN: 978-0-9861314-6-2

QuinStar Publishing – Dallas, Texas

DEDICATION

This book is dedicated to the most important people in my life. My deceased wife of 32 years Zee, my current wife Vikie, my deceased son Wim who tragically left this world at the young age of 27, my grandchildren; Kali, Tyler, Carlie and Edward and to the memory of my mother Gerry, my father Willy, and my brother Roy. A special acknowledgement goes out to my beautiful sister Jane who always inspired me as a wonderful devoted and loving mother to her children. To my brother Jim I want to say how proud I am of you for your indomitable spirit and strength to meet and exceed all of the challenges and barriers that life put in your way.

This is also dedicated to all of the wonderful people who made a significant difference in my life and were there when I needed them the most. Without their support, guidance, and unconditional love I would not have survived my often troubled but full life. They include Lt. Colonel George Prewitt and his beautiful wife Jane and phenomenal children Lori, Lisa and Phillip. I cannot forget my colleague and lifelong friend Alberto (Al) Capone who came through with financial assistance to support my son and me when I was destitute and did not have a pot to pee in.

To Doctor Sherry Buffington and Gina Morgan, head of Quantum Leap Systems, Inc. and originator of the CORE MAP assessment, who helped me discover the natural and environmental factors that made me who I am. As Sherry so aptly states in her literature and personally told me: *"Life is not a destination. It's a Journey. Make it positively delightful."* I further encourage anyone who feels lost to get her book: *Who's Got the Compass? I Think I'm Lost! A Guide to Finding Your Ideal Self, Your Path and Your Purpose.*

To Jim and Nancy Thompson, Blain and Linda Sheppard who helped, encouraged and kept my spirits up through my recovery from open heart and 360 radical back surgery. Jim never left my side and often fed me for three weeks while I recovered from the heart surgery; Blain for always watching my back in Viet Nam and continuing to do so today. You are 'my brother from another mother', Blain and I am eternally grateful for your friendship and love; Master Sergeant Mike Black who always inspired me to be a better leader and manager during my last four years in the Air Force. A special thank you to Mike for writing the introduction that follows from his personal perspective of my leadership and management style. Donna Black for her invaluable feedback from a woman's perspective.

Last, but certainly not least, Steve Fisher at NEC, and one of my dear friends who inspired me to develop, build and launch the NEC National Training Center in Texas. Without Steve's dogged and intense drive to obtain the financial resources and employer support, my training team and I would not have been successful in that endeavor. The advanced and modern technology Steve and I introduced, deployed and maintained will give NEC the valuable edge it requires to increase its business worldwide.

With the trepidation that I am forgetting so many other great people in my life, I apologize to all those great people who I have missed in this acknowledgement. You are not forgotten. You are always in my heart, thoughts and prayers and I dedicate this book to you as well, and to all the great people who have crossed my path, and whom I have had the honor and privilege to meet.

ACKNOWLEDGEMENTS

I would like to thank my wife and life partner Vikie for supporting me in my efforts to write this book. It has been difficult for her to deal with a veteran suffering from PTSD and numerous Viet Nam service related medical problems but she stood beside me all the way. Even though we have only been together a few years at the time of this writing, she never failed to be there to encourage me to write.

I want to thank my mother for her strength and surviving her terrible 4 year incarceration in the World War II Japanese concentration camps only to bring me into this world. I want to thank my father for teaching me to never give up, to seek and obtain my life's goals with a sense of honor and backed by good name and word. I also want to thank him for teaching me what *not* to do and how *not* to behave through his often terrible examples. I thank God that I was wise enough in my early youth to be able to determine the difference and, more often than not, choose the correct paths to follow throughout my life.

Thank you to Doctor Rita Fuhr Marowitz who initially inspired and encouraged me to write this book in 1976 while completing her English Writing class at Edwards AFB, CA., and to Dr. Sherry Buffington for her help in editing this book to make my life's work legible and readable.

Contents

DEDICATION...iii

ACKNOWLEDGEMENTS v

INTRODUCTION 1

FOREWORD.. 11

CHAPTER ONE
Portrait of a Bruised and Brutal Man
Willem (Willy) Johannes Christoffel Wetzel (1921–1975)............................ 17

CHAPTER TWO
Honoring a WWII Heroine
Hermina Gerritje Nyland (Gerry Wetzel) January 25, 1928 - April 6, 2009............... 33

CHAPTER THREE
The Enigma 39

CHAPTER FOUR
Living and Surviving on the Edge.. 43

CHAPTER FIVE
The Great Escape
Basic Training - Summer 1966 55

CHAPTER SIX
Back Into Battle
Viet Nam: 1967 – 1968 63

CHAPTER SEVEN
Coming of Age
The Cat House Adventure 73

CHAPTER EIGHT
The Siege of Dak To 79

CHAPTER NINE
The 1,000 Yard Stare Return to Da Nang 89

CHAPTER TEN
The Siege of Khe Sahn... 95

CHAPTER ELEVEN
Returning to the World and Going Home to Beaver Valley........................... 99

CHAPTER TWELVE
The Making of a Fighter... 103

CHAPTER THIRTEEN
Base Jumping.. 107

CHAPTER FOURTEEN
New Challenges and Horizons 113

CHAPTER FIFTEEN
A Leap Into Hell 119

CHAPTER SIXTEEN
A Plan for Dying
The End of a Wondrous but Tragic Life 123

CHAPTER SEVENTEEN
A Day in Infamy
Murder and Redemption 129

CHAPTER EIGHTEEN
Catching "King" Bass 137

CHAPTER NINTEEN
Duty and Difficult Transitions 141

CHAPTER TWENTY
Wim-Zee 155

CHAPTER TWENTY-ONE
The Good, The Bad, and The Ugly 163

CHAPTER TWENTY-TWO
Aircrew Life Support and Survival Training 169

CHAPTER TWENTY-THREE
A Bright and Rapidly Burning Star
Roy Eduard Wetzel, 1948 – 1995 177

CHAPTER TWENTY-FOUR
Retiring from the Air Force
1990 181

CHAPTER TWENTY-FIVE
Life as a Civilian: New Challenges 185

CHAPTER TWENTY-SIX
Zee's Final Years 191

CHAPTER TWENTY-SEVEN
Paying the Piper 199

CHAPTER TWENTY-EIGHT
New Beginnings 205

CHAPTER TWENTY-NINE
Just When I Thought It Was Safe The Challenges Continue 209

CHAPTER THIRTY
The Nightmares Continue 213

CONCLUSION
No Man is an Island 221

EPILOGUE
Lessons from a Hero's Journey 225

Official Stenographer's Transcript of Roy's Murder Trial
Beaver, PA Courthouse Commonwealth of PA vs. Roy E. Wetzel 229

About the Author 254

Introduction

Memories of Wim Wetzel, CMSgt, USAF Retired
Life Support Officer, Altus Air Force Base, Oklahoma

By Michael Black, MSgt USAF Retired

One of the first memories I have of Chief Master Sergeant Wim Wetzel was during a church service. As I recall at the time, we had received notice that our branch, the Aircrew Life Support Branch was going to be getting a "new" Life Support Officer. The odd part of this was that most Life Support Officers were officers and not enlisted ranks. I think, at the time, this was primarily because of many of the problems and issues we were having with personnel within our branch. At this point in time, we were in three separate buildings, the main branch located in building 194, the Chemical Warfare Equipment being located in building 447 and the Life Support training being located near the post office in building 129.

That particular day after a Sunday service, I asked one of our members, a Chief Master Sergeant Woody Hall if he knew Chief Wetzel and what he thought of him. Woody, as we called him at church, said "He will do wonders for your branch....but you'll either walk the line or you'll toe the line!" I wasn't sure how to take that, but at that point it made me kind of apprehensive.

Within several weeks, Chief Wetzel did show up and after brief introductions were made, he revealed his plan. He had told us that he would be around "to observe how we do our jobs" over the coming month or so, and that he normally did not like to make radical changes within a work place right off. He was very much true to his word, somewhat. What I mean is this…he did go from one area to the next and one section to the next, and spent considerable time "watching" and seeing "how and why" things got done the way they did. Shortly, it was "my turn" in the barrel. Chief Wetzel had come down to the survival training branch and watched as I instructed aircrews in continuation training. He had also spent considerable time watching how I did my job and my interactions with others. Although I do not know this first hand, I also believe, because of his evaluation of me, that he had also gleaned additional information from his discussions with others, and most likely our First Sergeant and Commander as well. I have to believe this as he knew quite a bit about me by the time his next phase was implemented.

The Chief's first request was for me to provide him with a personal note card for every Airman and NCO in the branch. The cards were to list each person's full name, spouse's full name, their birth and wedding dates, education levels, the names and ages of all their children and any hobbies and interests the family members had. After he had time to review each of the cards he asked me to schedule one-on-one meetings with each person starting with the lowest ranked Airman. He wanted these lower ranked individuals to know how important she or he was to the ultimate success of the new Life Support Branch. There was some initial hesitation by the first Airman to meet with the Chief but the concerns were immediately set aside within minutes after the visit started. After leaving the meeting the word spread immediately that it was a positive event and no one else had any concerns or hesitation to meet the "Chief."

Chief Wetzel then spent considerable time going back to each of the people he observed and gave them a brief evaluation of what he believed was their strong and weak points. I called this his "phase 2" of his introduction as our LSO. When he approached me, he and I sat down to a very sobering, yet positive evaluation of my skills and strengths. Chief Wetzel never left anyone with negative thoughts and always had a way about him to bring out the best in anyone. His observations about me went as follows, to the best of my recollection: "Your duty performance and knowledge are above reproach, and I am thoroughly impressed with your professionalism. You are the best people person I have ever seen, and I know this because you know every person in your unit as well as their families and everything about them. However, I have two words for you… "monkey" and "mother." See, every one of us faces problems in life and in our day-to-day operations, and our home lives. These problems are what I call "monkeys on our backs." We all have them. Now, it is our jobs as supervisors and NCO's to not only handle our own "monkeys" but to also help our subordinates handle their own "monkeys" as well. The problem I see with you is that you are being too much of a "mother" to be an effective supervisor. In other words Sergeant Black, you are so close and know your people so well that when they come to you with their problems (their monkeys) they know that you will take their "monkeys" on your back and thus alleviate them from solving their own issues... instead you handle the problems for them!

So now you have effectively removed the monkey from their back and placed it on your own, along with all of your other monkeys you already had. In this way, your subordinates never learn from their mistakes since you solve them for them, rather than helping them to solve their own problems or " monkeys". The sign of a good supervisor is one who not only stands up for their subordinates, but can effectively help them to solve their own problems so that they don't continue to make the same mistakes over and over again. Knowing when and where to refer someone for the proper help is as important as knowing how to solve the problem yourself. Sergeant Black, you are the best supervisor I know, but you need to quit being a mother to these people and help them to solve their own problems."

Chief Wetzel was totally correct that day and the amount of information that he had come up with in that short amount of time amazed me. He knew of years of things that had transpired within that Life Support Branch that I had to deal with, and how I stepped in on many occasions to protect and help those of my subordinates who had gotten in trouble. At the time I had thought I was doing them a favor, but in hind sight I could see that many of those instances would not have been repeated had I simply allowed my subordinates to manage their own" monkeys" rather than me "fixing" them or taking them on my own back!

What I learned that day from Chief Wetzel will forever stick in my mind. That was a lesson that would change the way I supervised and thus alleviate many potential problems down the road. The tact with which he approached me left me with a feeling of empowerment, and although changes had to be made in my style of supervision, Chief Wetzel was the very first supervisor who cared enough to be honest with me and to help mold me from a good supervisor to the best I could be. He cared enough to give constructive criticism when, where and how it was needed. Chief Wetzel, and the man Wim Wetzel, was always honest, open and up front in all of his dealings whether you were an Airman 1 striper or another Senior Non-Commissioned Officer like himself....and you could bank on the effectiveness of his advice. It was always tactful, tasteful and right on the money regardless of what it was that was needed to be said. I have yet to meet anyone as honest and forthright as him.

In the Aircrew Life Support Branch of the United States Air Force, it should be noted that the Life Support Officer (LSO) is "normally" a commissioned officer, and never an enlisted person or Non-Commissioned Officer (NCO) regardless of the rank of that NCO. Suffice it to say that we, the Life Support Branch as a whole, were all very surprised to find that Chief Master Sergeant Wim Wetzel (normally referred to as "Chief" or "Chief Wetzel") had been assigned as our LSO. What we did not know at the time was that Chief Wetzel, who had recently been reassigned back to Altus Air Force Base was considered to be an overage which meant that there was not a job or position available for him to fill. The base did not have a Loadmaster "Chief" slot to fill at Altus as his reassignment came as a "humanitarian" reassignment. This simply meant that the Air Force moved Chief Wetzel and his wife Zee close to home so that they could help take care of sick relatives.

The thing that a lot of people do not realize is that once you attain the rank of Chief Master Sergeant in the Air Force, you are considered a "manager" and can actually be placed in any capacity within any specialty, shop or branch and be able to manage it correctly. Less than 1 percent of the entire enlisted force in all branches of the military combined ever attain the rank of E-9, which is the highest enlisted rank that is attainable. Chief Master Sergeant is the E-9 position in the US Air Force. Because there were not any "openings" for a "Chief" slot at Altus, Chief Wetzel was given the option to "choose" which shop or branch that he wanted to be assigned to. Unbeknown to the Life Support Branch, he had chosen us because it was one of the largest "enlisted personnel" shops on the base and had many "negative" strikes against the personnel in it. For that matter, the Life Support Branch was considered to be the worst unit on the base at that time. To say that Chief Wetzel had his hands full was the understatement of all time and the Altus Air Force Base Aircrew Life Support Branch was in for a rude awakening!

After Chief Wetzel made his appearance at our Life Support Shop for the first time he subsequently spent time "observing" each and every person within the branch, especially the supervisors. He spent time talking and counseling with each person to advise them of some changes they could make to make them more effective and successful in their jobs. But just "talking and counseling" with the personnel within the branch would not be enough to bring about change, and change that was desperately needed at that time. Chief Wetzel knew this and started to implement some new policy changes effective immediately within the branch. First and foremost was an "Open Ranks" inspection in which Chief Wetzel would recruit one senior squadron commander at the full Colonel level to come down and perform the open ranks inspection each month right in the Life Support Branch. The first open ranks inspection was accomplished at Chief Wetzel's request, by the highest ranking officer on the base – the Wing Commander. This open ranks inspection was where the Commander from one of the base squadrons would come into our branch and would inspect the personnel, as they would line up (fall in) for inspection and inspect their grooming and uniforms to make sure they were within set standard of the Air Force requirements.

This "Open Ranks Inspection" served several purposes. First, it gave the personnel within the shop a sense of pride in how they took care of themselves and their uniforms. Second, the personal integrity of each member was challenged to look the best they could, as the "new" expectation was to be the best they could. Third, it opened up a sense of competitiveness and integrity as the best Airman selected each month would receive a Letter of Recognition and would be selected by the officer doing the inspection as the top member of the unit for the month. Fourth, it brought the Life Support Branch and its personnel into the "limelight" of the base as this was the only shop on base doing this, and taking pride in doing so. This also helped to get the shop personnel known throughout the base, in something other than a "negative" view as was previously the case. Lastly, the winner of the monthly inspection would also receive a three-day pass for her or his efforts. Pride was starting to emerge within the Life Support branch both in the job the personnel were doing and also in themselves. But as I said earlier, this was really only a beginning step in Chief Wetzel's comprehensive plan to turn this Life Support shop around and make them the "pride of the Air Force," not just Altus Air Force Base.

Within the first several months, I, as the Branch NCOIC at the time, started to notice that some of the supervisors were struggling a bit with some of the new changes. Now take into consideration, that these changes were not many, but the level of excellence required was one standard that falling below was not acceptable. The changes were not unfair and the standard of excellence was well within reach, and badly needed. The problem was, though, that none of us within this branch had ever had these standards imposed upon us, nor did any of us self-impose these upon ourselves. We, as a whole, meaning the Life Support Branch, had fallen into this level of "just OK" and that permeated our entire branch. Not so much in the performance of our duties, but more so in the performance of our personal lives. And unbeknownst to us, the rest of the base could see that by the high number of disciplinary problems and cases we had. Not a good reputation to have! But Chief Wetzel, being an "outsider" to our branch, could perceive these issues within the first week he was in our branch...he really did not even need to see the personnel files at the orderly room to know this. But the Chief's changes although needed badly, had a level of expectation with them that a lot of personnel were finding hard to achieve.

After several visits from my supervisors and seeing some of their struggles, I made the decision to call Chief Wetzel at home. "Chief Wetzel, this is Sergeant Black, do you have a minute that we can talk?" "Yes, Sergeant Black, I have told you I would take your calls anytime, day or night, what is on your mind?" "Chief, I know that these new changes and expectations are for our own good, but I am seeing many of my supervisors' struggling with them and trying to keep their heads above water, and I was wondering what to do about this!" The Chief then asked me if I knew where his home was located in Altus, and he gave me the address of his house. He asked me if I could come to his home and talk with him face to face - right now. And I said yes, and headed out the door to his home. At this point, only knowing the Chief for several weeks, I had this huge pit in my stomach, not knowing the outcome of this visit. Plus, it was the only time in my 20-year career that any senior officer, commissioned or not, had me come directly to his personal residence. I thought, "Oh man, I wonder if I just put my foot in my own mouth" as I was driving to the Chief's home.

Upon arriving, Chief Wetzel greeted me warmly and had a paper in his hand. He said, "Before we get into this conversation Sergeant Black, I want you to read something. This is a paper, a biography that I had written as part of my Master's degree dissertation. It is entirely true and factual, start to finish. I tell you this because even the professor questioned as to whether or not some of what you are about to read was factual or made up. It is all factual, and this will give you a better idea of who I am and where I come from, and what I really want to achieve while here in Life Support. Please take all the time you need to read and digest this, and then we can talk!" Now, in the paragraphs to follow, I am going to just touch on, and to the best of my recollection, some of what I read in this paper he gave me to read. To this day I don't think he had given this to anyone else…other than maybe his wife and professor. And, to this day, parts of what I read I will never forget. It spoke volumes to me as to "who" Wim and Chief Wetzel were, and the man he still is today.

My family is originally from Indonesia and we immigrated to America when I was 8. My father was a drill sergeant in the Royal Dutch Army known by the nickname of "Little Bear." He was captured as a prisoner of war by the Japanese. He was a master in Poekoelan Kung Fu and all of his children were also black belts in this style of martial arts. Our father expected perfection, in everything we did…whether in the practice of our martial art, school grades or sports. Anything less than perfection was unacceptable, and we would pay a heavy price by our father if we did not attain that. So the standard of acceptance growing up was nothing but perfection in all that we did. When I joined the Air Force, I remember making the statement in basic training that "Boy Scout camp was harder than this!" The drill instructor heard me and proceeded to make my life miserable. But regardless, for me it was easier than Boy Scout camp. Nothing would be harder than what my siblings and I endured during our lives growing up as his children."

At some point, Chief Wetzel's biography led to him going to the Republic of Vietnam as an Air Freight (Mobility Operations) Specialist. The paper described an incident when he and other Airmen were off loading a C-130 aircraft when they came under mortar fire from the Viet Cong. It further described how a mortar round landed close enough to blow him off his bright yellow forklift. The same explosion blew one of the Airman into pieces as he was jumping off the ramp of the C-130 aircraft. He further went on to tell that they finished off-loading the C-130 so that it could get to safety before the Viet Cong walked another mortar into it for a direct hit. The aircraft did get off the ground safely, but Chief Wetzel was permanently affected by watching another human being die so brutally.

As I continued to read this biography, I remember fighting back the tears…I did not want this Chief to see me that way, although further in our time together we would share many tears and joys. Then this biography became even more personal. In his biography, the Chief continued, "... because of my upbringing most things came to me in my military career much easier than most of my contemporaries. I took this attitude of "perfection" with me from my childhood and into my career in the Air Force. When many others could not seem to figure out a way to solve a problem, I had already not only found the way but had implemented the solution. When I ran shops and the C-141 Loadmaster School, or any units, you either led, followed or got out of my way. I was hard driving and expected and accepted nothing less than perfection. So throughout my career, making rank and getting assignments were relatively easy. As I learned in Boy Scouts you always leave a campground cleaner than you found it. Consequently following that philosophy, I always left units in better shape than I found them. However, the penalty for this approach to perfection also had a penalty to pay by leaving the units with few or no friends." This was the part of Chief Wetzel's biography that I was fighting hard to choke back the tears through.

The biography continued, "...Now, towards the end of my career, and probably my last assignment before retirement, I am looking back at my life and career and find that friendship has always been very important but elusive and secondary to my management responsibilities. I was assigned as the Life Support Officer to the 443rd MAW Life Support Branch/Shop here at Altus Air Force Base and I am about to make a major change in my life. I departed every military assignment in good shape and bolstered my career immensely. The successes were often at great personal costs to include a divorce. The changes I am going to make in my personal life, as well as my military career and with these new people in this floundering shop are life changing and significant. I don't even really know if I can accomplish, or even if my wife Zee can handle, this monumental challenge. But I feel that I must try. I hope that they will work and that through it all, I can help this organization and its Airmen pull themselves from the dust to rise and become the top Life Support Shop in the Air Force. And while doing so, that I can help some of these floundering Airmen not just in their careers but in their personal lives as well. I would hope not to leave friendless this time around."

There was a lot more to this biography, but these are the parts that really stuck out for me and made a huge impression with me. I had come to Chief Wetzel's home expecting him to be stern and tough and motivational, but nothing could have prepared me for what actually occurred. The visit opened my eyes that day and made Chief Master Sergeant Wim Wetzel human and a man as well as a figure to look up to. Reading that document did not taint my respect for Chief Wetzel, it solidified it. I could see the "methods to the changes he was making" not just for the reputation of the shop, but also for every person in the Life Support Branch as well as for their self-respect, and for his own life as well. We continued to talk and Chief Wetzel answered some questions I had about his biography and other concerns I had. Once I mustered up the strength, I said, "Chief, thanks for giving me the privilege to peek into this very personal part of your life. But I have to say, while your level of professionalism and perfection are up here at this line, and come very easy for you, each and every one of us in this Life Support Branch are struggling just to maintain a minimal level of your expectations. We do not have the background nor upbringing that you do, but we will, in time be able to achieve all of what you ask, and will continue to work to that end." Chief Wetzel looked at me and just stated that he'd give it some thought. I knew he would…he was a man of his word.

In the days ahead, Chief Wetzel continued to implement his plan and the changes, but in doing so, he arranged in such a way so as to enable everyone to attain these goals incrementally. Because of how and what the Chief did in the days that followed, he gained the loyalty and respect of everyone within that Life Support Branch.

I went home on leave to Erie, Pennsylvania for Christmas that following December. On Christmas day, I was at my brother's house and I asked him if I could use his phone to call the "Chief" and wish him a Merry Christmas, and he said "yes." My brother asked me whom it was I was calling, and I told him a little bit about Chief Wetzel, our new Life Support Officer. As I made the call, my brother was thinking about his name, and asked me to ask Chief Wetzel where he was from. Chief Wetzel stated "Beaver, Pennsylvania." When I told my brother, he almost fell out of his chair. Then my brother asked me to ask the Chief if he was any relation to Roy Wetzel or Master Willy Wetzel, who would come to local martial arts tournaments. My brother was into the martial arts in Erie, PA. Chief Wetzel said, "Yes, Willy is my father and Roy is my younger brother!" After the call ended, my brother and I reminisced about the tournaments we had gone to when I was just a teenager. It was incredible how Roy Wetzel completely dominated in every aspect or event that he entered in the tournaments. Roy normally was the top champion of these tournaments. I personally recall the first time Master Wetzel and his son Roy entered the first tournament that I competed in. Everyone in the entire place just stopped and stared as the Wetzel school students and competitors took their places! As always - the Beaver County School for the Oriental Art of Self-Defense dominated the tournament.

Bottom line for me, after the conversation on Christmas day, was that I KNEW every bit of what Chief Master Sergeant Wetzel had written and told me was the truth. I had never once doubted Chief Wetzel's word or his character. In the days and years that followed, Chief Wetzel would take the 443rd MAW Aircrew Life Support Branch from just floundering to stay alive to become one of the top Life Support branches in the United States Air Force. We never failed another surprise command inspection again and routinely achieved "Excellent" or "Outstanding" statuses for Operational Readiness Inspections and Evaluations. Whereas before the Chief arrived, we typically failed the major inspections and often quite miserably.

I can honestly say that I have never seen more love for this country than Chief Wetzel has, but over the 7 years under his command, I have never seen more love and humanity for his troops as well. Chief Wetzel always expected a lot but always gave a hundred percent more in return. Over the many years before his final retirement we spent a lot of time laughing, but also shed many tears when a single Airmen would be lost or would get themselves in a situation where nothing we could have done could have changed the outcome...whether duty related or in their personal loves. When Chief Wetzel retired from the Air Force, not only did he leave the Life Support Branch as the number 1 Life Support Branch, but there was not one of the Life Support personnel who did not have her or his career bolstered by what they accomplished because of leadership and mentoring. Every one of us within this branch was given the opportunity to realize that we were much more capable of levels of success than what we even thought we could attain because of the confidence he instilled within each of us. I look back now, on social media, and see many of those whom he mentored during his final Air Force assignment. They all are living very rewarding lives and retiring from very successful careers...all due to 1 role model and man who cared deeply for us all.

Foreword

I started writing this book in 1976, at the suggestion of my college English professor at Cerro Coso Community College, located on Edwards Air Force Base, California. At the beginning of Doctor Rita Fuhr Marowitz's writing class the students were given specific writing assignments for the semester, consisting of one paper per week for twelve weeks. One of the papers I wrote was titled "A Plan for Dying." It was about the death of my father Willy Johannes Cristoffel Wetzel in 1975, at the hands of my younger brother, Roy. Roy took my father's life in self-defense, as was proven in his murder trial. After reading the paper several times, my professor returned it to me with a score of A++ and she included her suggestion that I should think about writing a book. I considered it briefly before moving on with my own troubled life. This book will discuss how I faced my own demons and challenges to turn them into triumphs and successes. It is, in essence, a survival story.

Each time I started to write the book over the past 39 years my emotions kicked in and writer's block kept me from moving forward and making any worthwhile progress. It was just impossible for me to disconnect my emotions from the realities and suffering of the Wetzel family that led to Dad's death. The death indeed was a planned event, whether he planned it overtly or covertly. In order to tell the whole story, so that you might understand the events that precipitated the actions that resulted in his death, it is important to take you back to where the Wetzel family came from and where and how we ultimately settled in America.

Over the many years since Dad's unfortunate death, I picked up and set down my writing pen literally hundreds of times; a few words here and a few words there but nothing of any decent progress. I was just existing from day to day and year to year, waiting for my own time to leave this earth. To some, my story and ultimately my family's story, is one of pain and suffering without any hope of redemption or peace of mind. You would be wrong in making that assumption as you progress through the book because the ultimate result is a story of turning tragedy and pain into success and healing of the heart, mind, soul and body. No matter the depth of pain and sorrow someone experiences in life, everyone has it within him or herself to recover and be triumphant in the end.

In my case, I turned all of the negative influences of my father around and learned from them. I learned not to repeat the taught behaviors but reached deep within myself to find and use my natural God-given talents, to reach out to help others and to ultimately help and heal myself. Without knowing why or how, I made the decision to stop the vicious cycle of physical and mental abuse demonstrated daily by Dad. At the early age of thirteen I committed to never abuse someone else for my own benefit. Dad had also demonstrated some powerful and positive behaviors and rules of the road, and those I chose to adopt and replicate during my life. These include:

1. A man's word is a reflection of his name;

2. Fulfill your commitments, regardless of the challenges that may cause others to just give up;

3. Don't be ready to accept "No!" as the answer without speaking up and trying to have the answer changed to "Yes!"

4. Reach out to help others when achieving successes; and finally

5. "If you don't ask – you don't get!"

Every decision I made and every step I took after leaving home for my Air Force career and throughout the rest of my life was based on these simple but effective rules.

The Japanese definition for the word "Karate" means "empty hand." Dad refined the definition for the use in our Karate schools as "Empty Open Hand." It has remained that way since he started teaching in the USA. The "Empty Open hand" part of this book's title is a reference to Dad's overarching approach to life in general. It has meaning in our family Karate school's logo and patch in that there is no need to approach life with a weapon in hand, in the event that misfortune confronts you. Simply confront those challenges with the intent to overcome them. In the event that those challenges or opponents become overwhelming, back away from them but never turn your back. Regain your strength and think through how you might confront them from a different angle or approach. If necessary, reach out with your empty open hand and work out a compromise with your opponent. Only then, if that approach fails, should you consider using a defensive weapon. I lived by this motto or logo throughout my life. There were many times when a defensive weapon would have solved a confrontational issue but I chose to reach out with my empty open hand to offer compromises. In every case my opponents were surprised by this approach and returned the gesture.

Many readers of this book will be Karate enthusiasts who have heard stories about my father and the ultimate fight with Roy that ended in Dad's death. There are literally hundreds of stories on the Internet about the trial and the events that led to that fateful day and the events that occurred since then. So much speculation, untruths, innuendo, accusations and twisting of the facts exist out there that make me sick to my stomach. I stopped reading these stories and chat room crap when they became so offensive that it sickened my very being. It is my hope that this book will shed some light on the life that my father lived and how it ultimately caused him to "crack," for lack of a better term. Let there be no mistake, regardless of who reads this story, no one outside of my family knows what really happened behind our closed doors. The cruelties we suffered at the hands of a ruthless and overpowering man were never observed outside of our home. You only saw the public persona, as he wished for you to see him.

Finally, and regardless of what the public thinks it knows, this book is a story about the man who made me who I am, despite the negative influences he often demonstrated. I loved and still love my father and I pray that he rests in peace. This book is my attempt to say thank you Dad for making me who I ultimately came to be, despite the bad examples and because of the good things you taught me.

The purpose for writing this book, more than being a self-reflecting biography, is to transfer my feelings, emotions and deep seated angst from my brain onto paper and, hopefully, giving me some inner peace and you a new perspective on what you are capable of not matter what life has thrown as you. Whether anyone will be interested in reading about the Wetzel family's trials, tribulations, failures and triumphs is secondary to my intentions. When all is said and done one must ask whether our lives were just the norm for any family or grossly outside the norm. I submit that we lived far from the normal American family life.

Today I live for and enjoy each day to the fullest. Welding horseshoes into works of art has become my passion. Cutting firewood and stocking it up for the winter provides me with much needed exercise since the treadmill sits in the corner unused, Walking throughout our 120 acres of pine timbered land provides Vikie and me the solace, peace of mind and tranquility we both crave. The three dogs, our "Golden Years" children Dixie, Amber and Sassy accompany us almost everywhere we travel. All we really seek is to enjoy our retirement to the fullest and travel as often as possible.

I continue to suffer a great deal from PTSD and often wonder if I am not just a weak minded adult who lacks the strength of mind or character to forget Viet Nam. The nightmares are terrible and I wake up numerous times at night before waking up at 3 or 4 in the morning. The CPAP machine for sleep apnea provides some relief and stopped my outrageous snoring, but doesn't do much for the nightmares.

Being raised in a hostile home environment negatively affects all children and ultimately their own offspring. Only a strong person with moral character and a desire to change negative environments to positive ones can effect change in their future and that of their off-spring. PTSD is not just a combat-related malady or disease. Bad parenting, spousal and child abuse will also cause PTSD symptoms that can and will last a lifetime.

As a severe dyslexic it is hard for me to read anything regardless of the format. Writing is often difficult because my brain does not recognize what I put on paper. How I was able to achieve several college degrees amazes me – it was a struggle and only through the strength of will and self-determination was I able to succeed. In my civilian jobs I traveled across the country to give speeches at training conferences and conventions about twice a year. PowerPoint presentations were the norm. The dyslexia would strike at the worst times during presentations if I looked at the slides at all. In order not to sound as if I was mentally deficient or had a speaking impediment I always memorized the presentations and avoided looking at the presentation slides on the screen. If for some reason I looked at the slides to read them out loud the words and sentences would tumble from my mouth in the most jumbled and embarrassing manner. I tell the reader this so that you will know why and how it took me over forty years to write this story.

Willy Wetzel, my father, was not an evil man, but he may have been mentally ill as a result of his POW confinement and torture by the Japanese. Watching family and friends being butchered had to have a devastating impact on him. I know that when I experienced and witnessed combat personally that it has a way of damaging one's psyche and forever changing life as you once knew it. The butchering and cutting up of my grandmother in a dozen or more pieces by the Indonesian separatists forever hardened and changed Dad. His revenge was immediate and without regret as he led his men into the rebel village to kill every man they found. It did not matter whether any of them were innocent of the barbarity inflicted to over a hundred people on his parents' plantation. There is no doubt that he suffered from PTSD because of his time as a POW and the death of his beloved mother. I look in the mirror and often see Dad. Not only because we look so much alike but because I have lived my life so much like he did. I never expected to live beyond thirty because I looked danger in the face and rarely suffered from fear.

I survived so far in this life because of the survival tools Dad taught me. The good and bad things that he did gave me a special insight on what type of person I wanted to be and ultimately became. Very early in my teen years I set aside the bad and adopted the good behaviors to the best of my ability. When angered I walk backwards away because the alternatives to not doing so are very bad. We were taught at a very young age how to kill with one blow to specific parts of a body. Common sense and a desire to never hurt anyone always ruled my decisions in conflicts. Only once in my life did I strike out and hurt someone and that was in Korea. I regretted it then as I do today.

Roy, Mom and Dad are at rest and, God willing, at peace with one another. Mom loved Dad to the end and even told me so in the hospice facility before passing from this life. She often told me how good a person Dad could be when the demons did not take over. I experienced the goodness of my father many times and savor those memories today. I want to be remembered as a good person; the way I decided to remember Dad in spite of his shortcomings.

Rest in Heavenly peace and in God's loving and forgiving grace Mom, Dad and Roy! To my son Wim I say; "I love you so much and look forward to the day that we will be together again."

Willem (Willy) Johannes Christoffel Wetzel Leading the March

CHAPTER ONE

Portrait of a Bruised and Brutal Man
Willem (Willy) Johannes Christoffel Wetzel
(1921–1975)

But by the grace of God I am what I am:
and His grace which was bestowed
upon me was not in vain; but I labored
more abundantly than they all: yet, not I,
but the grace of God which was with me.
1Corinthians 15:10
King James, Cambridge Edition

Willem (Willy) Johannes Christoffel Wetzel (1921 – 1975) was an enigma who fascinated and puzzled many people in his short and troubled life. Who was Willy Wetzel really? What made him tick? How did he become the man so many people loved, adored, idolized, and greatly feared? These questions can be answered to a point but we will never really know all there is to know about the man I called "Dad". Dad had multiple personalities. He probably had more than two but only two distinct personalities matter in this memoir. The differences between his private family persona and his public persona were stark and as different as night and day. Our family knew him to be a very loving, caring and nurturing father one minute and a dark, cruel and ruthless disciplinarian the next. We lived in fear as he often threatened to kill all of us some day.

The public's view of my father was one of a very caring husband, parent, and loyal friend, highly disciplined, hard-working and extremely likeable. To this very day many of his public acquaintances still believe that their view of his public persona is the only one that existed. They were so brainwashed by his electrifying personality that nothing any of us could tell them to believe differently mattered. To give one perfect example of the public's view of my Dad can be described through a brutal beating that Mom suffered at his hands one Sunday afternoon when I was only ten or eleven years old. Mom was so badly beaten that she had a broken nose, both eyes were black and blue and terrible bruises covered her body. It actually was the straw that broke the back of their marriage.

We went to the Justice of the Peace (JP) in New Brighton, PA to file a restraining order and to have him arrested. The JP, unknown to us at that time, happened to be a good friend of Dad's. When we explained the incident to him his response was incredible. He questioned "Well what did you do to deserve to get the beating Mrs. Wetzel?" He told us to go home and to behave. Mom, at that moment, made the decision to file for divorce. I mention this incident at the beginning of this memoir because it is important for you to understand Willy Wetzel's absolutely disparate personality differences that shrouded our family's lives until and still continues long after his untimely but predictable and foreseen violent death. This was also the incident when I made a life changing commitment to never beat or strike any women or any of my children regardless of the circumstances. I have lived by that decision to this day.

Before moving forward in this chapter it is important to address where Dad and our family ultimately came from and how we arrived in America in September of 1956. Our family name originated from Aken, Germany as Von Wetzel. Our Great-Great Grandfather Willem Johannes Von Wetzel moved to Indonesia during approximately 1850. For reasons unknown to the family he dropped the Von from the Wetzel name.

Great-Great Granddad was recruited from Aken by the Indonesian (formerly Dutch East Indies) royal family as a mercenary soldier. He immigrated to the Dutch East Indies, married and had three sons. Little is known about the three children except my Great Grandfather Johannes Nicalaas Wetzel. My grandfather Willem (Wim), whom I was named after, was born on July 23, 1890. He died in 1963. He married my grandmother Erma Wilhelmina Catherinus who was born on September 24, 1901. Right after World War II she was brutally murdered by Indonesian rebels and separatists fighting for independence from Holland. She was killed along with about 100 of her housemaids and plantation workers on the family plantation on October 27, 1945. Her butchered remains were strewn around the family home. The people of the Dutch East Indies wanted and fought for their independence. The rebels were ruthless and killed many of the Dutch settlers in their quest for freedom. My grandmother was one of the unfortunate casualties, even though she was loved by everyone who worked on the family plantation the rebels did not care.

Upon hearing about the slaughter Dad gathered several of his soldiers and they went on a rampage to find and kill every rebel they could. All the bandits they captured were decapitated and their heads were imbedded on bamboo poles.

More about this later. My Grandmother adored Dad and did much to protect him from Grandfather's abusive treatment and wrath. As you will read later a psychiatrist at my brother's murder trial commented that Dad's entire life was significantly affected by hearing about my Grandmother's butchered remains. The psychiatrist stated under oath that he believed the tragic event ultimately caused Dad's mind to break and resulting in his attempt to murder my Mother and my siblings.

Dad was born in Lumajong, Indonesia on January 23, 1921. As the oldest son he was given the nickname of "Nono" which was a traditional name given to the first born son in Indonesia at the time. Dad had an older sister Pauline Elvira (Tante Pollie) and two younger brothers Richard Leonard or "Oom Tikkie" and Edward Benjamin "Oom Ben". At this wring Oom Ben is the only surviving sibling of my Dad's and lives in De Haag, The Netherlands.

Dad and his Father constantly clashed and just did not get along. At the very early age of 10 and as an escape from his father's harsh treatment and conflicts, Dad studied and practiced the Indonesian art of Poekoelan Tjimindie. The lessons were taught privately by a local Master of the art. As time progressed and his expertise in the art grew so did his rank to the 9th Degree. If the war had not intervened he probably would have ascended to the coveted rank of 10th degree or Master. A goal he regretted not achieving his entire life. He believed in and practiced witchcraft and voodoo ceremonies but studied the Bible and could quote it chapter and verse to suit his needs. He believed in the Yin and Yang and was an expert in moving from one to the other at will. For those unfamiliar with this belief it is a simple **Chinese philosophy and religion of two principles.** One negative, dark, and feminine (Yin) and one positive, bright, and masculine (Yang) whose interaction influences the destinies of creatures and things. Unfortunately he dwelled in the dark and negative realm (Yin) in his private life more prevalently than the other.

Dad was not a big man and was only five foot six inches in stature but he was unbelievably strong and agile. No one could touch him in a real fight or in competition. He was an active sportsman and good at every sport he played. As an accomplished heavy weight lifter he easily lifted weights far above what his peer lifters could. He was a soccer champion until he blew out his right knee thereby ending that passion. He could play tennis like no one else and reviled in his prowess on the court.

The teen years at home were hard on Dad. He was a rebel constantly looking for adventure, challenges and women. All of these caused the rift between him and Granddad to grow wider and more hostile. At the age of 17 (1938) Dad had enough of the conflict at home and joined the Royal Dutch Army as a sports and self-defense or martial arts instructor. Today he would be known as a Drill Instructor or DI at military boot camps. He was the ultimate military professional highly regarded and respected by his superiors, peers and subordinates. Dad was captured by the Japanese in 1941 and was sent to a Dutch prisoner of war camp in Japan. In 1943 he was sent via a prison ship from Japan to a POW camp in Thailand where he was assigned to hard labor to build the River Kwai Bridge in Kanchanaburi, Thailand. Two of the prison ships that sailed from Japan next to his ship were bombed and sunk by allied bombers. All of the prisoners and Japanese sailors were lost. Dad often told me how he and a couple of other prisoners killed a Japanese guard and buried him under several layers of fresh concrete within the bridge. He and his closest friends had a goal to kill at least one Japanese soldier upon the anniversary of their captivity. When the movie "Bridge on the River Kwai" was released I saw him shed tears for the first and only time in my life. The movie had a very strong effect on him and he watched it several times.

Dad was moved to several POW camps as a slave laborer including one near Saigon and others in Indonesia. He was finally released in 1945 and was allowed to continue his career in the Royal Dutch Army. He was reassigned to a post near Bandung, Indonesia where I was ultimately born in July of 1947.

My Uncle Tikkie was drafted by the Dutch military and ultimately captured by the Japanese. He escaped captivity and went home to get his brother Ben who was too young at 16 to be drafted. Ben and Tikkie remained together and in hiding for the remainder of the war. Both became policemen after the war.

After the war, the local chief of police released revolutionary prisoners for the sake of Independence. Since the rebels had butchered his mother Uncle Ben became extremely upset and left his job for about two weeks. During that time Ben discovered that the Indonesian rebels created a Black List containing the Wetzel name and any other Dutch nationals, which were all marked for death. He quit the police force and immediately moved to Holland. Oom Tikki remained in Indonesia until 1955. Not much is known as to how he was able to avoid being arrested because of the Black List.

Dad met Mom at a Dutch Air Force base dance soon after the war. Against my maternal Grandfather's wishes, she married Dad. I was not the first progeny of my Dad's loins. A previously conceived brother, right after the marriage of my parents, was forcefully aborted when he made Mom drink quinine and other jungle medications. He was not ready for nor did he want

Dad, Mom and Me 1947

children to impact his Army career, but I was born 9 months later on July 8, 1947. There have been times in my life that I wished that it had been me who was aborted, but as life turned out, God had a purpose for my survival and has blessed me with many achievements and gifts.

My maternal grandfather was the police commissioner of the region and his police force provided us with protection from the rebels. We continued to live in and moved around several of the army posts in Indonesia until 1951. Death threats and the Black List were catching up to us and Dad knew we had to leave. A local Indonesian friend advised Dad that the rebels were coming for us in the middle of the night. The friend arranged for us to be put on a little boat and warned that we could only carry small items. We left our house under the cover of dark and watched as local militia broke into the house and burned it to the ground. My brother Roy and sister Jane along with my parents and me were very lucky to leave in time. The small boat carried us to the nearby army base where we were under the guard of a full contingent of Army soldiers before being put on a ship to Holland. The Black list remained active with our family names on it until after the death of Sukarno. While I was in the Air Force as a Loadmaster Indonesia was the only place in the world that I could not fly missions into because of the Black List.

Sukarno, was the leader of the Indonesian Revolution. In 1945, Sukarno was declared President and he established the Republic of the United States of Indonesia. The Dutch finally recognized their loss and liberated Indonesia from their colonial control in 1949, when Queen Juliana of Netherlands proclaimed that Indonesia was free of Dutch rule.

The Wetzel Family and Siblings in Indonesia

We lived in Holland for five years and moved from Army post to Army post numerous times. Like many Dutch citizens during the post war recovery we did not have much. The Army pay barely sustained our nutritional needs. At the early age of 5 and 6 Roy and I arranged with a local farmer to help care for his livestock. In return he gave us goose eggs on occasion and allowed us to milk his cows and keep some milk to take home. After harvest he allowed us to go into his fields to pick any remaining turnips and potatoes to supplement our meager diets. Meat was not a staple that adorned our table often.

Regardless of the hard times, our family was generally happy and Mom and Dad got along beautifully. The corner grocery store owner gave us all of the left over coffee grounds from his store each day. We used them in a bed of food leftovers to grow worms that we used to fish in the canal we lived by, supplementing our family diet with fresh fish whenever the canal was not frozen in winter. We actually did wear wooden shoes. During winter we stuffed them with newspapers to help insulate them to keep our feet warmer. As we walked in the snow it would stick to the bottom of the shoes. We competed to see how high we could actually get the snow to build up. Dad made ice skates for playing on the canal. He became an accomplished ice skater and competed with the neighborhood men in races. Roy and I developed our strong work ethic and the deeply held belief that one takes care of their family regardless of the challenges you face.

Dad was restless and wanted a better life for the family. By this time my baby brother Jim was born and he knew that we had to leave for greener pastures. He applied for emigration to the United States even though he had seventeen years in the Army and could retire in three years. After about a year, we received emigration approval to America because we were sponsored by the United Methodist Church in Rochester, PA. Soon after receiving the emigration documents we boarded a ship named the SS Waterman out of Rotterdam, Holland. We literally left everything we owned behind in Holland and only took suitcases with our clothing and valuables.

Mom and my siblings and I loved and reveled in the 5-day voyage but Dad remained seasick for the entire journey until we sailed into New York harbor at the end of September 1956. I can only surmise that his illness stemmed from his memories of being stuck in the bowels of the slave ships. We sailed right past the Statue of Liberty as we entered the United States. What a magnificent and unforgettable sight that was and it still remains permanently in my mind's eye to this day. Dad reminded us that it was the American Army that freed him from the POW camp and that we owed our new country a debt. My allegiance and love for this country was born at that very moment and Roy and I promised him that we would serve in the military one day as a way to say thank you to our newly adopted home and country.

Life in America was not easy to say the least. The Methodist church provided us with a car, a home near the church in Rochester, a fully stocked refrigerator, clothing and a job for Dad at Westinghouse in Beaver, PA. We have never forgotten the kindness and generosity of the congregation and remain eternally grateful. Dr. Fisher was the pastor of the church and he ensured that someone from the church came to our home every day to help ease our transition. Our first Thanksgiving in America was a disaster and we all ended up in the hospital. The church provided us with turkey and all the trimmings. Never in our lives did we ever experience eating so much rich food. That evening we all became deathly ill and had to be taken to the hospital. We were so sick from the meal that we did not eat turkey for a couple of years.

Dad's job at Westinghouse required him to sweep the floor and clean bathrooms. He never complained because he knew things would get better with time. He did have to put up with racist comments from several of the people who worked there. Some of the employees often called him racist names like chink, slope head and zipper head referring to his Asian appearance and heritage. During a long span of many days one man harassed him constantly and ruthlessly until Dad had enough. The English language was a real challenge for him so it was very difficult for him to communicate in a clear and concise manner. On the last occasion where he had been harassed too long Dad dropped his broom and in the presence of numerous employees, stuck his finger in the guy's chest and said "You are dead!" Then he turned and walked away. Later that evening the harasser suffered a massive heart attack and dropped dead on the factory floor. Dad's reputation and mystique took off like the proverbial rocket.

Right before Christmas of 1956 the union at Westinghouse went on strike and since he did not have any tenure as an employee Dad was summarily laid off. We were broke and he had no benefits. He took every available job he could find in order to support the family. The week before Christmas he was paid $40 to hand trim 4,000 Christmas trees for a local tree farm. With bloodied hands, my Dad and Mom wrapped presents for us during the night before Christmas. It is a Christmas morning that set the basis for my life's belief that something good can always come from something bad. Our family was strong and we had a bright future in our newly adopted country. Oh! - If only we could have had a crystal ball and the ability to foresee the future.

Mom and Dad were hired by a local dairy delivery company about a block from our house. Their job was to clean the milk delivery trucks every night. It was a nasty stinking and gut wrenching job, and they hated it. Regardless, they cleaned these trucks better than anyone ever had before them. The owner recognized their work ethic and arranged for both my parents to be re-hired at Westinghouse at better and more substantially paying jobs.

My first job was delivering newspapers. I started out covering about a block, but before long I owned the whole territory. Snow, sleet or rain did not stop me as my work ethic became stronger each day. Watching Mom and Dad work tirelessly gave me the inspiration to do the same. The extra few bucks certainly helped the family budget.

Around that time, Dad started showing depression and anger control issues that manifested themselves in how he treated the family. In today's military environment it would be classified as Post Traumatic Stress Disorder (PTSD). Nightmares about prison, his mother's death and his childhood years haunted him to a point of near insanity. He began to drink heavily and could not control his behavior while drunk. Roy, Jim and I would get beaten for the slightest infractions. Jim especially was physically and mentally abused. None of us ever shed a tear or screamed out in pain during our beatings. But I would cry every time I watched either of my brothers get punished. Poor Mom would stand between us and Dad to ward off the blows aimed at us. She suffered so much but never complained.

One day I came home from school with an 84 on one of my report card grades. Unfortunately Dad was shit-faced drunk. He had emptied the refrigerator and thrown the food all over the kitchen and toppled the fridge onto its side with the door open. He grabbed my report and read it. Without a hesitation he yelled "Get your brothers and go up to your room NOW!" I complied knowing that a beating was to come since he demanded that a minimum grade would never be below 85.

A couple of minutes passed and he came to the bedroom with our border collie Duke in tow by a choker collar and chain. "I warned you about coming home with bad grades and now you will learn what will happen when you do not!" he said. He dragged the yelping Duke to the second story window steam heater and tied the leash to it. He opened the window and threw the screaming dog out of the window to hang by the leash and choking on the collar. After some time Duke stopped moving and was dragged back into the bedroom. After dragging Duke back into the bedroom he was kicked several times until he started moving again and came back to life. "This is what I can do to each one of you. Do not forget it and never bring failing grades home again!" We lived under the constant threat that he would kill all of us one day. We knew it to be factual and that one day one or all of us might have to deal with it.

One night during the winter Dad asked Roy and me to go with him to get gasoline for the station wagon. Since he still could not speak and understand English clearly it was not unusual for him to ask us. We drove to a town across the Ohio River from Rochester where the gas was a few cents cheaper than the 18 cents a gallon in Rochester. We pulled to the forward fuel tank and he got out to pump the gas. After just connecting to the fuel tank and pumping gas a car pulled up behind us and bumped against our rear bumper. The very large African-American guy in the car opened the door and started yelling at Dad to get out of the way. As soon as he realized that my Dad was not Caucasian in appearance he started calling him names. "Get the Hell out of my way you Gook!" he yelled. This guy had to be 300 pounds and well over 6 feet tall. Dad of course could not understand a word and shrugged his shoulder and pointed to his ear. For some reason this response enraged the obstinate aggressor even more. He came at Dad like a bulldozer and without a second of hesitation, Dad did a flying sweeping kick to the right side of the attacker's head. He hit him so hard that the left side of his head right next to his eye socket hit the fuel pump. His eye popped out of its socket and the guy hit the ground unconscious like a sack of crap. The fuel station owner saw the whole thing as did a local policeman who was sitting in his car monitoring traffic not far away. The policeman called for an ambulance and told Dad not to worry. I had translated to the policeman for him that he was afraid to be deported now. Unfortunately, Dad did get a $15 fine for disturbing the peace.

Because of the special tutoring I was receiving from Mrs. Were in grade school I was becoming very fluent in English and started to teach my parents to read and write in our new language. Dad had already decreed that no one in the family would ever speak anything but English again. That was very unfortunate because all of us could speak several Indonesian dialects and a couple of European languages. My method of teaching my parents the English language was through reading comic books and the newspaper or Krant (in Dutch). Mom was a fast learner. Dad not so much!

One day a news article in the Beaver County Times about a criminal beating a local policeman was written on the front page. After reading it Mom translated it for Dad. She suggested that he volunteer to teach the local police how to defend themselves from such gangsters and hoodlums. It was a suggestion that would impact the family immeasurably and for the remainder of our lives.

Dad and I made an appointment with the chief of police in New Brighton, PA and I translated his offer to teach Jujitsu and Karate to all of the police for free. The only thing he asked for was a building to teach in for free and for the police department to provide workout mats and a punching and kicking bag. The chief jumped on the opportunity. The news spread about this opportunity to every Beaver County police department and the Pennsylvania State Police officers in the Beaver Valley. Over the next three years Dad taught literally hundreds of police to defend themselves at no cost to them or the police departments. The classes were held in the National Guard Armory for many years. One day a policeman asked Dad why he did not start a school for the public and charge them for the training. He volunteered to help Dad with setting it all up.

While continuing to teach the free classes in New Brighton, Dad rented a building in Rochester, PA and started advertising in the local papers. Classes would cost $3.00 but if someone could not afford it and prove it – the classes would be free. It was a boom time for us and all the classes were filled to capacity. Roy and I started training when we were 8 and 9 years old. By the age of 10 and 11 we were teaching adults to defend themselves. I vividly remember my first adult student who was about 250 pounds. He made the sarcastic remark "What do you think you can do little man? Tell your Dad that I want a grown-up instructor!" Roy laughed and said "No – just attack him any way that you want and let's see what he can teach you." The guy came at me and tried to wrap his right arm around my neck. As anyone who knows anything about self-defense you use the opponent's momentum against him. He was so much bigger than me that I simply grabbed his thumb and bent it backwards and let his momentum and weight carry him over my small body. He hit the mat with full force and while still holding his thumb rolled over on top of him and gave him a simulate Karate chop across his throat. He needed no further proof.

Classes were primarily held on Saturdays and Sundays but the school was open every night for workouts and practices. Unfortunately Roy and I had to be there every night regardless to provide additional training to anyone who needed it. That was the way it was until I left home in 1966.

We did not participate in any school sports or activities during our teen years. People laugh when I tell them that I never held a basketball until I was well into my 50s when my second wife Zee tried to teach me how to play. When I was eleven the local youth baseball coach asked my Dad to let me play baseball. "As long as it didn't interfere with the Karate school responsibilities." He said. The coach assured him that it would not and Dad let me join the team. It did not go well!

At eleven I was the smallest member of the team and they could not fit me for a baseball uniform. I practiced in my normal street clothes and also when the first game was played. I begged Dad to come watch me play and he finally consented. Like me, he had no concept of the rules or procedures of the game.

My turn at bat came and I hesitantly approached the plate. The first pitch came and I missed the ball. The second pitch came and I hit a direct line drive to first base. My short legs got me about ten feet and the first baseman waited for me to tag me out. I looked over at Dad and could see him mouth the words "Dumb ass!" He left and I followed him to the car, never looked back or returned to the field. That was the end of my baseball career.

During those days in the 1950s you could only find Kung Fu training published in the back of comic books and the picture of the teacher in the add would always wear a black mask. Teaching Kung Fu in public was a no-no to the yellow mafia (Chinese). On a couple of occasions Asians would come to our school and sit in the visitor seats and watch quietly. Since there were always police present the visitors never said anything. Dad knew that trouble was brewing and told us to never be alone without him.

On one eventful night the three of us were driving home from the school when we were forced to the side of the road by a black limousine. Three men walked back to our car and told Dad to get out. They walked him to the back of the car and proceeded to threaten him and told him to stop teaching Kung Fu in public. Dad refused but struck a deal with them that they ultimately agreed to. The deal was brilliant and typical of his negotiation skills. Simply – Dad told them that he would only publish the training as Poekoelan Tjimindi which is the Indonesian style of martial arts. He agreed to never again mention Chinese in his advertisements. So the name of our school was permanently cemented as the "Beaver

County School for Martial Arts" and the logo was prominently displayed with the words Kenpo and Poekoelan. Since the dragon logo was not necessarily a Chinese symbol it remained a prominent symbol of our school's logo and remains so today. Our training motto for lack of a better term is *"Empty Open Hand"* which simply means that we can and will defend ourselves without the need for any type of weapons.

Over time the art of Kung Fu became a national phenomenon and accepted for public consumption by the Chinese. Bruce Lee and other movie stars displayed their skills in numerous movies. Everyone wanted to be a karate expert and schools flourished all over the country. Public competitions became the rage and there was a lot of money to be made,

Our reputation grew quickly and widely resulting in new schools opening in East Palestine, Ohio and Wheeling West Virginia. Two schools were opened in the Beaver Valley and some of our graduates were opening schools elsewhere in the country. The $3.00 monthly fee remained the same for many years. Free classes were still offered for those children whose parents could not afford the classes.

The family's public persona caused everyone to believe Dad was the exemplary father to his perfectly dressed, coiffured and behaved children. No one knew what it was like for us at home since we were always extremely well behaved in public? We were just the perfect children!

The private behind-closed-door family persona was a wholly different matter. This private Willy Wetzel also had two distinct and opposing personalities. One was the perfect caring loving and ample provider personality and the other one was the dictatorial abusive and terrifying father and husband. He had different expectations and standards for all of the four children in our family. But Mom suffered the worst of all during the entire marriage until she divorced him.

Mom was the obedient wife who followed two steps behind Dad at all times. Mom either loved Dad or perhaps she was just scared shitless all of their married. The regular beatings seemed to become the norm for her and she seemed to accept them as normal. She often protected us from his blows by stepping between Dad and us as he tried to beat us half to death. Black eyes, bloody noses and body bruises were easily covered with makeup and no one outside the home noticed or showed any concerns when they did.

I was the oldest and expected to always be perfect in whatever I did while being my dad's mirror image. Unknown to me at the time, I had a very low and below average IQ of 109. Additionally, I suffered from a lifelong disorder called dyslexia. I also suffered from severe bowel problems that caused me to mess my pants regularly. I had no control whatsoever and it would occur at the most inopportune time. That made me far from perfect and far from the mirror image Dad expected, but I will say this about him. Whenever the bowel accidents did happen, he would not embarrass me. He would simply pick me up and take me out of sight and clean me up, then hug me with uncharacteristic compassion.

Roy, child number 2, was to be the fighter of the family. He would be the one who could stand on his own and be unchallenged in competition regardless of the sport. Roy became a phenomenal Karate fighter and instructor. Dad and Roy rarely communicated and when they did it would end up in conflict. Dad had his goals for my brother but Roy was a man of his own and not about to cower to Dad's every wish and desire. His extremely high IQ was in excess of 160 which allowed him to do well in school without ever opening a book. His photographic memory maddened me since I had to work extremely hard for minimal grades. Roy never opened a school book for studies. He would open the book to the pages covered in the exams, flip through them literally photographing each page with his incredible mind and then pass the exams. His grades were always good thereby not giving Dad the opening to punish him for bad grades.

Jane, number 3, was the apple in Dad's eyes. He loved her unconditionally and protected her from any physical harm. But, I believe Dad harmed Jane emotionally as a result of the beatings and abuses she witnessed being inflicted on her brothers and Mom. We all dreaded hearing him say "Go get my belt or bamboo switch!"

Jim was the only child born in Holland. We all loved and took care of Jimmy but, from my personla observation, Dad seemed to ignore that he even existed. All that seemed to matter was that Jimmy was out of Dad's sight. I never ever heard Jimmy call him Dad, Daddy or father. To this very day Jim refers to him as Willy.

Beatings never resulted in tears from Roy, Jimmy or me when we received the harshest treatments. Shed tears came only came from me as I watched Roy or Jimmy being beaten. To this day I find myself shedding tears, even as I write this, for just remembering them receiving the beatings.

Life at home began to suffer more as the success of the school grew. Dad cintinued to cheat on Mom, and it is during this time that the physical abuses towards Mom accelerated culminating in their divorce. Dad could not leave it there though and arranged for Mom to be fired permanently at Westinghouse. Mom was destitute and we had to move into a housing complex collecting welfare in Vanport, PA. To make things worse Dad bought a house close to our poor housing apartment and moved there with his new wife. Velveeta cheese and dried milk and beans became our staple foods. Life was hard and almost unbearable for all of us. But it seemed to be worse for me as I became the butt of cruel taunts by my brothers. They equated me with Dad since I looked so much like him and inherited many of his mannerisms. Mom started telling me time and time again that I was too much like Dad and that I should move in with him. Dad used me as a go between with mom and brothers. I felt like a human ping pong ball.

At 15 years of age, I got a job at the Beaver County Humane Society. I loved the animals and the job, and dove into it with a passion and dedication I had never experienced before. We had dogs as pets when I was a kid, but Dad never liked them. They didn't like him either. They would growl or run in hiding whenever he came anywhere near them. Being around the animals made the job at the Humane Society enjoyable enough, but what made it even better was the fact that I was deeply in love with the manager's daughter. Her name was Marilyn but went by the nickname of Penney. Here nickname for me was Wimpy and I loved it. Penney would save my life one day and her Mother would be my salvation one day as well.

My Mother, Hermina Gerritje Nyland (Gerry) Wetzel
Watching Over My Siblings and Me

Mom's Idea of a Fashion Statement

CHAPTER TWO
Honoring a WWII Heroine
Hermina Gerritje Nyland (Gerry Wetzel)
January 25, 1928 - April 6, 2009

My mother was born in Jokjakarta, Indonesia. She had 4 sisters and 2 brothers. She was the second born daughter, a beautiful and striking red head who was tough as nails. Mom suffered through over four years in a Japanese concentration camp, spousal abuse throughout a 16 year marriage to Dad, 11 years of near poverty conditions – six of which trying to raise 4 children on welfare cheese, beans and dried milk. She had an infectious laugh and her favorite saying in stilted Dutch/English slang was "You don't want to get on my shithouse!" She always forgot the term as "shit list." Dad trained her well to always follow him by at least two steps. Even until the end of her life and through her second marriage Mom followed her men by at least two paces. It infuriated me when she did that to me and I always made it a point to walk beside or behind her.

The following information was given to me in her hand written letter which she penned before passing away in 2009. It is provided here verbatim.

World War II broke out and the Dutch tried to maintain the islands. A sizable group of Indonesians were demanding complete freedom from Dutch control. The Japs (sic) attacked in early 1942 and the Dutch army collapsed. Before long the Japs were in full control of the islands.

During the entire war the Indonesian rebels under the leadership of Sukarno collaborated with the Japanese to obtain their freedom and independence. After the Japs surrendered in 1945 Sukarno claimed control and claimed the new nation of the Republic of Indonesia. He gained control over a large part of Java and Sumatra. Allied troops consisting mostly of British India moved in to protect the Dutch population. The Dutch Nationalists resisted and a civil war erupted until November of 1946.

Dutch and Indonesian leaders tried to reach an agreement on the future government of the islands. Major disagreements continued and the civil war reignited. On August 4, 1946 both sides called a cease fire but Indonesian independence was not recognized until late 1949.

Mom's parents were born in Holland. My grandmother Antonia Johanna Wilhelmina Kok was born on November 8, 1901 in Diepeveen, Holland. She died of breast cancer on July 15, 1937. My grandfather Herman Nyland was born on December 14, 1897 and passed away from a heart attack in Holland on January 22, 1982. Mom flew to Holland to arrange for his funeral and to settle his affairs. While packing his belongings and cleaning out his closets, she discovered $25,000.00 in American currency in a shoe box; a point of interest that indicates how frugal he was during his entire life. It is important to note that he ate very little but always had cash in reserve in case of another war. He was a policeman in Holland before being transferred to Joc Jakarta, Indonesia in1926 as the head police commissioner and inspector of police. Every two years he moved his family as he continued to be promoted. He held senior police commissioner positions in Semarang, Java, Samarinda, Borneo, Makasan, Celebes and Holland. The family returned to Holland n 1932. Grandfather was again promoted to Chief Police Commissioner and transferred to Bandung, Indonesia. They lived there until WWII broke out.

The Japanese slowly infiltrated the islands by setting up small shops similar to 5 and 10 cent stores. No one knows how they smuggled weapons into the islands but the stores served as covers for storing them. Once war broke out the Dutch army collapsed in three months. Dutch soldiers were put into POW camps in Borneo, Siam, and Cambodia as well as throughout the Indonesian islands. Most were put on slave labor gangs to build roads and bridges.

Grandfather formed an underground organization and set up a radio station in his attic. He stored ammunition and guns in their water wells. Police motorcycles were dismantled and parts hidden throughout the plantation. His new Indonesian wife was afraid of the Japanese Gestapo or Kam Pai Dai (sic). She turned him in to the secret police and he along with 5 of his underground leaders were picked up and jailed. All of them were tortured and the Japs broke grandfather's back. The only reason the Japs did not kill him was because of his high level position in the police forces. He suffered with severe pain for the rest of his life because his captors refused to treat him. His wife committed bigamy and married an Indonesian man to hide in plain sight of the Japanese. Being married to a Dutch citizen as an Indonesian caused anyone to be considered as Dutch. All Dutch citizens were imprisoned. Thereby remarrying an Indonesian prevented her from being incarcerated.

Mom's oldest sister Leida (17) was picked up and shipped to Semarang, Java. Mom at the age of 12 was left to care for her 2 brothers and three sisters. Struggling to stay alive and always hungry Mom and the eldest Brother Hank (9 years old) sold all their belongings. Their stepmother told the Japs where my mom and her siblings were hiding and that they were alone. The Japs picked them up and handed them over to the Kam Pai Dai or secret police. They were all put into a concentration camp where they remained until the end of the war.

Life in the Concentration Camp was Routine:

1. 6 am the prisoners were required to honor the Rising Sun flag ceremony.

2. Exercise for 30 minutes

3. Work in the fields, compound and kitchens

4. Complete daily Japanese language classes

5. Attend church services as long as they were held in Indonesian or Japanese languages.

6. Bow to every Jap in a specific way. If the bow was unsatisfactory the prisoner received vicious beatings.

7. Breakfast consisted of a half cup of corn or sweet potato.

8. Lunch and dinner when provided consisted of 1 cup of cooked rice and leaves boiled in water. Sometimes 1 up of soya beans were offered.

During the entire time in concentration camp no one was given meat, sugar, butter, bread, coffee, candy or pop. The favorite pastime was talking about food and making up recipes.

There were no cats or dogs anywhere in camp. Stray animals were quickly dispatched and used as meat sustenance. My uncle Hank searched for snakes, rats, mice, grubs and any other food that could be fed to his siblings. He was assigned the responsibility for taking care of the Japanese livestock – pigs, ducks, chickens and goats. On one occasion when his brother and sisters were extremely malnourished and ill Hank killed a duck. The Japs found out about it because Hank plucked the duck on his way back to the tent where they lived. They simply followed the plucked feathers and found Hank with blood on his hands. They initially put him in a cage for 24 hours. He somehow escaped but was recaptured and put into a secure jail. He was beaten nearly to death and given electrical shock treatments with electrical wires attached to his ears, wrists and ankles.

The guards provided a small bar of soap that the children were required to use for bathing, washing clothes and washing their hair.

Coconut husks were provided for use as toothbrushes but toothpaste was not provided. Prisoners crushed rust particles into a fine dust then mixed with water to serve as toothpaste. After the war Mom suffered with severe tooth aches until we moved to America where she had all her teeth removed.

Japanese soldiers started to search all of the camps for women and girls to serve as comfort women for the soldiers. The school teachers hid Mom and her sisters when it was possible. When it was not possible to hide them they were taught to behave as if they were mentally ill. Their clothes were muddied and their bodies and hair were soiled with feces and soil. Because they fooled their captors so well, they were never forced to become comfort women.

Even though the war ended in 1945 the captives in all the concentration camps were not released until 1946. Allied aircraft dropped food and supplies into the camps regularly. Many of the prisoners overate from sheer hunger and died. My family was not permitted to leave the camps until relatives were found and claimed them. Eventually my Grandfather discovered their location and had them released. But it was not safe outside the camps either since the rebels fighting for independence were in full revolt. They killed every foreign national, especially the Dutch citizens that they could find.

Two teachers in the camp taught my mother and her sisters all they needed to pass their high school examinations. After their release they all completed their high school graduation exams.

Mom met Dad through one of his previous girlfriends, Lucy Hoff, at an Air Force dance. Dad was a recently released Army sergeant who was constantly moved to various Army posts to include Bandung, Semarang, Surabaya, Malang, Lumadijong and Jakarta. The family was always restricted to the camps for their protection. When it was decided to evacuate the Dutch nationals from Indonesia they were escorted to their boats by tanks and other heavily armored vehicles.

The boat trip to Holland lasted for 35 days. The trip transited the Java Sea, Milaca Straits, Bay of Bengal, Indonesian Ocean, Arabian Sea, Gulf of Aden, Red Sea, Suez Canal, Mediterranean Sea, Atlantic Ocean and the North Sea to Rotterdam Holland.

There were no provisions for babies and children. No milk or food was available and 3/4ths of the babies died enroute. Mom told me that I was always hungry and craved food even throughout my youth in Holland and America.

Adjusting to Holland was very hard on us all. The climate was cold and wet and the clothing was hard to get used to and the food was very different and bland.

Dad and Wim on the boat leaving Indonesia

In 1956 President Eisenhower opened a program to allow several thousands of Europeans to immigrate to America. Displaced persons, such as the Dutch Indonesians, were given special consideration. Dad applied immediately and we were accepted. I distinctly remember that the number one song on all the Dutch radio stations was "The Yellow Rose of Texas." It is still my all-time favorite song.

Mom and Dad in a Military Photo in Holland

CHAPTER THREE
The Enigma

The Womanizer

From a very early age, Dad loved and bedded many women. His sexual prowess and reputation in the bedroom carried with him throughout his life in Indonesia, Holland and the United States. How do I know? Some of those women told me so as he handed them off to me in my post high school years.

One of my aunts once told me quite forthrightly that if you have the Wetzel name, then you are a womanizer and have mistresses. The comment offended me as she made it in the presence of my second wife Zee. Unfortunately Zee believed my aunt and developed a significant mistrust towards me from that time forward.

A typical scenario where a handoff from Dad would occur is when I would come home for the weekend from Langley AFB, Dover AFB or McGuire AFB. All east coast bases were close to home. I typically arrived home for the weekends by 10 or 11 pm on Fridays. Dad would hand me a telephone number with a name and tell me to call the number when I arrived home. Sometimes I would and other times I would just ignore the request.

Whenever I did call I would make the decision to meet the woman or not based on the content of the conversations. When I did decide to meet them they would inevitably tell me about Dad and his prowess in the bedroom. Try living up to those standards as a young man. I took up the challenges and seemed to be successful since there were no complaints – at least towards me directly.

The User/Abuser

Dad made acquaintances easily; especially if someone could help him in any way. Notice that I did not say friends. If he needed help with anything he would find someone with the skills to do so and "befriend" them. Some of those relationships lasted for the remainder of his life while others went by the wayside after their usefulness to him ended. Those brainwashed students who stayed with him remained loyal to him until the end. One of his student "friends" even testified at Roy's murder trial that if "Willy wanted to kill someone he had the right to do so!"

Loyalty to Dad was always returned. He did so by putting his selected loyal followers into a small contingent of well-trained instructors. They became his private army of highly trained experts in Karate, in particular Jujitsu and Poekoelan. These men and women became his top black belt students and instructors who almost unanimously stayed with Dad to the end. In their eyes, hearts and souls Dad could do nothing wrong.

The karate school in New Brighton had taken off like gang busters. Dad was away from home more often since he also worked at Westinghouse. The only time we really saw him was when we were attending Karate classes or teaching Karate at the school. Since the beatings had come to a literal halt, we preferred it that way. The less we saw of him, the better it was for all of us.

The Master Teacher

Although I have painted a very bleak and unflattering picture of Dad in this writing, he also had great traits that I wanted to emulate in my life. Dad had the characteristics of a good father in the way he provided for the family. I chose to keep that trait. Dad was a great teacher in all things. I became a good teacher and some have told me I am a great teacher. Dad went straight to the point about his feelings and always told it the way he saw it at the time. I wear my emotions openly and those who know me will tell you I am a straight shooter. He taught me three key rules to live by to be successful.

1. Don't ask – don't get.

2. Volunteer for every dirty nasty job that no one else wants.

3. Be true to your word regardless of the consequences.

Characteristics that I knowingly chose to not accept are very clear. Watching Mom be beaten regularly made me choose never to beat or touch a woman in anything but in gentle and loving way. Friends to Dad were tools to be used for his own needs and desires. I have very few friends but they are not tools to be used for my own goals. I give and gave more to my friends and acquaintances than I have ever expected to receive in return. Dad had a public and a private persona. I am who you see every day whether in private or public.

Dad was a product of his upbringing and an abusive father who was abused by his father, and his father by his father, as far back as one can go.

I chose to break that cycle early on in my life and have lived a life true to myself, my first wife, my second wife Zee of 31 years until her death, and my current wife Vikie. I've not done so badly in the long term. The good traits Dad gave me in life have offset the bad ones. I am thankful for them and yes, I loved him, and still do.

To live is to suffer. To survive

is to find meaning in the suffering

Friedrich Nietzsche

CHAPTER FOUR
Living and Surviving on the Edge

Typhoid Fever in the United States and in 1964? Where did I get it? How? When? Are you absolutely positive? Why me? All of these and many more questions I would ask for several weeks to come while hospitalized in ICU for over 30 days. However, the knowledge that I ultimately survived one of man's deadliest diseases would not really dawn on me for several years to come. After all, there had not been a proven documented case of Typhoid in Pennsylvania since 1956. Then how could it be possible for me to contract this deadly malady in the USA during the sixty's? My only answer at the time was that for whatever reason – I deserved it! I ultimately found the answer, but before getting there, we must get some background information to make sense of all this.

Five years had passed since Mom and Dad divorced. The divorce was a stormy and nasty affair for all of us and especially for Mom. She suffered beatings that would have put any woman in the hospital but after all, Mom survived the Japanese internment camp. See the chapter about Mom elsewhere in this book. What was a beating from Dad now and then going to do to break her strength and survival spirit? Mom stepped in many times to receive the angry blows directed to Roy, Jim and me. Those actions only caused the anger within Dad to multiply and the blows became harsher. If his open hand blows did not satisfy him then any available object such as a belt, stick or bamboo reed would do.

We were poor and on welfare. We had plenty of Velveeta cheese to eat and milk powder to mix for milk since that is what the welfare food stamps primarily consisted off. The biggest problem was we could not eat or drink any of it since we were all lactose intolerant. Our diet consisted primarily of peanut butter and jelly sandwiches.

Racism

We had to move from our New Brighton home to a low income housing development in Van Port, PA. 50 "L" Street, our new home, was located on a turnabout at the end of the street. "L" street residents were a mixed minority lot. We were all poor, but it did not stop us from doing the best with what we had.

One of my neighbors and best friends was Adolph Ellis. He played for the Beaver High School Bobcats football team. Adolph, an African American, did not care where you were from or what color of skin you sported. God help you if you referred to him as an "N" word. One of our neighbor's teenage boys made that mistake and Adolph knocked him down, sat on his chest and pissed in his face. No one ever referred to him with that word again. Years later, Adolph was killed by a "Bouncing Betty" land mine at Dak To, RVN where I was assigned to support his unit. His combat buddies told me about his death the day after it happened. War really came home for me that day.

Our neighborhood in Van Buren Homes was eclectic in the various races and nationalities that lived there. Ours was the only Asian family and probably the only one that ever did live in the neighborhood. Even though we were Dutch-Indonesian and my mom was obviously Caucasian, with blond hair, her four children looked very Asian. Our neighborhood was at the end of a street that had many black families and our immediate neighbors were Italian. It was a rough neighborhood for us. For the first couple of months, I was beaten up quite badly on several occasions by some of the then racist kids in the "hood." Then, on one particular day, I came home very badly beaten, literally to a pulp. Both my eyes were bruised badly and my nose was bleeding profusely. Dad happened to be at the house when I walked in. He asked me what happened. After explaining that three boys had beaten me and called me a gook and other names, Dad cleaned me up. He called Roy and had us go to our small back yard where he taught us our first lessons in self-defense. His lessons were very specific in how to immediately disable an attacker. He spent a couple of hours making sure when we were done that day that we would never have to suffer beatings again. The one fighting rule that he insisted on, and I have followed that rule whenever a physical confrontation forced a response, "Do everything to avoid a fight, but when you are forced to fight, do so with a minimum of three

Roy Wetzel

targeted blows or strikes to your opponent."

The next day Roy and I went hunting for the boys that had beaten me up. It did not take long before finding them roughing up a black kid. Roy kicked one kid in the family jewels. The little punk screamed in pain grabbing himself and falling to his knees. Strike two was a hard slap to the face, followed by a punch to the sternum. I tripped my opponent as he tried to get away and jumped on his back and pummeled him with my small fists until he yelled, "I give up!" The third kid left the scene as soon as he saw his buddy go down, writhing in pain. Our reputation as the "Wetzel Boys" was firmly cemented in the neighborhood that day.

After that event we started Karate lessons and ultimately taught the art of self-defense at our family's schools. We gave numerous public demonstrations at shopping malls, television shows, Beaver High School and other public events.

The second time racism struck my family, was when I had a job as a lifeguard at the New Brighton municipal swimming pool. I had the job for about two months, when my cousin, Johnny Budding, from Dayton, OH came to visit us. Johnny had a very dark complexion; almost black in appearance. Some of my friends believed him to be African American. One day I asked him to come to the pool to swim, because the summer heat was sweltering and miserable. John came and was swimming for a while when the pool manager came over to me. He said; "How did that nigger get into our pool?"

My response was, "He's not a nigger, he's my cousin and I invited him to go swimming."

Without a second of hesitation the racist city official responded with: "If he is a nigger and he is your cousin then you are a nigger too. You are fired. And get your asses out of my pool!"

The third time I experienced racism was at the age of 17. I met a girl by the name of Rosemary or "Ree," at the Rollerena in East Palestine,

OH. She was a bit taller than me by at least 4 inches, but we hit it off immediately. Her father owned a prominent jewelry store in town and was well known in the community. I asked Ree for a date and when she accepted, we arranged for me to pick her up at her home the following evening. On date night I knocked on their front door, located in a ritzy neighborhood. Her mother answered, looked me over, and said: "Who are you and what do you want?"

"My name is Wim and I'm here to pick Ree up for our date!"

Her answer was cold-blooded and immediate. "We don't allow interracial relationships or marriages in our family. You can't see Ree, don't ever come back here again!" She slammed the door in my face.

Ree and I continued to date without her parents knowing for a few months, until one really bad winter day. It had been snowing several days, and the snow plows had created several high piles of snow that froze to chunks of solid ice which covered the Rollerena parking lot. Ree and I had spoken by phone and arranged to meet for a short date, for a burger in town. I was standing outside the building entryway when I saw Ree in her dad's brand new black Cadillac coming at a high speed towards me. She did not see the snow and ice chunks, as she crossed from the road onto the parking lot.

Ree pulled up and I got into the car. As she started to leave the parking lot I noticed that her engine oil light was on and commented to her that it should not be. I asked her how long it had been lit but she did not know. "Let's go!" she said and left the parking lot. Just a few hundred feet down the road, in a blowing blizzard, the engine coughed, sputtered and died. She had hit a huge chunk of ice at the base of the oil pan as she entered the Rollerena parking lot, causing all of the oil to drain onto the ground.

I asked her to stay in the car to keep her out of the bad weather, while I walked back to the Rollerena to make a fateful call to her dad. I told him that Ree was stuck on the highway and needed his help to get it towed. About ten minutes passed when he pulled up to the building to pick me up and take him to his daughter. He asked who I was and how I came to know about the car. I told him and received absolutely no response. We pulled up behind the Cadillac, and both got out. He went directly to Ree, opened the door and told her to get into his car. They left me standing there in total darkness and blowing snow. I never saw Ree again.

First Love

Van Port is where my life took an even more terrible turn that would ultimately and inexplicably mold me into the man I am today. I met and fell in love at the tender age of twelve with Marilyn "Penny" Krepps.

It was an unplanned and fortuitous incident on the school bus that allowed me to meet Penny. I was late in getting to the bus and all of the seats were full except one seat next to this absolutely gorgeous girl. Being extremely shy it was hard for me to ask if I could sit next to her. Penny evidently realized my discomfort and asked me to sit next to her. I promptly did and from that moment on for the next six years we were almost inseparable. The best part was that she lived within close walking distance of my house. On many occasions we walked home together rather than take the bus so that we could be with each other longer. I had found the "happy place" I so longed for in my tumultuous life and the possibilities for happiness in my life were now endless.

Penny was the first girl I ever kissed and I did it while I was sitting on my bicycle and she was sitting on her porch. I was so stunned that she kissed me back that I promptly fell off my bike. Soon after that Penny nicknamed me Wimpy. A name that only she could and would use for the remaining years we knew one another.

During this time, things at home were getting worse every day. Mom and my brothers and sister were so angry with Dad that they seemed to take out their rage and frustrations on me. It appeared that being the oldest son was reason enough to take revenge on me for Dad's transgressions. Whether it was intentional by my parents or not I was being used as a tool. I found out quickly what it was like to be a ping pong ball; bouncing back and forth between two hard and unrelenting wooden paddles, forever going back and forth. Unknown to me at the time I was being used as a whipping boy by both of them to satisfy and serve their cruel punishment on each other.

For six months I would live with Mom and then with Dad. And so it progressed, getting ever worse for five of the longest and most painful years of my youth. The results were always the same regardless of who I lived with. Penney was always there to help lessen the pain and misery. I would and could not have survived my teenage years if it had not been because of this wonderful and beautiful young lady.

Mom would say, "You're just like your Dad; you look like him, sound like him, act like him and even have the same thoughts. Sometimes I wish you were dead!"

Dad would counter by saying, "You are soft. No guts and all you can do is cry. You're a weakling like your mother. Why don't you go live with her?" He did not realize it but I only cried when he punished Mom and the other children and I never shed a tear when he wreaked punishment upon me.

As a direct consequence of this daily parental treatment, other things in my life were directly affected. My school work reflected my misery the most. Where I was a bright but slow learning student who worked extra hard for his grades, I was now getting Ds and Fs. With the wonderful exception of Penny, my moodiness caused many of my friends to stay away from me. Penny, God love her, understood what was happening to me and unknown to either one of us at that time; she would be instrumental in saving my life in the not-too-distant future.

As 1964 summer vacation began the misery at home become more unbearable since there was no escaping it. Thoughts of suicide crossed my mind all too frequently and the cacophony of overwhelming and mixed emotions served to confuse my mind even more. On one occasion I actually started to drive off a cliff overlooking my home town but stopped in time to ponder why. To avoid staying at home as much as possible I searched for a part time job.

I moved in with Dad hoping that things would change for the better. Dad had a friend and Karate student who owned a lawn mower repair business in Bridgewater and asked him to hire me part time. The owner agreed and allowed me to start work immediately. Since I was not and am still not mechanically inclined the job was frustrating but it served to keep me busy and allowed me to focus on learning how to fix small engines.

Then for an inexplicable reason that is unknown to me to this day Dad had me fired from the job. The owner could or would not look at me as he told me not to return to work. No reason was given for the termination but subtle comments from Dad about his dissatisfaction with me regarding other family matters led me to believe that he was behind the termination. Soon after the termination he asked me to move out and back to Mom's house.

Moving back to Mom's was the worst possible thing that I could have done. My brothers and sister let me know that I was not welcome there and started once again comparing me to Dad. Then the name-calling began making things even worse. My hair was very unruly and unmanageable during those days. The bangs fell naturally into a position that made me look a little like Hitler. Thereby that became my new nickname from my siblings and they used it rather often to ridicule me. I had an uncontrollable cow lick at the back of my head that made me look exactly like Alfalfa. It was great fodder for other cruel taunts and jokes at my expense.

Penny's Mom was the manager of the Beaver County Humane Society and offered me a job. My passion for the work was over the top and it was a natural fit that gave me a reason to keep going. No one could ever have taken better care of the animals under my charge. Additionally I rationalized at the time that at least the animals would accept me and that all they could ever do to hurt me was to bite or scratch. Those wounds will always heal.

My work days began at 4:30 am seven days a week. Each day lasted as long as I desired so it was a rare occasion when I would return to Mom's house before midnight each day. To my tortured mind the kennels were my true home and the animals were my family.

My dedication to the work at the Humane Society was unchallenged. My friends' cages were spotlessly cleaned and sanitized. To be absolutely certain of that I would crawl, with brush in hand, into each cage to thoroughly clean them. The toxic mixture of Clorox and Pine Sol did not help to make me feel better but it served to clean the cages. Unknown to me at the time I was slowly being poisoned by the cleaning mixtures in the closed confinement of the cages. Animal feces and urine stained my work clothes and every part of my exposed skin. Breathing in the toxic fumes and the animal defecation odors did not deter me. It did not matter whatsoever because I absolutely did not care. Relentlessly and with undying energy; I cleaned!

I missed regular meals but would now and then nibble on dry dog food to stem the hunger pangs. After a week or so the hunger pains disappeared and the thought of eating no longer crossed my mind. Over the first month I lost about twenty pounds from my already low weight of 108 pounds. Mom believed me when I told her that I was eating at the kennels with the manager and other employees. She did not question, or I doubt, noticed the significant weight loss. The Humane Society manager took it for granted that I was brown bagging my lunch. Only if she would have known that it was the same brown bag that I had been taking to work with me for weeks.

One Sunday afternoon, early in September – it struck me like a bold of lightning! Penny and I were watching television at her house. I was very hungry so she made me a bacon-lettuce-tomato sandwich. I took one bite when my body became wracked with unending waves of nausea and painful vomiting. Since my stomach held no appreciable amount of food I was struck by dry heaves and unbearable cramping pains. Then the vomiting ended as quickly as it began.

I was cold—Oh so cold! My body shook uncontrollably and relentlessly. Penny covered me with a blanket only to have me rip it away as beads of perspiration rolled from my forehead into my eyes. So it went for several hours; first hot then cold! Penny tried to take me home but I refused to go there. Her mother returned home at 5 pm and realizing how sick I was she immediately took me to Mom's house.

At home I was met with looks of disgust and anger from Mom. "Where have you been? You missed supper!"

"Mom, I don't feel very good!"

"Then go take a bath and go to bed!" she retorted with extreme anger.

As I climbed the stairway to the second floor bathroom I fainted and tumbled back down to the hallway. Only God and my family members know how long I laid there before regaining consciousness. When I did recover they were all watching television and Mom was still at the kitchen table. They believed that I had been faking the illness and had chosen to ignore my fall. I crawled back up the stairs, into the bedroom and fell into my bunk bed.

I awoke Monday morning with a high fever and unable to move to get dressed for school. Mom refused to believe that I was really sick and attempted to force me to get up to go to school. I was too weak to budge and she finally gave up and went to work. As the day wore on my mind lapsed into and out of total consciousness. It was as if my mind was no longer a part of or in control of my body.

Penny dropped by the house after school to bring my homework and Mom met her at the door. "Wim's upstairs in bed, still pretending that he is sick."

"But Mrs. Wetzel, he's not pretending. I want to go up to see him." With that said, she rushed past my mother and ran up the stairs.

"How are you feeling?"

I mumbled "Not very well!"

"I'm going to take your temperature because you're burning up."

The thermometer registered 106 degrees. "My God! Mrs. Wetzel, come here!"

"What now?"

"Look at this temperature and tell me again that he is not sick!"

For the first time my mother realized that there was indeed something wrong with me. She cried hysterically and hugged me, but to my burning brain it was just too late and I pushed her away. I fell into unconsciousness and remained that way for three days. Penney told Mom that if she did not take me to a doctor then she would get her mother to do it. Mom relented and took me to Dr. Tom Jones who immediately had me admitted to Beaver County General Hospital and put into isolation.

Beaver County General Hospital was to be my new home for over thirty days. Ice packs, ice baths and God only knows what other methods were used to bring my temperature under control. The fever reached its peak at 106.6 degrees before it fell. The medical diagnosis was Typhoid Fever. The doctors concluded that I had contracted Typhoid from an environment that was rare to humans. Due to my weakened body state because of inadequate nutrition over several months I had become exceedingly susceptible to picking up any kind of disease.

Anyone who came into my hospital room including the doctors and nurses had to wear protective masks and covers. The doctor excluded Penny because she had spent the many hours and days by my side and showed no symptoms of the disease. Mom entered my room when I was no longer in critical condition and I told her that I never wanted to see her again. She tried to make amends by visiting each day, but it made no difference to me anymore. I just did not care to ever see her again!

But I did; after thirty days and the loss of thirty pounds in the hospital, I returned home.

Upon returning home, the cruel taunts and comments from Mom and my brothers resumed. I was in such a weakened state that I had to crawl up the stairs to my bedroom and the upper bunk bed. How ironic! Typhoid, as deadly as it is, was my salvation for a brief period in my life. My safe place: the Beaver County General Hospital. After two or three days back home, I made the decision to run away or kill myself. Either option was preferable to my life's condition at the time. I waited for Mom to go to work and the kids to go to school the next morning. When I was certain that no one was home, I crawled down the water spout between the apartments in our building and broke into the empty apartment next door. I passed out for a while before leaving the apartment and walking to the Humane Society offices.

Mrs. Bryner looked at me and panicked. I must have looked like Hell. I told her very clearly that I was turning myself into the Humane Society and was never going home again. I would kill myself first. After telling her what had prompted my situation and why I was so unhappy, she promised me that no one would ever hurt me again. She took on the crusade to resolve the problems and took drastic actions that literally saved my life.

After putting me to bed, she asked me to wait for her return. Without my knowledge, she met with my Dad and read him the riot act. Without mincing words she told him what happened and that, if he did not resolve this problem, she would take legal action against him and mom to remove me to foster care. Dad did not hesitate to admit his contributions to the situation and promised to take me in and take care of me. He committed to never mistreating me again. Dad was good to his word and I moved in with him and my stepmother until I graduated and left for my 24 year Air Force career.

My stepmother made every effort to make me feel at home. Every morning she would insist that I have breakfast before going to school. To keep it simple in an effort not to burden her I always asked for oatmeal. That is what I ate almost every morning until I left home permanently. I avoided eating oatmeal for the rest of my life until recently.

For the remainder of my teen years and until I joined the Air Force life was fairly stable and normal. There were periods of major depression with thoughts of suicide now and then. Penney kept me grounded until her Mom got a job in Port Jarvis New York and they moved. Penney was such a beautiful person in body, mind and soul that she was selected as Miss Port Jarvis soon after moving there.

A couple of days after they left the Valley I again drove my car to a cliff overlooking my home town. I sat there for hours feeling a sense of loss and grief that were overpowering. I decided to end my life and backed the car up so that I could race over the edge to oblivion. I took a running start, but again stopped near the edge for reasons that I do not comprehend to this day. It did occur to me that there had to be something better in life than the pain and misery I and the rest of my family had suffered for so many years. I decided to live!

Wim Leading the March

CHAPTER FIVE
The Great Escape
Basic Training - Summer 1966

Mom had already taken the oath of citizenship a few years earlier allowing all of her children to become citizens automatically. However I would have nothing to do with automatic citizenship because I was going to do it my way and at the expense of my own efforts I already knew that on the same day that I became a citizen I would be eligible to enlist in the United States Air Force.

It was the "Ides of March" 1966. Julius Caesar was said to have been assassinated on this date in 44 B.C. by followers of Cassius and Brutus. Mr. George Wildman, my Explorer Post 488 scout master, my inspiration, mentor and friend, was my witness and sponsor for the oath of citizenship ceremonies. I drove to the Beaver County Courthouse and along with several other immigrants took the final oral exam given by the judge. With tears on my face and pride in my heart I swore the Oath of Allegiance as a brand new minted citizen of America. It was and always will be the proudest day of my life. American citizenship was my goal since first laying eyes on the Statue of Liberty as we sailed into New York harbor on the SS Waterman in 1956.

Why does the Ides of March stand out for me? It represents the day that I decided to take charge of my life and to get the heck out of my miserable no positive future existence for my life in PA. It was the best decision I ever made and have never looked back. Without another thought I drove to Beaver Falls to the military recruiting office and joined the Air Force on the delayed enlistment program. On June 10th Dad drove me to the Greyhound bus station and dropped me off. I got my freedom wings and flew out of the nest never to go back.

Everyone who knows me has no doubt where I stand regarding the honor of being a citizen of this great country. They also know that I do not and never will support illegal immigration. In my humble opinion, accepting illegal immigrants equates to insulting and denigrating all of those properly naturalized immigrants who became citizens legally following the law.

I am unabashedly loyal to our country and proudly show it in many ways. The flag flies high over my home every day and I smile with pride every time I see it there and in public. I still choke up when I hear the Star Spangled Banner or repeat the Pledge of Allegiance. Many businesses who have allowed their flags to fly in a torn, faded or other inappropriate state received a personal visit, phone call or letter from me reminding them that they should purchase a new flag and to destroy the existing flag in the appropriate manner. If they do not know how I will accept the flag and properly destroy it or give it to a local Boy Scout troop to ceremoniously do it.

Dad was against me enlisting because he wanted me to go to college to become an Industrial Engineer. Since he believed he could not achieve his own dream to become an engineer he set that goal for me contrary to what I wanted to do with my life. I could never make Dad understand that I had learning problems which prevented me from ever being what he wanted me to be. I fully believed that at the time, but time would prove me wrong. As it turned out, I can do about anything I set my mind to.

My dyslexia, which was not diagnosed in those days, would only to serve as a slight impediment or wall for me to deal with in my own way. Yes I could have become an Industrial Engineer but it was not on my radar screen as something to do with my life. My High School counselor had even said that I should not expect to achieve much in life nor to expect to ever be accepted in any college. She was wrong. Two weeks after entering Air Force basic training I received my acceptance letter from Penn State University. I showed it to by drill instructor who advised me that it could be used for me to get discharged immediately and would be my ticket out of Viet Nam. However, I had already made my life's career decision and ignored the letter. Only God knows what my life would have been like if I had accepted the discharge and gone on to college.

At 7:00 am on June 10th Dad drove me to the Greyhound bus stop in New Brighton. He did not say much but clearly indicated his dissatisfaction with my ignoring his wishes before driving away without even saying goodbye.

The induction physical was almost a disaster ending any hopes I harbored for enlisting. I passed every phase including the notorious finger wave and "Turn your head and cough!" instructions that everyone had to endure. The mix of new recruit candidates was something to behold. Guys who had been drafted came in dressed and made up like women to get disqualified. Some blatantly flirted with the medics hoping to be disqualified due to their gender choices. Others behaved in a way to indicate they were mentally handicapped, psychotic or anti-social. You imagine it and someone used it in a futile attempt to get out of the draft. The voluntary recruits just grinned, laughed openly or just ignored this weird behavior.

It was my time to be examined by the doctor who would make the final decision of my fitness to go to Air Force Basic Training. All went well until he said "Stand straight up with both feet flat on the ground as if you were at attention!" I did as directed. "You have flat feet young man. I cannot qualify you to enter the military. You will have to go home as an "4F" (unqualified for military service)."

"No sir I am not flat footed!" I stated adamantly. "Please check again?"

"Are you questioning my judgment?"

"No sir but I am not flat footed!"

The doctor checked again and repeated his diagnosis. "Yup - you are flat footed!"

Since we were in a room with many recruits and military medics I asked for permission to speak with the doctor in private. He consented and we entered a small secluded cubicle.

"Doctor I just became a citizen of the United States and I want to serve my country to repay it for what it has done for my family and me. Please do not write me up as being flat footed and destroy all of the dreams and hopes I have had to serve." I told him how my parents were Japanese POWs and that American soldiers had released them from the camps.

He was apparently convinced of my sincerity towards enlisting and serving, and said, "In that case let me check again. Curl your toes inward a bit as if you are trying to pick something up from the floor with them. Yes you are right! I misdiagnosed you initially and you are not flat footed! Please get dressed and move on to the Oath of Enlistment room and ceremony."

After getting dressed and about to enter the enlistment ceremony, the doctor pulled me aside. "Young man I appreciate what you are doing, but understand that there is a reason flat footed men do not serve in uniform. You will suffer greatly during the time you serve and I want you to remember what happened here today."

I thanked him profusely and acknowledged his warning. Boy! was he ever right, as I would discover during the next 24 years. The foot pain was always excruciating, but I never wavered or second guessed my decisions and actions.

My best friend in High School, Larry Welsh, enlisted with me under the Buddy Program and met me at the swearing-in ceremony. The Buddy Program ensured that we would be able to enlist and go to Basic Training together. The recruiters failed to tell us that the Buddy Program did not continue when we graduated from Basic Training. We both took the oath together and could not wait to get on with our new lives.

We were given our written orders to fly to Lackland AFB, TX for Basic Training. Since I was the oldest on the list of new recruits they assigned me the responsibility to keep everyone together on the trip to report to basic. Upon arriving at Pittsburgh International Airport we were notified that due a major outbreak of Spinal Meningitis at Lackland AFB and that the recruits were being sent to Amarillo AFB located in the panhandle of Texas. It was the first time many of us flew on a commercial flight and we were all excited. Those were the days that male passengers still wore suits and ties and women still dressed in pretty dresses. Passengers were all polite and well-behaved in those days and the stewardesses were still all very attractive and highly professional. We flew to St. Louis where we had to stay the night waiting for our flight to Amarillo. Oh what a night that was going to be.

I doubt there were any exceptions but almost everyone in my group had never been so far away from home without parental guidance. We let it all hang out so to speak. Downtown was wide open for the wide-eyed, finally free from family bondage and wildly curious teenage recruits. We all went downtown as a group without knowing we were in the less than acceptable part of town. Burlesque houses and strip joints lined the street.

"Let's go to a strip show!" someone yelled and everyone responded in the affirmative with a "Hell yeah – why not?" We did not have a clue what a strip show looked like but we were about to find out.

We paid the cover charge as we entered a burlesque show instead. All of us were a bit disappointed at first because we did not see any bare "titties." But it became clear soon enough that the show was going to be great. The bawdy jokes and raucous behavior on the stage were beyond anything anyone of us had ever experienced. We laughed so hard it hurt. No one regretted seeing our first burlesque show and all of us would remember the experience years later.

The flight to Amarillo was absolutely horrible. Many of us were sick because of the extreme turbulence and could not wait to land. Upon landing in what appeared to be in the middle of nowhere we wished to be able to turn around, get back on the plane and go home. The place was awful!

An Air Force bus took us directly to the base and into Hell incarnate! Our Drill Instructors (DI) met us and began the ritual torture in preparing us for our new lives and possible careers. But nothing they did fazed me and I got into a lot of trouble over the next three months for laughing or grinning at our various predicaments. Nothing they could throw at us would come near to what Dad had put us through. Our Drill Instructor (DI) asked me directly "Are you having fun yet Boy?" I was later to regret making the offhanded comment "Boy Scout camp was rougher than this!" Because of the comment, extra pushups and latrine duties became the norm for me during basic training.

Our barracks were the old World War II style where anyone could see outside by looking through the spaces between the planks in the walls. They were stifling and without air conditioning. The summer temperatures in the panhandle of Texas routinely exceeded 110 degrees in the shade. Without AC in the barracks they became even more unbearable. But we were alive and still healthy unlike many of the Airmen who had the misfortune of going to Lackland instead.

Basic was over before we could actually realize and we all received our new base and unit assignments and our new job titles and codes. Larry became a welder at Offutt AFB, Nebraska and I was assigned as an Air Freight Specialist at Langley AFB, Virginia. So much for the Buddy Enlistment program and thank you Sergeant Recruiter!

We both received a transfer leave to go home to Pennsylvania before reporting to our new assignments. We received our "Blue Tubes" containing our personnel records and ticket home by train, bus, or plane. Larry and I received train tickets and were taken to the train station in Amarillo. The ride home was extremely long, about two days, and the food was expensive. Since we had no idea of the cost for our meals Larry and I went through what we had very quickly.

We arrived in Chicago for a layover and train change and we did not have a penny between us. We were starving as we wandered aimlessly in down town Chicago in our brand new Air Force uniforms. As we crossed one of the bridges crossing the canals in Chicago a strong gust of wind blew my Air Force wheel hat off my head and it flew gently upside down into the river. As we watched it float away I asked "What else can go wrong Larry?" We both laughed hysterically and I prayed out loud that my recruiter would not see me out of uniform.

We had no place else to go and without any money for food returned to the train station. While walking around the station, our hunger from not eating for most of the day was taking its toll. Drastic times require drastic action, or so I was always told. Dad's rule of "Don't ask, don't get!" got its first chance at being put to the test.

As I looked around the station at the many people rushing to catch their trains I spied what in my mind appeared to be a nice guy who was well dressed. I walked up to him and said "Excuse me Sir, do you have a minute?" Sure, what can I do for you Airman?"

I introduced Larry and myself and bluntly explained our situation and that we needed some help so we could get something to eat for the rest of the trip home. "We realize you don't know who we are but if you can loan us a few bucks for food I promise to repay you with interest as soon as we get home."

He introduced himself as Al (Mark) Payne from Fox River Grove, Illinois and asked how much we needed. Without hesitation he gave us the money and said we do not need to pay him back. We insisted on doing so and asked for his address which he ultimately provided. In good faith I gave him my home address, telephone number and military ID number. Thanks to Al and his generosity in helping two total strangers in need, Larry and I finally were able to eat.

Immediately upon returning home I told Dad what had occurred and he gave me a loan to pay Al back. Al, his family and I stayed in touch through letters for many years. I still remember sending them anniversary cards every year until we finally lost touch. But Al, if you happen to read this, I thank you again for your kindness to two strangers. Your actions affected how I treated strangers and friends for the rest of my life and I am forever grateful.

Military leave at home was good but I could not wait to report to Langley AFB, VA. The trip again to my first assignment was by Greyhound and I arrived at Hampton, Virginia at the terrible time of midnight. There was no way to get to the base except to hitchhike.

Upon arriving at the base the Security Police directed me to the Air Freight terminal and told me to report to the Charge of Quarters (CQ). I did so and the CQ promptly told me to throw by duffle bag into the corner and go to sleep. There was no place to eat and again I was extremely hungry from the bus trip and hiking to the base. Then, and throughout my career, it seemed that I was always hungry.

A Tech Sergeant happened to be making the rounds and found me in the corner and asked what I was doing there. I told him and asked "Is there anything to eat around here? I'm starving!" He told me to get up, grab my bag and to follow him. He took me to a small room containing a cot and told me to crash there. "It's my rack he said but I won't need it again tonight. I'll be back soon with something for you to eat."

A half hour passed and he returned with a plate of something I had never seen before and it looked less than inviting. "Eat, get some sleep Airman and report to me at "oh eight hundred." I am your new boss and my name is Tech Sergeant Avery."He left and I gingerly ate the strange concoction on my mess plate before throwing it up in the trashcan. I was just introduced to my first Air Force breakfast of "Shit on a Shingle" for the first and last time in my Air Force career.

Processing into a new assignment in those days was a lengthy affair that often lasted two weeks or longer. New recruits made less than $100 per month. One of the first things we did, was set up our pay and allowances to include any allotments for family members or debts like car payments. I set up an allotment for half my monthly pay to be sent to Mom. That allotment remained in effect for my first four years in the Air

Force. I cancelled it in 1970 when I discovered that Mom was using the money for cigarettes and alcohol, while her refrigerator remained empty.

I restocked her refrigerator on several occasions and even bought ceramic plates and silverware to replace the paper plates and plastic ware she was using. In 1973, I paid for her and my sister to move to Hawaii to live with my new wife Debbie and me. We arranged for her to become my Air Force dependent so that she would get a military ID card and all the privileges that came with it.

Initially things went well . Mom regained her health and was happy. However, as time went by Mom became more and more homesick for Beaver Valley and the rest of our family. Though her move to Hawaii was intended to be beneficial, it turned out to be a mistake. Their stay lasted for 6 months until we mutually agreed that she should return to the Valley and I bought her one way tickets to Pittsburgh and drove them to the Honolulu International Airport. I was not angry and neither was Mom. We were just sad that things did not turn out the way we had hoped. She ultimately remarried in Rochester, PA and moved to Florida with my stepfather and retired until her passing.

CHAPTER SIX
Back Into Battle
Viet Nam: 1967 – 1968

The story of my Viet Nam experience cannot be told without it starting at Langley AFB, Virginia, where I met the guys who would share the war with me for the year we spent there. Blain Sheppard, Gary Torres, John Becker, Bill Brice, Carroll Rhodes, Eugene Cammarota, Dave Moody and so many more Airmen from Langley went into the combat zone together, prepared to deal with whatever we had to do to support the war. Some of us stayed together, being deployed across the country, as three man mobility teams in support of combat operations.

We were the mobility guys who loaded and unloaded the cargo aircraft and helicopters, while often under heavy mortar attacks and gun fire. We had no protection as we drove the yellow Air Force forklifts and K-loaders on the open flight line. In essence, we were always sitting ducks and the targets of sniper fire. Air freight mobility personnel are the unsung heroes of Viet Nam and our current combat zones in Iraq and Afghanistan. Without these combat mobility men and women; food, ammunition, weapons, tanks, helicopters and beer could not get to the troops. Yet these men and women are typically overlooked by the news media and even the soldiers and marines they support.

But I am getting ahead of myself again. Langley was our training ground where we learned to operate the various combat loading and support equipment. We also learned to build the mobile pallet handling systems, build mobile cargo conveyor systems, build airdrop loads for simulated cargo supplies, rig airdrop mass pallets and vehicles and making honeycomb for airdrop loads. We recovered airdrop loads and equipment from drop zones in Blackstone, Virginia and at Langley, including ones that landed short into the ocean, just short of the drop zone on the base, and on one occasion from the swimming pool at the Officers' Club at Langley.

Camaraderie was important, enabling us to be accepting of different personalities from every walk of life. We were a microcosm of American society representing values and ideas that often conflicted with the norm. Initially it was hard because some of us were raised with deeply ingrained prejudices, going back many years in our families. Those who adjusted survived, while those who did not or could not adjust, found themselves unwelcome in our ranks.

Stupidity and immaturity presented themselves in many ways in our months at Langley. One particular incident is firmly burned into our minds. One Sunday night, an Airman in an adjacent barracks came back from a weekend at home. He was bragging to his roommate about a pistol he had brought back with him. The Airman was sitting on his bunk, next to his buddy's bunk, and was opening the top of his duffle bag. The clasp of his duffle bag got entangled with the trigger of the pistol, and as he pulled on the pistol grip the gun went off, shooting the other Airman in the head, killing him instantly. The shooting was deemed to be accidental, but the Airman with the pistol was discharged from the Air Force.

Jokes and hazing incidents occurred frequently, and I was the recipient of one, during a late night combat exercise on the asphalt flight line at Langley. We had just unloaded one of the C-130s and were awaiting the arrival of the next one. Some of us sat on our forklifts, while others either sat or lay on the black tarmac. I noticed what appeared to be an oil slick or some other type of leak from the forklift I was resting against. I made a comment to no one in particular that the forklift was leaking fluid. A couple of the guys looked at the leak and tried to find the source. Gary Torres said "Stick your finger in it, Wim, and see if it's oil." As I slowly rubbed it between my fingers, I said, "It doesn't feel like oil." Gary responded with a blank look in his face and said, "Put some more on your finger and taste it, to see if it feels or smells oily, or if it may be hydraulic fluid or MOGAS." I started to do just that when my sixth sense kicked in, and I looked directly at Gary. He laughed sarcastically and walked away. The liquid was his pee. He had peed against the tire on the opposite side of the forklift, which flowed downhill to where I was sitting. Everyone laughed uproariously! I never took anything Gary said, at face value, after that.

At the insistence of several civilian friends, I started a very small Karate school. Bill Bryce constantly harassed me to show him some

Karate moves, but he didn't take the time to attend the classes. This went on for weeks until finally one day, during a field exercise, he asked one time too many. In front of all the guys I told him to attack me in any way he chose. Bryce came at me directly from the front, and from a standing position I jumped up and completed a cross legged, scissor kick across his upper body. Bryce flipped over, under the grasp of my legs and landed on top of his head. He never asked for another demonstration for as long as I knew him.

We lived on the second floor of an open bay barracks that could accommodate about 20 people. There was no privacy and personal belongings had to be locked in assigned storage lockers, which were provided. On several occasions someone stole money or other personal belongings, left on the bunks or in the foot lockers. Thefts from a fellow soldier, airman or marine were never, and are still not, tolerated. We had to find out who the culprit was, but all of our efforts failed.

After returning to the base from a weekend at home in Pennsylvania, I opened my clothes locker. Our lockers were not lockable. My Karate uniform and belt were gone, along with a couple of other items. I gathered a couple of my close friends, and we opened every locker until we found my belongings. We were able to identify the Airman who was stealing from us and decided to take matters into our own hands. We found him napping on his bunk and threw a blanket over his body, and as a group, pummeled him senseless. This was a process known as a blanket party. Someone opened the second floor window and we threw his mattress outside. At some point during the process of kicking him out of the barracks, he broke most of his fingers and one thumb. A couple of the guys pushed him down the stairs and he ran away to the First Sergeants' office. The First Sergeant came to the barracks to investigate what happened and how the thief was so severely injured. Collectively, we explained the theft of our belongings and that the Airman must have broken his fingers while falling down the stair well. The First Sergeant said "Hmmm that explains it! Carry on Airmen!" This meant the investigation was over and that we could go about our business. The thief never returned to the barracks and none of us ever saw him again.

Just six months after graduating from Basic Training in late February of 1967, orders to Viet Nam arrived. Most of us received them at the same time, allowing us to stick together overseas. Gary arranged for most of us to meet at his parents' home near San Francisco, since we would all deploy from Travis AFB in early March. Everything we had all heard about the love and open hearted welcome of an Italian family was demonstrated by Mr. and Mrs. Torres. This short visit with them has remained in my memory as one of the fondest times in my entire life. Mr. Torres not only arranged for us to go deep sea fishing in Oakland Bay, but he paid the expenses for the entire group of guys. We had a ball catching some of the biggest striped sea bass we had ever seen.

Mrs. Torres and the other wonderful women of the family and friends cooked a sumptuous and delicious Italian meal that was beyond description. You not only felt the love they gave to us all, but you could also taste it in the wonderful food prepared for us. None of us wanted to leave when the time came to do so.

Before reporting to Travis AFB, I spent some leave time at home. Some of the Karate students pulled me aside, telling me that my Dad had bragged about me joining the Air Force. It was a satisfactory feeling, but it would have meant more if he had told me that himself. My dad's advice prepared me for Viet Nam, which helped to keep me alive and bring me back home. As a Japanese prisoner of war for more than 4 years, he learned many things, which enabled him to survive those horrific days. He advised me on how to evade capture, should I find myself alone in the jungle. Some of the very special, dangerous defensive and offensive killing moves he shared with me, engendered a sense of self-confidence that boosted my passion for going to Viet Nam.

Then he hit me with the 'coup-de-gras'. "When I take you to the airport to fly to 'Nam,' I expect to never see you alive again. In essence you will be 'dead'. You in turn must approach the tour in combat as the end of your life. Do not expect to come home again, but live each day as if it is your last. Volunteer for anything and everything, especially those things that can cause you to be killed. If you are to survive and return home alive, instead of in a body bag, you must do as I say! Do you understand?"

"No Dad, I don't understand!"

"Trust me," he said. "If you go over there looking over your shoulders and around every corner expecting the worst, the worst will happen to you. Don't look over your shoulders, look only ahead and do whatever must be done so that you can come home in one piece, instead of in a coffin."

It was sage advice that I ultimately took and appreciated as the war went on. He was absolutely "dead-on correct."

On March 15, 1967, our Boeing 707 landed at Saigon in the middle of the night. It was so late that there was no place for us to go and check in to get to bed. As each of us stepped out of the open passenger door, we were hit right between the eyes with two very distinct and unwelcome senses. First, the heat was tantamount to sticking one's head into an oven. The second attack on our youthful senses was the overwhelming stench of Viet Nam. It was like diving directly into the holding tank of an outhouse. To say it was gruesome and overwhelming would be an understatement. Our clothes were immediately soaked with sweat, after stepping onto the tarmac.

Man! I had to take a leak badly. The Air Passenger Specialist pointed me to a bathroom and I ran to it as fast as possible before I peed my pants. Trying to hold my nose and pecker at the same time was a new trick for me, but I succeeded. Through my watery eyes I spied an old Vietnamese woman cleaning the open urinal trough next to me. She casually looked at me, then at my pride and joy, while grinning the black and red toothed Betel Nut grin, typical of old Vietnamese women in the country. I followed her eyes down to her focal point and noticed a tiny bug climbing along the limp staff of my penis. "Oh, God!" I said out loud, to no one in particular. "I've been here only ten minutes and I already have crabs!" It just turned out to be a local bug that obviously liked small packages.

We slept under the wings and tail of the B-707 that night, as the base was hit by a Viet Cong rocket attack. None of the incoming rockets or mortars fell near to us, but

Total Rocket Attack Destruction 1967

it was a direct and stark reminder that we were now in a real combat zone. For the next two weeks we were all put on "Casual Status", while the Air Force decided where to send us.

Our orders finally came, and most of us were sent to the 15th Aerial Port Squadron in Da Nang AB. Da Nang was still in the buildup stage, and almost everyone was assigned to live in 12-man field-style tents. The 12-holer, open to the public, toilets were the hardest to get used to. There was no privacy at all and the shy ones among us, including me, waited until the darkest time of night to take the one crap a day.

The squadron's First Sergeant asked for a volunteer to clean the latrines and to paint the Quonset Huts that served as our showers and bathrooms. I followed Dad's advice and volunteered. It took over a week to clean and paint without any help. The effort paid off as I was the only Airman out of the group to be promoted on the first selection.

Over the next two months we learned about the different functions and jobs that anyone of us could be assigned to while stationed in Da Nang. I was initially assigned to the motor pool. The motor pool assignment gave me some special opportunities, learning how to drive new vehicles and getting them entered onto my military driver's license. My previous certifications for the rough terrain forklifts, the tracked K-loader, the M-151 wrecker, and numerous other combat vehicles would become extremely handy during the various assignments I fulfilled in mobility operations. Being certified on the 58 passenger bus, while initially beneficial, proved to be a curse rather than something to be proud of as you will read later.

My next on-the-job training assignment was to the air freight section, where I learned how to load a C-130, C-141, C-9, C-123, Boeing 707, C-97 and numerous other civilian and military type aircraft. Each aircraft presented different challenges for loading them. The C-97 in particular, required the tail section to be disconnected and hinged to the side so that the K-loaders and the various sized forklifts could access the cargo compartment. The vertical space was extremely limiting, and most of us could not stand completely upright while loading. That, combined with the heat and humidity, made this the most miserable aircraft to load. My favorite aircraft was the C-141, which I envisioned would be the aircraft that I would fly in the future as a loadmaster. It was a fairly new cargo airplane fondly named the Starlifter. It was a beauty to behold and an easy aircraft to load and unload.

The "Ranch Hands" were the C-123 aircrews that sprayed Agent Orange (AO) and other chemicals throughout Viet to kill jungle foliage and trees. Unfortunately, as many military personnel would find in later years, it caused them to have many agent orange-related medical problems. It wasn't unusual, during the unloading process, for the poisonous liquids to spill on us. Little did we know of the future consequences to our health, by not routinely disinfecting ourselves and our clothing. On one particular occasion, a forklift driver was loading a drum filled with the chemical onto the ramp of a C-123 with a 10K forklift. During the process, his forks punctured the drum and sprayed all of us with the fluid. Rather than stopping to clean it up, we offloaded the damaged container and proceeded to load others, not knowing what the ultimate ramifications would be years later. In between aircraft loading of the chemicals we would sit on the 55 gallon barrels that we had just emptied. Residual AO on the barrels soaked into our clothes and underwear. Almost everyone I knew back then, me included, suffered with prostate cancer as a direct result of that simple and innocuous habit.

One fateful night at 2:30 a.m., I was provided the cargo manifest for a C-141 cargo load that was inbound for offloading. I was standing near the edge of the loading/off-loading cargo area and was prepared to inventory the cargo load. I watched as the C-141 landed on the main runway and turned almost immediately, after stopping onto the taxiway. The aircraft stopped for a moment to get permission to cross the parallel runway, then started to cross over to the parking ramp, where the offload crew and I were standing. We heard the high pitched scream of a fighter jet engine racing down the takeoff runway just before it impacted the C-141, between the number two engine and the crew cockpit.

The Navy A-6 intruder blew up instantaneously, upon impact, and forced the C-141 to turn about 90 degrees in line with the runway. During the taxi process, the Loadmaster had already opened the rear clam shell doors and the ramp, where he was standing near the cargo doors, when the fighter collided with the Starlifter.

Remains of the C-141A hit by A-6 Intruder

Every crew member in the cockpit was killed almost immediately, but the Loadmaster survived and we watched him jump off the aircraft ramp and run away upon landing on the tarmac. Just prior to the A6 hitting the C-141, the pilot ejected and survived this horrific tragedy.

I was in shock and froze in position as both aircraft blew up and caught fire. Shrapnel blew past us and one blast knocked us to the ground. We were standing less than a football field's length from the accident scene. For a few moments we could not move, as shrapnel continued to fly in every direction. Finally, upon realizing that we were all in danger of being killed or wounded, we made a dash for the protection of one of the open but protected fighter aircraft bunkers. The aircraft burned for several hours, consuming all of the fuel, cargo and mail onboard. We told the fire fighter responders that the Loadmaster had jumped from the aircraft and ran away. They send a search party to find him. When they located him, he was still running around in circles at the end of the taxiway.

I believe the most painful responsibilities that anyone of us had, was to load and unload the hundreds of body bags, containing our military men and women. Unfortunately, many of the Marines and Army soldiers were cavalier in the way they handled these body bags during the loading and unloading processes. An empty 5 ton Marine truck backed up to the ramp of a C-130 that had just landed from a remote site. It was loaded with numerous body bags. Two Marines jumped onto the C-130 and two remained on the M35. Rather than gently transferring the bodies to the truck, the Marines on the C-130, in cadence with one Marine at each end of these body bags, simply tossed the bodies onto the trucks. The Marines on the truck stacked the body bags like cord wood. Several of the airmen and I lost our cool watching this display of complete disrespect towards our dead soldiers. We warned them that if they threw another body onto the truck we would kick their asses. The Marines looked at us and laughed, knowing well that they could probably beat us hands down, but instead, began to unload the bodies showing them more respect.

Another very disturbing aspect, relating to our duties on the flight line, was to load and unload Viet Cong POWs. Their heads were covered with bags similar to sandbags and their hands were tied or shackled behind their backs. Each VC was tied to the person in front or in back of him as they shuffled from the aircraft to the holding area, where they would squat in the typical Vietnamese fashion until someone came to pick them up. On one particular occasion, Blain Sheppard and I observed a 25-foot K-loader backing up towards a white picket fence surrounding our headquarters building. A single POW was squatting with his back against the fence out of sight of the person guiding the K-loader. Someone yelled "Stop!" but it was too late. The flatbed of the K-loader struck the fence, shattering several of the fence posts. A fence post shard penetrated the prisoner's left ear and exited the right ear. The K-loader driver was directed to pull away so that aid could be rendered to the prisoner. However, no one but the squadron commander's Vietnamese secretary appeared to be interested in helping the dying prisoner, so we all went about our business.

We were never bored, since every day brought something new, exciting, horrific or otherwise, into our young lives. The only respite we experienced was taking a bus or some other vehicle to China Beach for rest and recreation whenever possible. It was during one of those trips to the beach that caused me to completely change my perspectives and beliefs about our reasons for being in Vietnam. It was a minor thing, but never-the-less, changed my whole viewpoint on the war and the Vietnamese people.

As we were returning back to the base one day on the back of the 2½ ton truck, some of us were handing out candy and C-ration snacks to the children chasing our truck. As I reached over the tail gate of the truck to give a candy bar to one of the kids he threw a rock at my head striking my glasses and shattering them. "You little bastard!" I yelled, while wiping the blood from my forehead. That was a turning point in my attitude about the war and why we were there and how I approached doing my job for the rest of my tour.

Shortly after the incident I was interviewed by a CBS news reporter about my opinions regarding America's involvement in Nam. I just told him that I supported my country but did not believe that we should be there.

Nee and Nam Taking Lock of Hair

CHAPTER SEVEN
Coming of Age
The Cat House Adventure

DaNang AFB Viet Nam 1967 and prior had a military approved whorehouse. Whether any official military spokesman will acknowledge it today or not does not matter. We all knew it existed and many of the guys frequented its mysterious rooms and sowed their teenage seed in the previous valleys of the unknown.

Then one day one of the holier than thou military members sent a letter home to his Mama telling her of the house of ill repute. Mama in turn notified her Congressman who immediately sent a Congressional Investigation team to the base. After confirming its existence the establishment was closed permanently.

So now what were the horny GIs going to do for relief and physical recreation? How was I ever going to find out what Dad had told me about the Asian women's physical attributes to be true? All I knew at the time was that I was "horny" and something had to be done about it.

DaNang was off limits to all military personnel because much of the city was under the night control of the Viet Cong. There were a couple of small Army units down town but other than them no one ventured there without official business and armed guards.

My buddies and I had been "in country" for a month working our asses off in the searing Southeast Asian heat. The workload was exhausting and often times deadly. In just this first month we witnessed F4, B52, F105, C-141 and other aircraft crashes. Death was everywhere and not always at the hands of our enemy. Security Police and others pulling guard duty at night were often bored and played quick draw contests. In just one month we had three such deaths. We were loading literally hundreds of GI KIAs in body bags from Marine Corps and Army trucks onto the C-130s and C-141s returning home to Dover AFB. The rotating 12 on and 24 hours off work shifts were tough to manage and our body clocks were all screwed up.

The heat, the monsoon downpours, the rocket and mortar attacks, the awful stinking military uniforms and the ever reeking diesel and aircraft fuel fumes took their tolls on everyone. You could not get away from it anywhere on the base. The ever present foul odor of human feces and urine saturated the air emanating from the open binjo (sewer) ditches around us also served to drain our senses.

It was all just too much for any young person to absorb without some relief.

It was the middle of April and the ten of us who arrived together were still getting settled into the daily routines in the 15th Aerial Port Squadron. I was assigned to the motor pool as part of my on-the-job training program and scheduling the base transportation vehicles including the Blue buses. I was horny and my hormones were raging when the thought came to me that I could sign out a bus with the excuse of having to go to one of the Army posts in town. After all it would only take me about 5 minutes to do my business. That included two minutes to get undressed and two minutes to get dressed for my return.

Ben (his real name is not used here) was my assistant in the motor pool. It was his job to fuel and wash the vehicles. I broached the subject and my ideas with him and he thought it was a "great" idea. "Let's do it man!" he said.

I signed the 58 passenger Blue Air Force bus out to myself and Ben signed on behalf of the Motor Pool Sergeant as authorization to leave the base. We put on our combat helmets and gathered our M-16s, got on the bus and drove to the main gate. The Security Policeman stopped us, inspected the paperwork and let us through the gate.

We had no inkling of where we were going. We saw an Army PFC walking down the road and he flagged us down. He asked for a ride but we had no idea of how to get where he wanted to go. Now instead of two geniuses on the bus we had three. Ben told him all we wanted to do was find a cat house, make a short visit and return to the base. Like any GI worth his salt he knew exactly where to go and proceeded to get us there. Fear never crossed our minds. There was no hesitancy in doing what we were about to do. "Just get us there Dude!"

Within a few minutes the "Grunt" (a nickname Air Force guys gave to Army personnel) suggested that we park next to a warehouse type

"U" shaped building that seemed to stretch out forever." We entered the building and were immediately met by "Mama San."

"How long you stay GI? Wat chu want?" she asked.

"We want numbah' one quickie!" we responded.

"10 dollah' each" she said.

The grunt and I reached into our pockets and quickly came up with the 10 dollah' each and handed them to her. Ben reached into every pocket and turned them inside out. His wallet, with the exception of his military ID and Status of Forces (SOF) card, was as empty as our collective brains.

Since we were only making $87 a month in military pay plus $55 a month in Combat Zone pay $10 was a lot of money in "them there days." But I reached into my wallet and loaned Ben the $10.

Mama san took us to three separate cubicle type rooms separated only by curtains. Each room had a cot type bed, a wash bowl and folded clean sheets. At least the sheets appeared to be clean – but by then who cared?

The five minute visit stretched to 15 minutes, then to an hour. We were having a ball so to speak. The first thing I did was take close look and verify whether or not the Asian women's vaginas were different than "round eye" women. Dad had told me to look for myself to verify that oriental women were built so that they have to lay on their sides for men to be able to have sex with them. I looked and verified that the answer is 'No!'

It was party time and the "business girls" brought in some rice wine. We could still sense the odor of gasoline from the GI gas cans where the rice wine was fermented. It may have been aged at least a week. But then who cared? Two hours quickly passed and all of us had a good buzz going.

Then it happened! The lights started flashing and bells started ringing. Mama san was running down the narrow hall screaming "Quan Canh", "Quan Canh", and "Quan Canh" – "di-di mau" –"di-di mau! Loosely translated it means- "Military Police – Get the Hell out of here!"

It took a couple of minutes to sink in but my new Vietnamese friend was shoving my clothes and boots at me and telling me "di-di mau"! Ben and I were now hastily donning our uniforms and trying to exit the building. The Army grunt grabbed his clothes, rifle and boots and rolled under the bunk. His girl used the blanket to hide him and left the room.

Ben and I parted ways looking for an exit. I ran from room to room until Mama San stopped me and pointed to an opening in the wall adjacent to and above one of the beds. I climbed up and she closed the panel door behind me while still screaming "di-di mau!" the whole time.

I was scared shitless when the panel door closed behind me putting me in complete darkness. Once my eyes adjusted to the darkness I could see a sliver of light every 10 to 15 feet or so shine through the cracks in the wall. Ever so quietly and gingerly I felt my way along the long, narrow and twisting passage way. It seemed to go on forever but I'm certain it was only minutes when I found a partially opened panel. I pushed it wide open and without looking jumped through it landing immediately on a kitchen table where Mama and Papa San were eating lunch.

After their initial surprise and my shock they began to laugh and pointed me to another panel on the adjacent wall in their little kitchen. I exited the room without hesitation and started my strange journey again. It was lighter in this new corridor and in the distance I could see what appeared to be a door. Unhesitatingly I ran to the door and stopped to catch my breath. The heat in the corridors took my breath away but until this moment I had not noticed until the sweat poured into and burned my eyes.

Gingerly pushing one of the exit panels I peeked outside to see if there were any military policemen in sight. Not seeing one I left the corridor and slowly hesitantly walked with my back along the building until I could see the back part of the bus at the corner. After waiting a few minutes and catching my breath I turned the corner just in time to see an Army MP come around from the front of the bus with Ben in hand cuffs.

Exhausted and relieved it was one of our own guys I slumped to the ground waiting for the inevitable hand cuffs. I laughed and determined that only God knew what was in store for us. Since I was the only person with a bus license they had me drive to the Army post for initial processing. Then I started to laugh and could not stop. Some irrational thought that this was a hilarious situation just took over any rational thoughts I had left.

Ben and I were put into a holding cell until our First Sergeant could be called to pick us up. He arrived after about two hours and just shook his head and said "What were you dipshits thinking?" There was no answer!

"Wetzel – you drive the bus and follow me back to the base! Major Brown (our unit CO) wants to meet with you ASAP and you can kiss your ass good bye!"

Major Brown was ticked off beyond description but he was also short-handed. He gave us a choice between an Article 15 and a Court Martial. After a quick discussion with the First Shirt and following his strong recommendation we chose the Article 15. For the non-military reader an Article 15 simply means non-judicial punishment. A slap on the wrist that is meant to get your attention and a warning to sin no more.

My punishment besides the Article 15 was a suspended bust from Airman Third Class to Airman and a $90 fine. Later on in my otherwise illustrious career I would regret this error in judgment. This one blemish in my Air Force records would disqualify me for nomination to become Chief Master Sergeant of the Air Force. Ben received an Article 15, a $90 fine and an immediate reassignment to Saigon. I never saw Ben again after that day. And, by the way Ben, if you are reading this, you still owe me $10.00 plus interest!

Two C-130s Parked Nose-to-Nose
Struck by Rockets Dak To

CHAPTER EIGHT
The Siege of Dak To

One thing for sure about the Air Force, once you've been trained to do your job, it does not fool around in getting its money's worth. They send you out with the tools to get it done. For the remaining part of our tour, Da Nang would remain as our home base, regardless where they sent us for mobility support. The responsibilities we had as young Airmen were tremendous. Yes, they deployed us with an NCO in most cases, but at times we were sent to a remote location without that "adult" supervision.

The two specific NCOs who positively impacted and set the tone for my career the most, were Staff Sergeant Hampton and Tech Sergeant Glenn Lutz. Both would eventually achieve the highest enlisted Air Force ranks of Chief Master Sergeant. They led by example, taught me well

Glenn Lutz and Me

and helped me develop skills that prepared me for future leadership and management positions in the Air Force. TSgt Lutz wrote my first airman performance report and entered the following words in the performance summary. "I would, if ever asked or given the opportunity, follow Airman Wetzel anywhere including into combat."

Bien Hoa, **Hue Phu Bai**, Dak To, Khe Sahn, Saigon, Monkey Mountain, and other locations throughout the country had relatively short runways that required air freight and mobility support. In most cases, we were sent to these sites in small mobile teams for the length of time necessary to support the combat troops with ammunition, food and other items. In every case, without exception, we were left to our own devices for obtaining places to sleep and eat. C-Rats were the norm and we brought our own initially, until our supported Army or Marine units provided them. Sleeping quarters were tents that we either brought with us or again were supplied by the units we were assigned to. At two sites we used the cargo loading pallets called 463L pallets and fashioned them into shelters tied together with chains. Each new experience at any one of the locations would add new tools to our individual tool bags and they would become extremely handy over time. We learned to make do with whatever we had or were given to us.

My first extended length assignment was to Dak To for 30 days. Those ultimately became 60, then 90, then 120 days and finally 210 days. Adolph Ellis, a high school friend and Beaver Bobcats football player, was killed by a Bouncing Betty land mine near Dak To. The mine killed him instantly, as I was told by one of our Army buddies who witnessed him stepping on the mine. Adolph and I grew up together on the same street in VanPort and he was a great and loyal friend.

The events at Dak To, over my seven month duty tour, were too many to tell about but I will cover some that still stand out in my memory today. Initially, on arrival at Dak To, we were billeted in an open pavilion type building with three of the four walls open to Mother Nature. We noticed a sweet sickening odor emanating from every part of the building. The Army guys told us the building was used to store dead bodies until they could be shipped out in one of the aircraft. The bodies often laid there for days in the overwhelming, stupefying heat, causing them to decay rapidly. The odor penetrated all of our personal belongings and clothing, so that we could not escape it any time. It is a smell that no one can or will ever forget.

After a week or so we were provided a tent. The monsoon rains came and the floor of the tent would flood, soaking all of our belongings. We five-finger discounted several wooden cargo pallets and used them as a floor to get our belongings off the ground. We surrounded the tent with concertina wire, as if that was going to stop anyone from throwing a hand grenade into the tent. In the middle of one night, a C-130 landed unexpectedly and the Viet Cong rocketed the base immediately. Without a second thought, we grabbed our helmets, flack vests and M-16s and ran out of the tent to unload the aircraft. I had forgotten about the concertina wire surrounding the tent and was immediately wrapped up in it shredding my clothes, cutting my bare skin, causing me to painfully bleed everywhere. The guys freed me from the painful razor sharp wire and we went out and did our job. This was the first time I was wounded in combat and could have been awarded the Purple Heart. I refused as I would the next three times that I was wounded in combat. Little did I know that this was dumb ass decision number 1.

During July, the base came under more frequent attack from the hills surrounding it. We decided that we needed a bomb shelter, so we dug one next to our tent. It was very small and could barely hold two or three guys at any one time. We stored it with ammunition, hand grenades and flares. None of us had combat training, but we were not going to go down without a fight, if it came down to that. Our tent and our bomb shelter were right next to the ammo dump, but we thought nothing of it. Then one day, we got hit really hard and the ammo dump suffered several direct hits, causing it to blow up. Everything was leveled and several people were killed within moments. Our bomb shelter suffered a direct hit and was completely destroyed, but thankfully we were all on the flight line unloading and loading the support aircraft. Two C-130s were also blown up that day, causing numerous casualties.

As I was walking between two C-130 aircraft that were parked face to face on the ramp I watched as a rocked slammed through the vertical stabilizer of one C-130 and impact the ground right in front of an Army officer. He was blown apart and disappeared right in front of me while body parts flew in every direction. I believe that if he had not been the one to take the impact of the explosion then I would have been killed instead. Both aircraft were destroyed. Our tent and our bunker received direct hits and were destroyed along with the ammo dump. For several weeks after these events we had to sleep in the open air morgue located on the cargo ramp. The horrendous smell of death permeated the air and walls in and around the structure making it almost impossible to sleep. We palletized hundreds of body parts of the Army soldiers that were killed in the massacre at Dak To and loaded them aboard the outbound aircraft.

The Air Freight guys were most likely to be wounded or killed on the flight line since they drove yellow painted forklifts and K-Loaders while wearing white tee shirts. None of us were issued camouflaged clothing in those days. During one mortar attack I was getting on my forklift to prepare to unload an incoming C-130. As I got on the forklift a mortar round exploded nearby and a piece of shrapnel struck my right hand in the joint between my index and middle finger. It was extremely hot and hurt like Hell. Again I chose not to be submitted for a Purple Heart.

At one period of time I was the only Air Force person physically assigned to the base and was attached to the Special Forces A-Team. It was one of the most rewarding periods of time in my entire career. The A-Team commander really took good care of the entire team as well as me. He welcomed me aboard without question and assured me that the team would take good care of me.

Late one afternoon I was walking back to the safety of the A-Team compound from working the flight-line when we came under a precision mortar attack. It was like being in the movies where the enemy was targeting a specific person or group and walked their mortar rounds towards the target. In this case it appeared that I was the target. Rather than dive for cover I responded to one of the A-Team members in one of their fox holes and ran towards him and dove headlong into the bunker. It turned out that the soldier was the team medic. He asked "Have you ever fired a mortar round?" My response was "No – but this seems like a good time to learn!" He showed me how to remove the appropriate number of sand bags from the mortar and how to remove the safety pin. The number of sandbags on the mortar determines the distance the mortar will launch to. The safety pin was installed at the head of the mortar under a lot of tension. The medic told me to be careful when removing the pin to avoid injury. He then told me to remove four bags of ballast and to remove the pin and hand the mortar to him. I immediately responded, removed the sand bags and in the process of removing the safety pin sent in straight through my hand. It was extremely painful but I kept on handing new mortars to the medic. The engagement only lasted a couple of minutes and I completely forgot about the pain until it was over. There was hardly any blood but the medic removed the pin and said "You just got the Heart (Purple Heart)!" Without a second thought I said "No – that the wound was not bad enough to warrant it. To this day I regret not being put in for that award.

The siege of Dak To lasted a long time and hundreds of our troops lost their lives and limbs there. The decision was made to send most of the mobility guys back to Da Nang. Someone had to stay behind to guard our equipment, K-Loader and forklifts, so I volunteered, along with SSgt Hampton. He may have known, but I had no clue about what was going to happen that night. As we settled down for the night, sleeping on the forklifts, we were hit hard by the Cong. The word came that the base was going to be overrun that night and we were warned to expect the worst.

A handful of infantry soldiers were assigned to protect us. Intense does not fully describe the events of the night, as one attempt after another, by the VC to overrun us, failed. "Snoopy, the Magic Dragon" C-47 aircraft flew circles overhead all night firing down at the VC surrounding us and the base. We survived the night and no one among us was killed or injured and our extremely valuable equipment was undamaged.

During the day we continued to unload the never-ending line of C-130s, coming in with resupplies of ammo and other required equipment and staples. In between aircraft, SSgt Hampton asked if I could help the Army marshal and guide the Huey gunships landing all over the tarmac. With some quick training from a helicopter crew chief, I was able to accomplish my new skill very quickly. They trained us to load fresh rockets onto the helicopters so they could return to the battle. Almost every helicopter brought back dead or wounded soldiers, which we helped to unload as well. This cycle of supporting our cargo aircraft, moving our dead and wounded, arming helicopters and returning mortar fire lasted over three days. We took 5 or 10 minute combat naps when we became too exhausted to work. We worked without sleep or rest beyond "Combat Naps" for over 72 hours.

On one scary occasion, I was marshaling helicopters in for landing and rearming, when I came within a couple of feet of being blown up by one of the rockets. It was the practice for helicopter marshals to point the copters down range away from runway and the pilots to "safe" their weapons. This meant that before actually touching down, the marshal had to point the helicopter into a direction that, in case of a problem with the de-arming process, any munitions or rockets that might actually fire would not kill or injure anyone. During this particular incident, I had directed the turn of the copter to about 10 – 15 degrees off my right shoulder, when the pilot accidentally fired one of his rockets. It happened so suddenly that it was impossible to react but the rocket missed me by about 15 feet and impacted the berms on the firing range.

This key battle reached its intensity over a 72-hour period, when none of us received any rest or sleep. Cold C-rats were the norm and we had to eat them while working. Ammunition, fresh troops and all sorts of new combat equipment came in relentlessly. The support aircraft came in one after another, almost like a train. Engine Running Offloading (ERO) was the norm, so that the aircraft were offloaded more quickly, allowing them to depart the base and readying the runway and parking ramps for the next one. The heat from the idling engines during the EROs, literally caused our watches, jewelry and the brass bracelets many of us wore, to burn our hands, arms and necks. The Air Force mobility guys did not have combat fatigues and worked openly with white t-shirts on brightly painted yellow forklifts and other cargo loading equipment. All of us were sitting ducks for snipers, but none of us were wounded as a result. The thought never really crossed our minds, as we took it in stride and worked on relentlessly.

At the end of the 72-hour fight we were able to get some sleep. I had forgotten one of the basic rules regarding how to leave your sleeping bags, upon leaving them for work each day. It was bad practice to leave your bag unrolled whenever you left it, to prevent creepy critters from going into them. Being exhausted and a little absent-minded, I took off my clothes and boots and jammed my body into the sleeping bag. Almost immediately, I screamed in pain as something at the bottom of my bag bit into my big toe on the right foot. I reached over in pain and wrapped both my hands around my ankle thereby trapping whatever it was latched around my toe. A couple of the guys helped by using their boots to beat whatever it was to death. When the critter stopped moving I dragged it, still attached to my toe, out of the sleeping bag. It was a huge rat, and we had to pry its teeth off my toe with a combat knife. The medic treated my toe and told me to be more careful in the future. The thought of rabies crossed my mind briefly but were set aside as I passed out from exhaustion.

A few days after the battle ended, we were told to report to the 173rd Airborne Brigade commander's tent. Upon arrival, we came upon a surreal scene, as numerous brigade officers and senior NCOs came to attention. Without knowing why we were told to stand at a specific location and directed to stand at attention, Brigadier General Schweider awarded me the Army Commendation Medal for Meritorious service, because of our actions during the battle at Dak To. It should be obvious how much I loved the Air Force, but no accomplishment in my entire career meant more to me than receiving the Army Commendation Medal during and as result of supporting the Army in combat.

The killing of civilians around the base continued every day, causing many children to become orphaned. Among those were five children ranging in age from 4 to 9. Their names were Bai, Minh, Siu, Nam and Nee. Bai was the oldest and Nee was the youngest but they were far more mature than any typical American kid at the age of 10. They were alone in the world, since all their families were slaughtered by the Cong. One day they came by our tent begging for food. I was hesitant at first, remembering how that kid had thrown a rock into my face at China Beach. But as I watched the guys start to feed them, my softer side started to melt and I proceeded to help also.

We could not get rid of them after that. For the remainder of our tour at Dak To, they slept nearby, ate our food, shined our shoes and actually guarded us when we slept. They had no hygiene skills whatsoever. They stunk and their breath was horrendous, since they did not brush their teeth. We taught them how to remain clean and even how to brush their teeth regularly. On slow days they would take us down to the river to swim and bathe in the red, fast moving waters. Bai, and a couple of the older kids, would stand guard on the shoreline with our M-16s. None of us had any doubt that they would be able to use those weapons if needed, to protect us and the other children.

I contacted Mrs. Charlotte Vento in Beaver, and asked if she could obtain any clothing for children from her church. Her sons, Mike and Bob, were high school friends and fellow scouts for many years. Mr. and Mrs. Vento were more than friends to me, since they took the role as adjunct parents, knowing that I was lacking proper parenting at home. Mrs. Vento took the challenge with a passion. She gathered the women at the church and collected boxes full of clothing, hygiene supplies, toys and food to send to us. We finally had to ask her to stop because we had no place to store the stuff and all of the local kids were now adequately clothed. Thank you Mom, for your letters and support during my tour in Nam and for being there throughout my teen years, when I needed you so much, helping me to stay grounded.

A C-130 landed at midday and taxied to the terminal. The cocky young loadmaster approached me and said "What do you have for us Airman?"

"We have a wrecker, its driver and shotgun rider to load for urgent redeployment. The total weight is just over 35,000 pounds."

"Load them up then, let's go!" he said rudely. I thought, "What an arrogant asshole."

After loading the vehicle and drivers, the loadmaster said "We have room on the ramp for more cargo. Do you have anything else that we can haul out of here?"

I said "You are already at gross weight with what you have!"

"I have room for more," he insisted.

"We have a jeep and its driver, but you are already close to being overloaded and I can't give you more."

"Who's the loadmaster here? What do you know about what I can load or not load?"

One more time I told him "No."

At that time, the aircraft commander walked up and said "What's the holdup here? Let's get her closed up and get out of here."

"Captain we have room on the ramp for more cargo but this Airman will not give us any more. He has a jeep and driver going to the same place as the wrecker and we can take them."

"Are we good for the extra cargo load?"

"Yes sir!" he replied.

"Load it up Airman!"

Exasperated at the treatment and disrespect being shown by the crew, I said "Okay, but only if he will sign the Form F, stating that he was briefed about the overload condition."

Form F is a document that is required to be completed for every aircraft, and basically certifies that the aircraft is within weight and balance standards for flight. We loaded the jeep and driver and the loadmaster gave me a copy of the completed Form F, as required by Air Force regulations. "Wait a minute Load." I said. Then I wrote a statement on the back of my copy, in essence saying that he had been briefed by me that the extra jeep and driver put the aircraft over gross for the takeoff and runway at Dak To on this date. Then I insisted he sign and print his name before departure. He did and walked away.

By this time several of our Army buddies and all of the Airmen gathered along the flight line to watch the departure of the aircraft because we all knew it was not going to get airborne. It taxied to the end of the runway, revved up its massive engines and rolled slowly down the runway. It was quickly obvious that as they were running out of runway that the aircraft might not be able to get airborne. She labored to get into the air, near the end of the runway, but rose only a few feet before striking a bulldozer, killing the driver and throwing the shot gun rider unconscious to the ground. The aircraft disappeared into the valley at the end of the runway and we expected to see a fireball at any moment. We waited breathlessly for what seemed an eternity before seeing it slowly climb up and away from disaster.

The aircraft declared an emergency and was diverted to Saigon where it landed gear up. The damage was significant but no one was killed or injured. The nose landing gear was ripped off as the aircraft hit the bulldozer and a significant part of the bottom of the aircraft was ripped away during the impact.

A few days later, an Air Force investigation team arrived and ordered me to testify about what had happened. They accused me of lying to the crew about the actual cargo vehicle weights, convincing them that they were under gross weight with each vehicle. They threatened me with court martial actions. At that time, I presented them with my copy of the signed Form F and showed them the statement on the back. Several of the guys, Army and Air Force, testified on my behalf and stated the facts as they saw them that fateful day. The investigation was concluded and I was exonerated. The pilot and loadmaster were both disciplined and that was the end of that story.

One late afternoon, after an exhausting couple of days supporting the Army units, I was relaxing in the Green Beret compound, when a helicopter landed, bringing Martha Ray, the famous comedian. Ms. Ray was part of the Bob Hope tour group and was out visiting various Green Beret units throughout the war zone. She was especially loved and admired by these valiant soldiers. She

Remains of the bulldozer hit by the overloaded C-130 killing the driver.

was about to leave to visit another unit, when she saw me sitting alone at a table. Ms. Ray came over, sat next to me and said "How are you doing Airman and why are you here?" Then she put her arm around my shoulders and gave me a fantastic, never-to-be-forgotten big hug. We spoke about ten minutes before she hugged me again, kissed my cheek and said goodbye. My spirits soared and all of the tired bones and muscles felt rejuvenated and I was ready to get back to work. What a phenomenal experience that was!

I had been in Nam for about six months and had never received the first letter or care package from home. It was especially disheartening to go to mail call every day and watch everyone receive letters and packages from home. It appeared to me that Dad was serious about considering me to be dead after taking me to the bus station. I just had not expected the same from my mother.

I happened to meet a Red Cross representative traveling through Dak To and asked her if she could help me. After explaining that I had not heard from anyone at home she assured me that the Red Cross would take appropriate measures to fix the problem. True to her word, she contacted the Red Cross office that was closest to my home in New Brighton, PA and advised them to contact my mother. Coincidentally the Red Cross office was only two blocks from our house. Within a few days after contacting Mom and Dad I received letters and a care package from them. Problem solved and my spirits soared,

Almost seven months had passed at Dak To and it was time to return to Da Nang for a well-deserved rest. It was tough to leave the kids behind. They had become an extended family for us all. There is a belief in Viet Nam that if you depart and leave friends behind they will cut off a lock of your hair as a keepsake. We were unaware of this ritual until the kids all came to us with a pair of scissors and asked us to let them cut our hair. We gave our permission and they all took their mementos, hugged each one of us and walked away, never to be seen again. I cannot help but believe, if for nothing else but my sanity, that after all these years these boys survived the war, married, had children and told stories about their American friends.

CHAPTER NINE
The 1,000 Yard Stare
Return to Da Nang

During the months of October or November 1967 I was waiting with several other Air Freight Specialists at the Da Nang cargo terminal to offload ammunition. Two C-130 aircraft taxied in with what we believed to be ammunition/explosives. A Marine Corps 2.5 ton truck backed up to each aircraft. As the ramp and door opened we discovered that both aircraft were loaded with body bags. The stench was overwhelming causing several of us to vomit uncontrollably. We unloaded the bodies onto the trucks to deliver them to the morgue. As I was offloading one of the body bags my offloading partner was standing on the ground while I was on the cargo ramp. As I raised my end of the bag the drain plug came loose and body fluids poured down onto the face and body of my partner causing him to drop his end of the bag. He convulsed in vomiting causing a chain reaction that resulted in all of us getting violently sick. The Marine in charge of the trucks advised us that almost everyone that was killed was about our age, the late teens or early 20s. The smell of death, the blood and other bodily fluids pouring out of the bags and feeling the pain that their families will suffer still haunts me today.

It was Christmas at Da Nang and we were all having a great time partying. We had all become pretty callous from our experiences during the previous months, and all of us were ready to go home soon. Personal count-down calendars were posted on everyone's lockers for the world to see. A small artificial Christmas tree adorned with bulbs and lights was put on the refrigerator in the corner of the tent. A Santa Claus doll was hanging by the neck nearby. Everyone was pretty drunk but we were all glad to be back together and in one piece. New barracks were being built at a rapid pace, allowing us to move into more comfortable billets. We were also eagerly awaiting the opening of the new dining hall. C-rats and food at the field kitchen were coming to an end soon.

We finally moved into the new two story barracks and settled into our new digs. The new dining hall was scheduled to be open in the morning.

In the middle of the night Da Nang was hit hard by rocket attacks. We all scrambled to get to the safety of the bunkers. One guy rolled out of his bunk in the dark and ran smack into one of the barracks central support posts, knocking him down. He got up, started running and hit the same post again, but this time was knocked out cold. He received a Purple Heart for his "combat" injury.

A rocket hit a few feet next to our barracks and skidded under a 2½ ton truck parked there. The truck probably saved many lives, as it took the brunt of the explosion, flying straight into the air and landing upside down on top of our barracks.

No one benefitted from eating in the new dining hall because it took several direct hits and was destroyed. After action reports indicated that the new barracks and dining hall were targeted with the help of some Vietnamese civilians working on the base. We should have known, since all of us had seen the barber and other civilian workers pacing off distances all over the base. It was also curious that whenever the base was hit the barber and others did not report to work that day.

When Roy arrived in Nam, I met him at the passenger terminal. We spent a few hours together before he left for the DMZ and met up with his Marine unit. Before leaving, I promised him that I would find a way to get up north to visit him soon. He just laughed it off and said "How do you think you're going to pull that off?" I did not have an answer at the time, but I knew that day would come.

Two months later, I received a three day pass to visit Roy at a location called the Rock Pile close to the DMZ and caught a ride on a C-130. When I arrived, I was able to hitch a ride on a small convoy heading to the area near the Rock Pile. The driver of the jeep told me that he doubted that I would be able to see Roy because the unit he was assigned to was under heavy enemy fire and the forward operating base was surrounded. It did not stop me from seeing my brother, as the driver dropped me off near a small communications tent the size of about a 4 x 6 outdoor shit house. A single radio operator manned the tent and told me to have a seat. After a few minutes he asked what the hell an Air Force airman was doing there.

I told him that my brother Roy was with the 3/9 and I was there to visit with him and to possibly help him get a pass to come to Da Nang for a few days. He advised me that the unit Roy was assigned to was in a fixed pitch battle and that many of the Marines assigned to the unit were already dead. He promised that he would do whatever was possible for me to at least talk to Roy on the field radio. I waited for what seemed to be hours, when the radio operator told me that Roy was pulled back and ordered to return to base. I was exhausted and collapsed into an available seat and waited.

About an hour later I heard the rustling of the tent door and turned around to see Roy leaning against the door tent pole, with his M16 sling around his elbow and the end of the barrel resting on his boot. Roy's right leg was bleeding and his combat fatigue trousers were soaked in blood. I rushed over to him, put his arm around my neck, and helped him to a chair.

"You saved my life, Wim! Most of the guys are dead or wounded and your call came just in time. We won and the CO told me to go visit with you and that he would see us both later." The stench surrounding Roy was indescribable. I could smell death, blood, mud and God only knows what other odors emanated from his clothing. I told him to rest and the radio operator called for a medic to dress his wound in his right thigh.

Not long after, a Marine Captain came to the tent, introduced himself and asked "What are you doing here?" I advised the Captain that I was based in Da Nang and wanted to try to get permission for Roy to come back with me for a short pass. He said "This is a bit unusual and I've never heard of such a situation before. Corporal Wetzel has earned a few days off and he is cleared to go back with you for three days."

Catching a ride back to Da Nang from Dong Ha was not a problem. I called ahead and contacted one of my buddies at the passenger terminal, who arranged for a seat to be set aside for us both. During the boarding process, we find out that there was only one available seat and one of us had to be bumped from the flight. I looked for the loadmaster and found him in the snack bar buying a sandwich and drink. I explained the situation to him and that the other passenger was my brother, who just received a three-day pass to Da Nang. The loadmaster told me that if one of us would sit on an ammunition pallet then he would set up the seatbelts. I asked the loadmaster to assign the seat to Roy and to allow me to sit on the ammo pallet. The return flight to Da Nang was uneventful, but I could not help but think what would happen if enemy ground fire penetrated the ammo pallet I was sitting on.

During the next three days, Roy was treated like a celebrity. I asked Roy if he would like to take a shower before the barbecue began, because he smelled nasty and looked even worse. Our shower consisted of a 12-man open walled bay, without a privacy wall. I gave Roy shampoo, soap and a clean white towel. After about 10 minutes, Roy came out of the shower drying off his back with the white towel. I cannot describe how smelly the formerly white towel became. Roy's back was still caked with mud. He told me that he had not bathed in about three months. I retrieved another white towel and told him that I would help scrub his back until it was clean. I did not think about it at the time, but could have guessed the rumors that would start about two GIs bathing each other in the shower.

Roy's boots and socks were unusable again, so we threw them in the trash. After wrapping him in a clean towel, we walked back to the 12-man tent. During our absence, the guys barbecued several steaks. The beer cooler and the party lasted way past midnight. At some time during the evening, Roy's wound began to bleed again. We treated it as best as we could, set up a nice clean cot with fresh sheets and a pillow. Within 5 minutes Roy fell sound asleep.

During the night, Roy had several nightmares, which somehow opened the wound again. The formerly white sheet was soaked in blood, which was dripping onto the floor. We rushed him to the base hospital, where the wound was properly treated and dressed. Over the next two days we had a ball, spending time together, before it was eventually time for him to return to his unit. It was at this time that we realized the Captain had not given Roy a written three-day pass. That pass was required to obtain a seat on the aircraft heading north. Then one of the guys came up with the brilliant idea, "Why not dress him in an Air Force uniform and let him use your ID card? Since we have open-ended mobility orders, no one in the passenger terminal is going to challenge his right to travel."

I thought, "Why not, I've done worse things since arriving in this shit hole called Vietnam." I told Roy what we were going to do. I gave him one of my uniforms, emblazoned with my name and gave him my ID card. Since it was the only card I had, he had to return to me immediately after landing and gave him a pre-addressed envelope. As planned, Roy processed through the passenger terminal, boarded the aircraft, and returned to the DMZ. After the C-130 departed Da Nang, a horrible thought occurred to me. If for any reason the aircraft crashed, killing Roy, the casualty unit and the Red Cross would notify my mother that I had been killed in action. That thought stayed with me until I received the envelope containing my ID card. If given the opportunity to once again to be with Roy, under any circumstance, I would take that chance.

Back in DaNang on December 25, 1967 several of us were at the Special Forces compound located at the North end of the runway. We were loading and offloading the Caribou aircraft located in this classified area. An F-4 Fighter was attempting a landing but apparently had a hydraulic problem as we were told later. The pilot tried to abort the landing and take-off with afterburner but failed. The aircraft failed the take-off as it roared over our heads and exploded in midair. Both pilots ejected safely but they were too low for the parachutes to open. Both crew members impacted the ground in front of us and were killed instantly. This was the most horrible Christmas Day for all of us as we barely escaped with our lives and watched two of our fellow Airmen get killed.

On another occasion we watched a B-52 bomber come in for an emergency landing. The bomber was hit by enemy rockets during a bombing run over Hanoi North Vietnam. The rockets severely damaged the aircraft's hydraulic system and disabling its ability to lower the landing gear and flaps for landing.The crew was able to manually lower the landing gear but was unable to do anything to manipulate the flaps for landing. Flaps are critical to landing an aircraft, especially the massive and ungainly B-52. Blain and I watched in horror as the aircraft touched down past the runway's half way point and bounced several times. The aircraft bounced one last time right over a guard shack at the end of the runway barely missing the shack and the Marine guard in it. It landed in the perimeter mine field and exploded in a huge ball of fire. The aircraft burned for a long time and the fire fighters could not get to the crew because of the exploding mines. Everyone on board was killed in the explosion, or at least that was what we all believed. At some point the fire fighters heard a banging and someone screaming near the tail of the aircraft. It was the tail gunner who was trapped in his turret just outside the minefield. They got him out and to the base hospital. He was the only survivor.

Direct Rocket Hit on Our Bunker

CHAPTER TEN
The Siege of Khe Sahn

During January and February of 1968 I was assigned to Khe Sahn, RVN to support the Marine Corps during the siege. The flight into and landing at Khe Sahn was surreal. As any GI who ever landed in a hot combat zone will attest, the adrenalin high is so intense that you do not notice that your asshole puckers up so tight that it sucks the combat seat halfway into the colon. The C-130 flight I arrived on came in from a high level above the runway and executed a steep spiraling combat landing to avoid coming in a normal, slow, straight in approach. Some of the Marines refused to sit during the landing and stood up holding onto any part of the aircraft or the web seating.

There was no in-processing or orientation to the new assignment. We were replacing the Air Force support team on the ground as a normal rotation. They could not wait to get out of Khe Sahn fast enough. The team lead gave me some cursory instructions on what to expect but then stopped and said: "Shit – you'll figure it out. Just get us out of here now!" We finished off-loading the aircraft, loaded the dead and wounded and the aircraft departed the base.

Our stay at Khe Sahn was eventful, exciting, terrifying and for some very life changing. The sights and smells of death were all around us 24x7. During my first assignment I was driving my forklift loaded with a heavy pallet of Class A ammunition to the holding area when an enemy rocket hit the ground nearby and exploded. The concussion blew me off the forklift and I landed unconscious and badly bruised next to the forklift. I don't know how long I laid there. The Marines that were nearby thought I was dead and while the mortars and rockets were still raining in on us they stayed in their bunkers.

At some point I regained consciousness and got back on the forklift that was still running with the ammo on the forks and finished the offload. For the remainder of my life I suffered major headaches from what I believe was caused by the explosion. Today this type of injury is referred to as Traumatic Brain Injury or TBI. This truly was the occasion where I fully deserved the Purple Heart and by not seeking medical treatment at the time I have continued to suffer terrible headaches.

The very next C-130 that landed had been shot up badly during its landing approach. Fuel was pouring out of the wings as it taxied in. The cargo ramp was already opened during the taxi in so that the aircraft could be evacuated. As we jumped on the ramp to help evacuate the wounded passengers I slipped and fell on a pile of intestines, body parts, fluids and blood that had come from a Marine who was gutted from the groin through his head by a 50 caliber round that came through the cargo floor. We carried the human remains out while two Marines used a water hose to wash the body parts off the aircraft onto the tarmac.

During another on load of outbound cargo I was the forklift driver assigned to load the aircraft. The guide instructed me to lower the pallet onto the aircraft ramp, back out and upon his signal push the pallet onto the aircraft floor because it was too heavy for two loaders to push it. Just as I pushed the pallet upon instructions to do so the onboard air freighter slipped and his right foot boot became jammed between two cargo floor rollers. The impact of the heavily loaded cargo pallet being pushed by my forklift caused his foot to be severed at the ankle inside his combat boot. Even thought it was not my fault I have lived with the knowledge that someone was permanently crippled because of me.

In addition to loading and unloading the support aircraft our primary assignment was to recover the low-altitude parachute extraction system (LAPES) and airdropped supplies from the drop zone. The LAPES were dropped onto an auxiliary dirt runway, close to the main runway. It was an extremely dangerous job, because we were out in the open and perfect targets of opportunity for snipers. However by the grace of God alone, none of us were killed or wounded during these LAPES recovery actions.

Drop Zones or DZs typically are specifically identified areas where the airdropped supplies and equipment would impact. At Khe Sahn, the whole outpost was a DZ with supplies, in many cases, landing randomly anywhere. The Air Force mobility teams accomplished these jobs out in the open while under enemy fire all over Viet Nam. In many cases, the Marines and Army personnel we supported stayed in their fighting positions or in the relative cover of their bunkers. This is not meant to be a criticism because they were doing their jobs, protecting the bases and outposts just as we were. The only point I intend to make here, is that these vital combat support actions by our Air Freight Mobility Teams were rarely, if ever, acknowledged by the military. The gals and guys in Iraq, Afghanistan and so many other hot areas continue this legacy today, also are rarely acknowledged in public.

My bunk was located in the Air Force's command bunker, near the center of the base. A 105 MM Howitzer was positioned directly on top of the bunker and it was fired constantly. After a few hours in the bunker at night, the sound of the Howitzer did not even distract us. Upon entering the bunker for the first time, I immediately noticed that a photograph of Anne Margaret was posted on the refrigerator. Yes, a refrigerator! Only the Air Force would arrange for a standard sized refrigerator to be taken into combat.

A few days after landing at Khe Sahn, we were in the middle of conducting an ERO of five ammunition pallets, weighing about 25,000 pounds. There were two sets of roller conveyors required for this operation and it took two guys to connect them. During the process of hooking up the roller conveyors one of the "cherry" (new guy) mobility guys was experiencing difficulty hooking the roller conveyor onto the end of the cargo ramp. Three of the four guys had completed their task and moved to safety while the "cherry" was still having difficulty with his connections. The loadmaster, during EROs, is required to wait for a signal from the offload team, before releasing the restraining locks from the pallets and notifying the pilot to add power, so the pallets can roll off of the aircraft. He did not wait after seeing that the two mobility guys from his side of the aircraft had moved to the safe holding area. He released the 463L pallet locks and directed the pilot to taxi.

The new guy saw the first pallet rolling off the main cargo floor towards him and tried to stop it with his arms. The first pallet hit him just above the knees and pinned him to the ground sitting on his chest. The second pallet struck the first, then the third, fourth and finally the fifth. As each pallet hit the offloading train, the guy's body slid a few feet because of the impact of 25,000 pounds of ammo. He remained conscious, waving his arms in the air and screaming. Screams clearly heard above the din of the running engines. Screams that still ring in my ears today. I was pre-positioned with my Jolly Green Giant forklift and moved immediately to pick up the edge of the pallet sitting on his chest. The guys pulled him out from under the pallet and the medics took him away, loaded him onto the next departing aircraft and never to be seen by us again. The loadmaster and the aircraft that caused the accident, apparently never knew what happened, because they taxied to the end of the runway and conducted a combat takeoff and left the scene.

Accidents at Khe Sahn happened every day. Some were just plain stupid, like the Airman who was playing with a pistol that a Marine had captured from a VC. He was unfamiliar with the weapon and somehow shot another airman in the left side of his face and blowing out all of his teeth through a huge hole on the other side.

The final day before I left Khe Sahn, the base was hit hard. The Air Force Forward Air Controller (FAC) on the ground was sitting in his jeep controlling traffic. He had us stack three stacks of 25 – 463L cargo pallets around his jeep in the shape of a large "U". A rocket landed on the tarmac's pressed steel plating (PSP) and skidded along the length of it and imbedded itself under one stack of the pallets, before blowing up and scattering 463L pallet shrapnel everywhere. The FAC escaped uninjured only by the grace of God.

On that same day, later in the afternoon, I was moving a cargo pallet from an aircraft to the cargo holding area near the fence. An F4 fighter came in low from behind me and dropped a huge bomb, targeting something just outside of the perimeter, but it landed short just outside of the fence line. The shock wave blew me off the forklift and I went completely deaf for about an hour. My ears rang and I could see people talking to me but could not hear a word. This was the second time I was blown off my forklift and I was ready to get out of Khe Sahn.

It was my time to rotate back to Da Nang. I went to the bunker, grabbed my stuff and flew out on the first aircraft leaving the outpost. While our replacements were exiting the aircraft, we boarded it without saying a word, sat down, buckled our seat belts and departed for the relative peace and safety of Da Nang. My return to the United States countdown calendar had 15 days remaining. The impact on my body, mind and soul as a result of my time at Khe Sahn were suppressed and literally forgotten for many years. But one day the memories would come back to haunt and torture me horrendously.

CHAPTER ELEVEN
Returning to the World
and Going Home to Beaver Valley

Blain and Gary were the first to leave Da Nang for home. The rest of our troop left on March 15, 1968. We tried to stay in touch, but were mostly unsuccessful. Blain and I still do stay in touch regularly and have spoken seriously about going back to Nam to revisit some of the locations we were assigned to. Hopefully, others who shared those days with us will want to go also.

Going Home to the World

Bai, Minh, Siu, Nam and Nee: if you survived the war and happen to be reading this, I want to thank you all for allowing us to help take care of you, thereby helping us to maintain our sanity and sense of humanity during those days. One of my proudest achievements was being awarded the Navy Marine Corps Presidential Unit Citation with a "V" for valor for serving at Khe Sahn.

Upon returning to my Dad's house in Vanport, PA, I immediately fell asleep on his couch. I had not slept or rested since leaving Viet Nam, 30 hours before. At noon the siren alarm at the fire department across the street went off. Without thinking and just reacting I rolled off the couch and with my right hand lifted it off the floor and tried to crawl under it. Dad grabbed me and lifted the couch off my back. A few days later I tried to pick up the couch but was unable to do so by myself. Sudden noises still continue to get my attention over 40 years after leaving Viet Nam.

It was good to be home again but the transition from combat to the peace and tranquility of the Beaver Valley was not smooth. The first person I actually went to visit on my second day at home was Mom. She

99

had moved to Beaver and rented a second floor apartment that could only be accessed from the outside through stairs. I had called her before leaving Dad's house to tell her that I was on my way. The last thing I wanted to do was just knock on her door and surprise her after being gone for a year. I knew her well and knew that she would pass out from the surprise.

As I pulled up to the house and parked across the street I saw her standing on the landing outside the apartment. Roy was standing next to her and I noticed something very strange. He had a cast on his right leg going all the way up to his underarm. His left arm was in a cast that extended 90 degrees from his body at the shoulder. My first thought was "What the Hell?"

Mom came flying down the stairs, ran across the street and gave me the biggest hug I had ever received from her. She was sobbing and laughing at the same time causing me to cry as well. Roy hobbled down the stairs contrary to my request to stay there and that I would come to him. We met on the sidewalk and the three of us hugged, cried and laughed. It must have been a sight to see by the people driving past us.

We spent the rest of the day catching up. Roy's body cast was from his last wound in Viet Nam that caused him to be evacuated to DaNang and ultimately to Yokota Air Base in Japan. He described what happened in great detail.

A month after he left me to go back to the DMZ the North Vietnamese conducted a surprise attack at the Rock Pile. Mortars and rockets announced their initial attack. Roy was helping two brand new replacements getting settled in to the Rock digging their fox hole when he heard incoming rockets. Without a second thought he pushed them down and started to cover them with his body. It was too late when the rocket hit the ground. The shrapnel from the explosion hit Roy in the right hip and the concussion threw him quite a distance from the foxhole.

Roy never lost consciousness and did not feel pain until the Medics started to work on him. A medivac helicopter was called to evacuate Roy and the other wounded Marines. The UH-1 Helicopter had two stretchers on each side of the chopper. Roy was put onto the second tier stretcher and secured with his lap belt. As the helicopter left the ground and some distance above the ground enemy fire struck and severed the stretcher support strap near Roy's head and he felt as if he was falling out of the helicopter. He reached up and grabbed the door rail of the chopper with both hands and locked on for dear life. He held on all the way to Da Nang AFB where it took two medics to get him to release his grasp of the door rail.

After receiving initial medical care at Da Nang, he was evacuated to Yokota where he received intense and long term care and rehabilitation. The shrapnel had destroyed most of his muscles in the right hip and the doctors advised him that he would probably never walk again without a cane or other assisted device. They tried to give him crutches, but he refused to use them and threw the cane against the wall. Roy remained at the hospital recuperating for several months before being sent home in the body cast.

So what happened to your arm I asked? Mom told me that after coming home he visited her just the same way I did. As he was leaving the apartment and going down the stairs he tripped because of the body cast and tumbled down the stairs breaking his arm and collar bone. He laughed as I called him a dumb ass.

Roy asked if I wanted to go with him, his girlfriend Cheryl and a couple of the guys from the Karate School to the East Palestine, Ohio Roller Rena. Prior to going into the service we had been hired by the owner to be bouncers on the weekends. Many high school students went to the place and often caused fights to occur, especially after football games on Friday nights. We did not make many friends as a result of the many fights we broke up over about two years. I begged off because I had other plans. It turns out that I should have gone with them.

Soon after appearing at the Roller Rena some of the attendees noticed Roy's casts and decided that it was a great opportunity for them to exact some revenge. They waited for the right opportunity and it came when Roy had to go to the bathroom. Since he needed support while going to the restroom he used one of the stalls instead of a urinal. As he was leaning against the wall passing liquid someone struck him from behind knocking him down. The force caused him to rotate during the fall and sit on the toilet. The attacker came in for a second hit when Roy kicked him in the balls. He pulled himself up of the toilet and with his good arm reached up to the door frame above him and kicked the second attacker in the chest knocking him to the ground. The guy recovered and got off the floor and ran out of the restroom. Roy called out "Duke – Help –

get him!" Duke was one of our lead instructors and was standing just outside the bathroom waiting for Roy to finish.

A third attacker had been waiting for his opportunity to get to Roy and he ran out at the same time as the second guy. Duke held on to the second guy as the third ran past him, out the door into the parking lot and locked himself in his car. He evidently could not get to his keys and frantically tried to find them. Roy had recovered and was going after the punk. He hobbled out to the car and banged furiously on the car window. Being unsuccessful he grabbed one of the instructors by the shoulder and with his good leg kicked the driver's window to break it. He reached in to drag the guy out when the police arrived. The guy in the car was lucky to be saved by the arriving police. You just did not screw with Roy anytime – body and arm casts could not stop him.

After leaving Viet Nam, Roy started having debilitating grand mal seizures that required him to take medications to control. The seizures struck without warning. One day while working out at his Karate school, he was struck with a very bad seizure. As he fell to the floor mat, he bit off half of his tongue. The separated tongue flopped on the mat as he writhed on the floor. His instructors called for an ambulance and did what they could to keep him alive. Someone recovered the severed tongue and wrapped in a cloth and covered it with ice in an attempt to save it. The doctors were able to reattach his tongue and saved his life again. I returned home soon after the incident and he was still unable to talk while the wound was healing. Roy communicated with me in writing notes and explained that his worst experience was not being able to breathe as the part of the tongue that did not get severed retracted into his throat cutting off his ability to breathe. Roy was again "one tough Dude."

CHAPTER TWELVE
The Making of a Fighter

I visited the Karate School to see how things were going there. Dad had expanded the number of locations to three with one located in Weirton, WV and one in Ohio. One of my former students had asked to see me before I left Beaver Valley for my next assignment to McGuire AFB. Following is a short story about him.

Who would have known that the short, chunky and overweight weakling sitting before me, cowering in his mother's protective arms, would one day stand up to challenge me to hand-to-hand combat? What happened, little Butchy, to make you so cocky and self-assured?

Tom Becher was his real name, but his friends and the bullies who beat him, called him Butch. His mother brought him to my father's Karate school when Butch was eleven years old. He was recently beaten up rather brutally by some of his neighborhood's bullies. He demonstrated courage during the beating but lacked the ability to fight back. His mother wanted us to do something to prevent the beatings to her child from happening again. Her comments that day still ring in my ears, "Make him tough and make him strong!" It almost seemed she was expecting us to melt him down and pour him into a Superman mold.

The other instructors were pretty tied up with their students and could not have any more challenges added to their work load. Dad decided to lay this challenging task into my lap that day in 1964. He often did that with younger students and the women in our school. It seems I had an affinity towards teaching students who the other instructors did not want to or choose to work with.

The kid was eleven years old, four feet and eleven inches tall and almost equally as wide; or so it appeared to me. It seemed as if he rolled from place to place instead of walking. It became readily obvious that if I could slim him down and toughen up his body while strengthening his self-confidence that there was a fair chance of making him into a fighter. Butch would help tremendously because what he lacked in fighting skills and physical stamina he more than made up for in courage. Butch's desire to accomplish the seemingly impossible task of losing weight did more to make a lean fighting machine out of him than any other factor. He worked out harder and unlike any of my other students ever did. When directed to do twenty-five pushups Butch would do forty or more every time. This driving force applied to every task or exercise I assigned him. "Perfection" became his personal motto.

Butch had been laughed at and beaten up enough to last him a lifetime and no amount of shedding his blood, sweat and tears would be too much for him. His focus to excel was monumental and inspirational to all of us who watched him grow and mature. His fellow students grew to respect him a great deal and his tutors bragged about him constantly. Butch was going to be a champion fighter and everyone knew it. Other instructors and students talked about it openly and extensively in and out of Butch's earshot. Butch ignored them and went right ahead without further prompting or encouragement from me to become one.

It was during his first three tournaments when Butch really began to blossom and shine as a fighter. The Northeastern Karate Conference of 1967 brought Butch his first championship trophy. The Nationals in Pittsburgh, PA that same year also netted him top honors. Ultimately, the Grand-Nationals in Lake Erie resulted in Butch winning the Grand Championship trophy for his weight class. From that moment on there were first place honors all the way. Unfortunately for me I was in Viet Nam during this entire time and unable to watch him achieve these honors.

I had been serving in Viet Nam for a year before being able to visit home on leave in the spring of 1968. Upon arriving home my first stop was the Karate school where Butch was the first person to welcome me home. However, I did not recognize him at first. He was now well over six feet tall and his shoulders were twice as broad as mine. It took me a while to realize that Butch – chunky Butch – was standing before me looking down at me and resting his massive hands on my shoulders. I was shocked beyond description and stared in disbelief.

Butch jokingly and outright challenged me to a sparring match. Even though I was exhausted from the thirty-hour trip home from "Nam" I could not allow the challenge to go unanswered. All of the students and instructors were staring and expecting nothing less from me. Dad commented that I should go home and rest first and then come back another day. But I was up to the challenge and for the sake of my "honor" I accepted it and, though I ultimately won the hard fought match, it was oh-so-close. Butch had come a long way and was taught well. The unpleasant thought crossed my mind, "Did I win or did Butch let me win?"

My greatest and fondest memory of Butch came later that day as I watched him teach other students what he had learned from me. It further warmed my heart when Dad told me that he always sought out the weaker, younger students, and the students who, on initial observation, appeared to not possibly have a chance at becoming Kung Fu fighters, to be taught by me.

Butch had come a long way and matured a great deal in body, mind, spirit, and had developed a great love for the arts of self-defense. He was now the teacher and I proudly called him Mas Butch. Hey Butch! Who's that chunky little boy sitting in the corner cowering in his mother's protective arms?

Looking for Love

A close friend from Beaver Falls High School invited me to come watch him play in a school football game. Since I had never been to a game before I accepted and went to the game in my Air Force uniform. By the way – I wore it all the time because I was so proud to be in the Air Force. I was 20 and a combat veteran and had the medals to prove it.

Before the game started, I walked around the field and noticed the cheer leaders practicing their routines. One especially attractive cheerleader caught my eyes. I asked my buddy who she was and to introduce me. Being a rather shy and self-conscious person in those days I would or could not walk up to a beautiful girl and introduce myself. Her name was Jerry Meyers and I was smitten. This was the first girl or woman that I dated seriously since Penney and I had stopped communicating with each other two years earlier. I was always, and still am, a one woman at a time type of guy. Penney had written me a letter asking me to move on with my life since she had fallen in love with someone else. There was only one time period when I broke the "one girl" rule over a three year period of time. But that is another story.

Jerry and I clicked immediately and we spent every available moment together for the next year. Every weekend, holiday and official military leave opportunity I drove home from Dover to be with Jerry. We were in love, or at least I believed it was "we."

Wim, 1969

CHAPTER THIRTEEN
Base Jumping

Dover Air Force Base, Delaware

My first assignment back in the CONUS was Dover Air Force Base and to the Aerial Delivery (AD) shop. Unfortunately AD was co-located in the same hangar that was used as the morgue for all returning KIAs from Nam. We packed parachutes literally 4 feet from the KIA body processing line. It still sickens me today remembering that the morgue workers would eat their lunches standing or sitting next to the bodies they were processing. The stench of the bodies and formaldehyde hung over us like a dark sickening cloud every day.

Quite frankly I do not recall much about my tour at Dover other than I learned how to become a good airdrop rigger and parachute packer; skills that would serve me well during the rest of my Air Force career. I went to Fort Lee, VA to train and become a certified parachute rigger or "Red Hat".

I was promoted to Airman First Class or E-4 shortly after arriving on the base. Being promoted to E-4 in less than 4 years was almost unheard of in those days. Some guys retired as E-4s at 20 years. My tour at Dover was very short and I received an assignment to Kwang Ju, South Korea exactly one year after returning from Nam.

Before leaving for Korea I went home and asked Jerry to marry me. I had asked her father for permission in the old fashioned way and he and his wife gave me the blessing to ask her. Jerry accepted and we planned to be married upon my return on mid tour leave from Korea.

Kwang Ju Airbase, South Korea

It was May 1, 1969 when I arrived in Kwang Ju. I will never forget the day because the temperature was reported at about 20 degrees below zero. Again that was in May or what we in the USA call spring. After reporting to Korea the Air Force started a new examination process for promotion called the Skill Knowledge Test or SKT. I received score of 95 on the exam and along with good performance evaluations I received my promotion orders to Staff Sergeant or E-5 soon after. I sewed on my stripes exactly 2 years and 10 months after joining the Air Force. I was in competition with several other Airman for this promotion at the time. Guys that were considered to be my friends became cold and distant and most stopped talking to me. Unknown to me at the time but was told later in my career that I was considered to be an ass kisser and hard ass perfectionist. I admit to being a hard ass and perfectionist but I have never kissed anyone's ass to get ahead in life. Regardless, that reputation baggage followed me for the remainder of my 24 year career.

It was a bad time to be in Korea. Race riots broke out everywhere especially in Seoul close to the DMZ between North and South Korea. The business girls – otherwise known as prostitutes – and other business and bars refused to do business with African American soldiers and airmen. The racial discrimination problems were also exploding back home. The blacks had enough and started riots at the bars in town and set a big part of downtown Seoul ablaze. We were confined to the base in Kwang Ju until things settled down. They didn't for the remainder of my 13 month tour.

I do not tolerate alcohol in any form very well. One beer will get me drunk and I lose my memory when drinking champagne. About 4 months into tour in Korea I received a care package from Jerry's mother. It was a pleasant surprise initially until I opened it and found Jerry's engagement ring and a short "Dear John" letter from her breaking off the engagement. I was shocked and hurt. I walked off the job and went to the NCO club and got shit-faced drunk.

My boss followed me to the club to find out what happened. We talked and got drunk together. At some point I had to take a leak and pushed my chair back from the table. The chair bumped into a chair at another table behind me angering the guy sitting in it. He got up, turned around and grabbed me by the collar and jerked me out of my seat. My instinctual reaction was to turn around, while grabbing his wrist, twisting it over causing him to bend over and exposing his elbow allowing me to forcefully strike and break it. My boss grabbed me and dragged me out of the bar. Security Police arrived shortly after. After hearing the explanation that I was defending myself from attack they released me to return to work.

I was given an Emergency Leave to go home and settle my affairs. This typically would not have been considered a justification for an Emergency Leave but my boss wanted me off the base until things calmed down. I was facing the possibility of a court martial. Since I worked in the Air Freight and Transportation unit it was an easy process getting me an Emergency Leave flight back to the states.

Things did not go well at home and I found out that Jerry had met another guy and they had become engaged to be married. I returned to Korea after a two week leave. Upon my return I found out that the guy who I hurt had dropped the charges against me because he actually started the fight. The rest of my 13 month tour in Korea went smoothly until I received my Permanent Change of Station (PCS) orders for my new assignment to McGuire AFB, NJ to the Base Supply Squadron.

I was in the barracks when I received my PCS orders. Immediately after reading the assignment to McGuire and worse yet reading that I was going to Supply I swore, made a fist and punched the wall. Unfortunately there was a nail sticking in the wall with about two inches exposed. The nail imbedded my fist between my middle and fourth finger. I screamed in pain as I jerked my hand back bleeding profusely. All I had ever heard about McGuire AFB was that it was a shit hole and a terrible place to be assigned. Worse yet I was going to be assigned to a Supply job. I could not have thought of a worse job to go to, considering my combat support experience. This comment in no way is meant to disparage Supply personnel because of the significant role they play, it just was not for me. My first 4 year enlistment was coming to an end in another year so I decided to get out of the Air Force after finishing my tour at McGuire.

McGuire AFB, New Jersey

"You don't ask – you don't get!" Dad's words kept coming back to me as I was traveling back to the CONUS and McGuire AFB. The day before reporting to the Supply squadron I took it upon myself to see the Aerial Delivery Squadron commander. His name was Captain Johnson; a massive human being and one of the most professional and imposing officers that I have ever had the pleasure and honor to meet.

Without an appointment I knocked on his office door and reported to him as "SSgt Wetzel requesting to meet with you – Sir!" He asked me to come in and tell him what I wanted. I explained that I was returning from Korea and was assigned to Supply. I gave him a list of my qualifications to include all of the combat vehicles and equipment I was certified to operate, my experience in AD and my combat experience at Viet Nam to include the sieges at Dak To and Khe Sahn. I clearly explained how my skill would be wasted in Supply and that I wanted to work for him in AD.

"You got balls SSgt Wetzel! I think you will fit nicely in my unit. Report to me in the morning. I will make some calls and see what I can do to arrange for you to work inn AD. I cannot promise you anything so be prepared to go to Supply if things do not work out as I expect. You are dismissed."

I thanked him profusely and promised him that he would not regret the help. I saluted and did an about face and left his office with a huge smile on my face. I knew in my heart that Captain Johnson would be successful in getting approval for my transfer. I do not know how he did it or who he contacted but when I reported to him the following morning he shook my hand, handed me a rigger's red hat and welcomed me aboard the team. I was ecstatic and once again promised that he would never regret going to bat for me.

I loved my three year tour at McGuire AFB. It was a great base to be assigned contrary to all the negative things I had heard about it. My roommate, Ken, suggested that I learn to skydive so that we could go into competitions. He took my buddy Tom Householder, who lived near my home in PA, and I out to the local sky diving center and we became certified.

On my first static line jump from the Cessna172 I was so excited to jump that before the jumpmaster actually told me to jump I had already done so. Fear never entered my thoughts. My first landing was in a 5 foot high pile of manure in a farmer's pasture. A parachute landing fall or PLF was unnecessary. The jump school owner made me ride in the back of the school's pickup truck on the way back to his training center.

My second jump was not so free from fear or trepidation. I exited the aircraft and stood on the aircraft tire and held on to the strut waiting for the pilot to cut the engine power and the instructor to tell me to jump. The engine went to idle and the jump order came. I was holding onto the strut for my dear life. It took the instructor several attempts to break my hands free of the strut so that I could fall free before the aircraft stalled. Once free and away from the aircraft I was once again relaxed and enjoying the drop. We all jumped three more times to obtain our certifications. During my remaining time at McGuire I recorded 35 parachute jumps.

Ken signed us up to compete in the annual Combat Control skydiving competition at Hurlburt Field near Panama, Florida. To my pleasant surprise and Captain Johnson's support the Air Force provided us with temporary duty orders to attend the competition. We jumped out of Huey Helicopters and a C-130. Although we did not win or place anywhere in the competition it was another experience of a lifetime.

My last freefall sky diving experience was disastrous as I watched a fellow diver die. We were at Perris drop zone near the Salton Sea, CA and decided to do a couple of jumps over the sea. The jump plane climbed to 17,500 feet with six jumpers. I was the fourth jumper leaving the aircraft and freefell to 2,500 feet where I opened my chute. The person who jumped after me continued to freefall. I expected that he would open his parachute at about 2,000 feet but he didn't. We watched in horror as he impacted the ground at 120 miles per hour. It was determined that he committed suicide. I sold my parachute and never jumped again.

Wim, the Pilot Living the Dream

CHAPTER FOURTEEN
New Challenges and Horizons

When I was eleven my Dad gave me a ride in a Cessna 150 for a birthday present. The flying bug bit me that day and I made up my mind to become a pilot one day. That day came after I became a C-141 Loadmaster and started collecting flight pay and could afford the training. I joined the McGuire AFB Flying Club. I will admit that I was a slow student and even considered quitting the training program. I did not solo until the 10th hour of training and my first solo landing was aborted and I had to go around. For any pilot reading this, keep in mind I was trying to land a Cessna 150 on a 10,000 foot Air Force runway. I never got lower than about 5 – 10 feet the entire length of the runway. Finally, I landed and completed three successful solo stop and go takeoffs and landings.

On November 10, 1972 and the 17th hour of my training I was cleared to go on the first short cross country flight to Millville, NJ. The weather was awful. Lots of humidity and cloud cover with the dew point spread of 2 degrees. I had a bad premonition telling me not to fly. I expressed my concern to the chief flight instructor, but he insisted that he had confidence in my ability to make the 100 mile round trip.

With trepidation I drove to Base Operations and filed my flight plan. My takeoff was smooth and I leveled off at 3,500 feet. Clouds were well above me but there was a great deal of visible moisture with rivulets of rain striking the wind screen. Twenty minutes into the flight I looked behind me and McGuire was no longer in view. Forward visibility was limited and getting worse. Suddenly the aircraft engine started to vibrate and the propeller turned slower and slower. It did not stop, but I sensed that it would if something was not done quickly. I pumped the throttle several times thinking that the engine was not getting fuel. The engine revved up and the propeller sped up, causing the RPMs to return to normal. I breathed deeply and began to relax. Then suddenly the engine vibrated badly, stuttered and the propeller stopped turning. Nothing happened after pumping the throttle and trying to start the engine. I freaked out but had the sense to put the aircraft into its best glide speed.

I remember clearly saying three times: "God help me, God help me, God help me!" I picked up the microphone and transmitted "Mayday – Mayday – Mayday – Cessna 23414 over southern New Jersey with total engine failure.

The tower at the Millville, NJ airport responded immediately with "Cessna 23414 what is your location?"

"I don't know. Visibility is almost zero and my engine quit – Over!"

The tower directed me to follow specific microphone keying procedures so that they could determine my location.

I was at about 2,000 feet looking out and below only to see nothing but scrub trees and brush that is common in southern coastal New Jersey. I repeated "Dear God please help me!"

I looked out the pilot door window and down again. I saw a small house with a pasture behind it. My decision was immediate and I started emergency landing procedures. Descending with the best glide speed I flew downwind, base and final with flaps down for a soft field landing. On final approach I pulled the carburetor heat and powered down for the landing. The main landing gear touched down and the engine screamed to life, startling me. There was enough room to take off but I said, Hell with it, and came to a full stop. I sat there in shock for quite a while until I heard someone banging on the passenger door and cussing at me. I reached across and opened the door. The farmer was furious at me for landing on his property and continued to cuss me out. His wife told him to calm down and asked me what I was doing there.

I was shaken up and could not speak but opened the door and got out. After a couple of minutes I explained what happened. The farmer and his wife asked me to come into their home. I asked them to let me call the airport tower to let them know I was OK. The local area FAA flight inspector answered the phone. He asked me to tell him exactly what had happened. His immediate response was "You had carburetor icing!" My response was "What is carburetor icing?" His response was "Who is your flight instructor?"

Seventeen hours of flight time in my log book and my instructor never told me about carburetor icing. He had assumed that I knew what it was since he had taught me the landing preparation procedures but did not teach me "why" a pilot had to use the carburetor heat lever for landing.

The FAA inspector sent a mechanic to my location that was only 15 minutes away from the Millville airport. The mechanic cleared the airplane for flight after doing an engine test run. He asked me if I could take off using a soft field landing departure. I told him yes. He advised me that the airport was due west of my current location and that I would be able to see it from about 1,000 feet. After a quick call to the tower and speaking with the FAA inspector I was cleared to take off. I thanked the farm couple profusely and departed. My 15 minute flight was uneventful.

The FAA inspector met me on the tarmac and helped me refuel while teaching me about carburetor icing. The weather had cleared and he gave me specific instructions on how to return to McGuire AFB due north of the airport. He entered his clearance in my logbook, I thanked him and departed. My return flight was uneventful and I landed at McGuire without any further incidents. After landing I received a call from Ground Control directing me to report to Base Operations immediately after putting the Cessna in the hanger.

The Base Operations officer, a civilian, was livid. My flight instructor was standing there with a confused look on his face and asked me what happened. The Base Ops officer said "Never mind that! Why did you depart without approval and NOT filing a flight plan?"

"I had approval from my flight instructor and I did file a flight plan with the Sergeant."

"We do not have a flight plan for your flight on file so you took off without filing!" he stated.

I looked at the Sergeant and reminded her of our earlier discussion and about handing her my flight plan. She removed the vertical folder from the top of the file cabinet looking for my flight plan. It was not in the folder. We looked everywhere and finally found it behind the file cabinet. The Ops officer apologized and I went home. I had decided my flight career was over and did not fly again for over a month. Once I recovered from the poor flight experience I met with my instructor who convinced me to start again. I obtained my license at 76 hours which is pretty extreme for getting a Private Pilot's license. Over time I obtained my commercial and instrument ratings and finally achieved the pillar of my civilian pilot certifications, single and multi-engine instrument flight instructor ratings.

Roy was my first passenger after I received my Private Pilot's license. I rented a Cessna 150 from the aero club and flew cross country to the Beaver County Airport in Beaver Falls, PA. Roy met me to drive me home but I asked him to give me the honor of being my first passenger. He just flat out refused, but would not tell me why. That Sunday I had to return to McGuire AFB and on the way back to the airport, I was able to convince him to take a short ride around the Valley with me. He was visibly nervous if not afraid. That was shocking to me because Roy was fearless.

We buckled in, taxied out and took off. Roy was shaking and sweating profusely as we climbed out. Not even 200 feet off the ground he said "Get me down! Get me down! Can't you see the tracers? Get me the fuck down now!" and he reached for the door handle to open the door. I grabbed his hand and yelled that I would land immediately but he had to calm down or we could crash. He closed his eyes and refused to open them as we climbed to the pattern altitude and started to fly downwind for landing. As we turned to base and final he said "I'm going to throw up."

"Not in my airplane you're not!" I yelled as I reached across and unlocked the window and shoved his head out. He lost his cookies outside just in time. We made the final approach and landed. Soon after and while still taxiing he jumped out of the door and ran to his car. He did not fly again for several years. Only the opportunity to go hunting and fishing with friends in Canada got him through the memories, trauma and fear of falling out of the helicopter in Nam.

A Dream Comes True: Basic Loadmaster School

About 6 months into my assignment, I applied for Loadmaster school. In those days you had to have Air Freight experience to be selected for cross training to Loadmaster. With the help of Captain Johnson and John Burkhardt (my supervisor) I was selected for cross training. Basic Loadmaster School was a two month course at Sheppard AFB, TX. I flew through the training with a passion that was unequaled during my short career in the Air Force. Just short of completing the first month I decided to ask the school Superintendent if I could somehow take a bypass test to avoid going through another month of training. At this point I had aced every exam and felt that I could do the same with a by-pass exam. The Superintendent advised me that there was a bypass test but no one had ever passed it. Regardless he gave me the chance to take it. I passed the exam with flying colors and graduated with honors at the half way point of the course. As far as I know, no one else had ever, or since then, accomplished this feat.

I called Captain Johnson with the good news. He told me that I was not expected to return to the base for another month so that I could go home for a thirty day leave. I did so and discovered that he never charged me for that leave time.

Upon reporting back to McGuire I volunteered to fly the C-119 known as the "Flying Coffin" in Florida. No one could even get on this aircraft unless you wore a parachute, but thanks to the Air Force, I was selected to fly C-133s at McGuire. The C-133 was nicknamed the Flying Silo. It had a history of self-destructing in flight and crashing. Regardless I was excited to start my new assignment. I reported to the 18th flying squadron chief loadmaster who promptly advised me that my assignment was changed to flying the C-141A. All of the C-133s had been permanently grounded since they had just lost another one in the Atlantic Ocean the previous day. All they found of the lost aircraft was seat cushions and other floating debris.

My instructor loadmaster was TSgt George (Clutch Cargo) McCluskey; a huge and very outspoken man with a reputation of being "a one of a kind!" Clutch and I became good friends and he taught me well. We were scheduled to fly my first training mission the next morning at oh-500 (5 am). He told me to report to him right after being alerted by base operations. I did and we got on the crew bus to prepare my first C-141 mission. To my surprise the tail number of the C-141 ended with the numbers 133.

Flying and being trained by Clutch was a unique experience. Clutch was my instructor for my first over water mission to the Pacific bases. This first mission transited Elmendorf AFB, Alaska, Yokota AB, Japan, Kadena AB, Okinawa, Clark AFB, Philippines, Anderson AFB, Guam, Hickam AFB, HI and a return home to McGuire. During our trip through Clark AFB, I turned 24. Clutch and the enlisted crew decided to celebrate my birthday in style. I won't get into the seedy side of the 24 hour celebration but I can tell you that I got so drunk that I passed out. Clutch carried me over his shoulder back to the room in the hotel and made sure I was laid on my side on the bed. He wanted to make sure I did not choke on my vomit if I laid on my back. Clutch and one of the

Flight Engineers actually slept in the chairs in the room to ensure I was going to be OK.

Eight hours from the "Bottle to the Throttle" was the rule. Crew members were not permitted to fly for many hours after drinking. Unfortunately, I was still passed out when the alert call from Base Operations came. I was unfit for flight duty. Clutch and the engineer cleaned me up helped me get into my flight suit and carried me out to the crew bus. We arrived at the aircraft before the pilot and co-pilot. Clutch once again carried me over his shoulder up the crew entry door and up the cockpit ladder and put me in the crew rest bunk. He covered me with a blanket and found a way to keep me out of the pilots' view. He conducted the preflight and the cargo on-load and responded on my behalf any time the pilots tried to contact me. I will never know how he and the other enlisted crew members kept my condition secret from the pilots. We took off from Clark and flew to Anderson. I regained consciousness upon landing at Guam and as far as I knew no one but the enlisted crew knew anything different about my fitness to fly the mission.

Clutch was a great instructor who often implemented unorthodox methods to get his points across. During my training for airdrop qualification I could not control the queasiness of the low level terrain following flights and constantly threw up. Clutch got tired of my running to the latrine and tied a large blue garbage bag around my neck. Until I became used to the rough and turbulent flights I wore the trash bag around my neck. The Army paratroopers thought it was the funniest thing they had ever seen on airdrop missions.

Clutch was known to speak his mind regardless who he spoke with; General officers included. Many of his colleagues had doubts that he would ever be promoted but Clutch fooled them all as he steadily climbed the ladder to the highest enlisted rank of Chief Master Sergeant. I owe a great deal of my success as a Loadmaster directly to Clutch.

My primary assignment at McGuire was to the Airlift Control Element (ALCE) Team. This significantly limited my flying duties but gave me a wealth of experience in supporting combat and other missions across the globe.

CHAPTER FIFTEEN
A Leap Into Hell

My roommate at McGuire was a Combat Controller and a favorite amongst the women at McGuire. It was a rare occasion when I went back to the barracks at night when he did not have a girl in bed with him. It was especially disheartening to hear him having sex literally every night. He offered to introduce me to some of his girlfriends but I was not interested. I was still not over Jerry and my disappointment in that relationship.

I went to the Airman's club even though I was an NCO. The first person I met there was a very attractive Air Force Recruiter. Her name was Cricket Schum. Cricket was a gorgeous, bubbly and a very energetic woman. We started dating and eventually became engaged. The engagement lasted about a week but our friendship continues on to this day. Cricket would ultimately introduce me to my first wife.

In July of 1972 I received PCS orders to the 61st Military Airlift Wing ALCE team at Hickam AFB, HI. I decided to drive across the country to San Francisco, CA to catch my flight to Honolulu. On my route I planned to drive through Decatur, IL to visit Cricket at her parent's home. I planned to stay for a couple of days before proceeding to California. Upon my arrival in Decatur Cricket told me she had arranged for a blind date for me with her best friend. I was hesitant but finally agreed to meet her. Cricket drove me to her friend's home to introduce us to one another. Her friend was Debbie Horenkamp. As we drove up to Debbie's house we saw her standing on her porch. Something inside me said "That is the girl I am going to marry!"

Debbie and I clicked instantaneously and the sex was unabashedly phenomenal. We never mentioned or discussed any further contacts or relationships during this time since we only had three days together, but somehow I knew that we would meet again. During our time together we saw the Steve McQueen and Ali McGraw movie "*The Get Away.*" Debbie had a bit part in the film as an Army soldier going on leave through the

San Antonio train station. Unknown to me at the time that I met Debbie she was actually in the Army but had been AWOL or absent without leave for over a month, and the Army was looking for her.

Enroute to San Francisco I had to report to Travis AFB to attend C-5 Loadmaster training school. Since my new assignment at Hickam required me to plan and load the C-5 I had to know how to load them and to complete the Form F Weight and Balance Forms.

Hickam AFB, HI

I reported to my new boss MSgt Howard Berg in August 1972. The ALCE team's mission was to support all contingences in the Pacific region and it was a busy and exciting time. Viet Nam was winding down and we were supporting all of the missions going into and out of the war zone. I was assigned to train the Marines at Kaneohe MCAS and the Army Transportation soldiers at the 173rd Airborne Brigade on how to load plan cargo loads on the Air Force C-141 and C-5 cargo aircraft.

My immediate supervisor was a complete asshole and a racist from Mississippi. I will use a fictitious name since he hated me enough to sue me for mentioning his name in this writing. I will refer to his as Jimmy-John. After being introduced to him Jimmy-John referred to Asians as zipper heads. He asked me where I came from and I responded "from Pennsylvania."

"No, he said. Where are you from?"

When I told him that I was born in Indonesia Jimmy-John turned away and muttered something about working with zipper heads. Fortunately I only had to work for him for nine months before he rotated back to the mainland. But while I reported to him he made my life miserable. His departing shot before leaving for the CONUS he wrote me a horrible performance evaluation. MSgt Berg rewrote the evaluation in a most favorable way and forced Jimmy-John to sign it.

Debbie and I stayed in touch by phone and letters. Cricket called me to let me know that Debbie was AWOL. She went AWOL because her NCO and a couple of the women in her unit were lesbians and were harassing her. Debbie reported it to higher ups but they refused to believe her. The women threatened her and Debbie felt that she had to get away and went AWOL.

I called her and talked her into turning herself in and to get her record straightened out. Hesitant at first she finally agreed to face her punishment. As it ultimately turned out, several other soldiers came to her defense at court martial and let the board know that they had also been harassed. The charges were dismissed and her record was cleared. Debbie returned to active service and was promoted to E-4 at Fort Bliss.

I received orders to go to Norton AFB to attend the NCO Leadership School. While there I asked Debbie to come to the graduation ceremony and banquet. I bought her the airline ticket and picked her up at the LA airport. I graduated with honors and we celebrated with my peers and our wives and girlfriends all night.

Sometime during the night I asked Debbie to marry me. She accepted and we set a date for her to come to Hawaii. It was at that point that I learned that she was in the Army and would need to arrange for a transfer once we were married. There was so much unsettling information about Debbie that a smart man would have discovered before asking someone to get married. Affairs of the heart have not been one of my strengths. But for some stupid reason I had the distinct impression that I had to be married before my 27th birthday and to start a family.

I returned to Hickam and received permission from the squadron commander to get married. Permission was required during those days. Howard and the rest of the ALCE team offered to arrange for the wedding details and the reception. I gladly accepted the offer and ultimately regretted doing so.

Debbie arrived at the Honolulu airport three days before the wedding. We checked into a hotel in downtown Honolulu and never left the room except to eat.

The base chaplain officiated the wedding. The wedding reception was held at the squadron and the room was packed with my peers and civilian friends. The decorations were shocking and pretty much foretold the future of our union. The punch bowl was a toilet and the snacks were served in wall mounted plastic urinals. The reception dinner meals were served in hospital bedpans and the drinks served in hospital bed men's urinals.

There was no honeymoon since I was sent on a thirty mission two days after the wedding. I saw Debbie about seven days over the next 3 months. During my absences she was having affairs with several guys and had started taking drugs. Worse than that, she was prostituting herself at the Pearl Harbor naval base.

Debbie's reassignment orders arrived and she was assigned to the Fort Derussy Army post in Honolulu. We started planning and working on having a baby. It did not go well. Debbie had an ectopic pregnancy 3 months after we were married and miscarried. Doctors determined that her ability to have children was improbable without special medical assistance that would be very expensive. Debbie applied for a discharge from the Army and it was approved.

My job required me to travel about 23 days a month. My constant time away from home caused a tremendous amount of distress between us and the marriage began to disintegrate.

I was on an assignment for a month at Clark AFB to train the Philippine Air Freight team members on load planning. I was conducting a class when the classroom telephone rang. It was an alert phone so I had to answer the call. I responded as SSgt Wetzel. The caller did not identify himself but said "I need to speak with Tech Sgt Wetzel." I responded twice more as Staff Sgt Wetzel. The caller finally identified himself as my First Sergeant and stated "No I'm talking to Tech Sgt Wetzel. You just got promoted to Tech Sgt. Congratulations!" I told the students what just happened and they congratulated me. I was extremely happy with the news when the First Sergeant said; "Just a minute. Your wife is here and wants to talk to you."

I expected to hear her say congratulations, which she did. Then she followed the comment with; "I hope you are happy since that is all you care about. Good bye. I am leaving you!" She hung up leaving me flatfooted and shocked.

CHAPTER SIXTEEN
A Plan for Dying
The End of a Wondrous but Tragic Life

I tried to continue the class without much success and was released for the remainder of the day. The First Sergeant called me back and advised me to return to Hickam on the first available flight. Howard supported that order and I returned to Hickam. When I arrived at our on-base housing I opened the door to an empty house. Even the dog was gone. The telephone was disconnected and I could not call Debbie.

The next day I went to the base credit union to get some cash only to find out the accounts had zero balances. I tried to get cash through the three credit cards we had only to find out that they were maxed out. Debbie had purchased First Class tickets to return to Decatur. She left me bankrupt and financially helpless.

Howard asked me to move into his house since I had to vacate base housing. He was worried about me and wanted to help. While staying with Howard I suffered a complete mental breakdown. I overdosed on sleeping pills that were taken with a half a bottle of Vodka. I remember lying down on the bed before falling into a coma.

For some unknown reason Debbie called Howard and asked to speak to me. Howard told her I was in bed asleep. Debbie in a panic, according to Howard, yelled go into his room and wake him up. Make sure he is OK. Howard complied and found me unconscious. He called for an ambulance and I was transported to the Tripler Army Hospital. I remained in a coma for three days and awakened to see Roy sitting next to the hospital bed. My First Sergeant was standing at the foot of the bed and said he was glad to see me alive and recovering. He also said "We are processing you for medical discharge and red-lining your promotion orders." My Air Force career was essentially over.

I refused to accept the news and told him without hesitation that I did not accept that action. Not only would I stay in the Air Force but I will get my promotion. One of the major reasons I was in this predicament was his failure to take care of his men. He had known about Debbie's behavior and failed to tell me about it.

I was assigned a mental health specialist at Tripler for thirty days. She did a complete mental evaluation that included the way I was raised at home. Her report to my commander was pretty conclusive that I was not trying to commit suicide. My overdose was a way for me to reach out for help.

During my recovery I received a call from Roy who had returned to Pennsylvania. It was Sunday March 16, 1975 around 18:20 Honolulu Time.

Roy said: "Are you sitting down?"

I answered "No!"

"Sit down! I have something to tell you. You need to sit down for what I have to tell you - so sit down!"

I lied and said; "OK! I'm sitting."

"Dad is dead and I killed him!"

"What did you say?"

"Dad is dead and I killed him!"

Before I could respond a stranger answered the phone and said; "Who is this?"

"I'm Wim. Roy's oldest brother. Is what Roy just said true, and who are you?"

"I'm Chief Colaluca, the Center Township Chief of Police and, yes, your father is dead and it appears that Roy did take his life. From what I can see it appears to be self-defense. Wherever you are - you better get home quickly!" Chief Colaluca hung up before I could respond.

Our lifelong fears about Dad's death threats finally came to fruition. His horrible and insane plan had finally come together. Roy was the best trained to defend himself from Dad. As yet I did not know that Mom was the first target.

I called my First Sergeant immediately and advised him of the call. The "Top" said he would confirm the emergency with the local Red Cross but for me to pack my bags and to get ready to go home.

The next two hours passed agonizingly slow and my brain waves shot into overdrive. I had known this day was coming from the time I was a pre-teen in Pennsylvania. All of us - my brothers and sister - knew it was going to happen eventually. Now we were going to have to deal with the reality of the crises at home.

The phone rang. "This is Tech Sergeant Wetzel."

"Sergeant Wetzel - this is Base Operations. Are you packed and ready to travel? We have a C-141 ready for take-off for Travis AFB and ordered it to return to the holding area and prepare for an ERO (engine running on load). Base Transportation is on the way to your quarters to pick you up!"

"I'm packed and will be waiting outside. Thank you very much Sir!"

I don't know what strings the First Sergeant pulled to arrange for this action but I would never forget it nor adequately pay the Air Force back for it.

Upon arrival at Travis AFB I was immediately whisked off to a waiting taxi heading for San Francisco International. Airline reservations to Pittsburgh were already made and paid for. To this day I do not know who made the arrangements or who paid for the ticket and taxi. All I know is that "the Air Force takes care of its own!" was no longer just a casual comment.

As my flight descended for landing at Pittsburgh International its path coincidentally took us over Beaver Valley, down the Ohio River and directly over Dad's house at 450 Jefferson Avenue in Vanport, PA As I looked down at the house I felt a sense of relief and like a heavy load was lifted off my back. For the very first time in my life while coming home to the "Valley" I felt absolutely no fear or premonition for bad things to happen there. The fear of losing my life at my father's hands was gone for the first time. God help me! I had a sense of peace that previously eluded me all of my life.

My flight landed at about eleven am and a Karate student friend was waiting for me. We shoved my bags into the trunk and immediately headed home. I asked him to take me to the police station first so that I could see Roy. Words cannot adequately describe the terrible condition Roy was in.

His jail cell reeked of smoke and other odors that were not identifiable. The top of the mattress on his cot was burned to a crisp. Apparently another prisoner had lit the mattress on fire the previous day and the jail staff had yet to replace it. Roy's right arm from the wrist to almost his elbow was red, swollen with portions of his skin peeling off.

The jail guard had brought Roy a pot of boiling hot coffee and while handing it to Roy spilled it on his right arm. The skin literally boiled off part of his forearm. He was in obvious shock and in terrible pain. But Roy, being Roy as those who knew him well, just gritted his teeth and soldiered on. He was shirtless and it appeared that he had razor cuts all over his chest, arms, neck, back and face. We ultimately counted 56 such cuts better described as slash wounds.

His jaw appeared to be dislocated and his cheeks were horrible swollen. He opened his mouth wide and showed me what appeared to be four long scratch marks at the back of his tongue and down his throat. "He tried to tear my jaw off!" Roy said.

His right thigh was bleeding and there was a slash type hole in his pant leg at the site of the bleeding. It was the place where Dad buried his pen knife deeply into the thigh to the bone. Apparently it was the last action Dad took before expiring during the fight.

Tears welled up in my eyes because a feeling of helplessness overwhelmed me and I could not hug him. I fought back my failing emotions and gathered myself to give Roy the confidence that I would help him through this.

"Judge Beryl Klein set my bail at $15,000 and wants the cash before I can go home. Where am I going to get that kind of money Wim?" Roy asked.

"I don't know Roy but I will get every penny and get you out of here as soon as possible. I promise! What do you need now?"

"They won't let me take any of my seizure meds or the other medications the VA provides me."

"I'll take care of that before I leave. We'll get through this Roy so try to get some rest. I'll get you a new mattress and clean sheets."

After calming him down, getting his medications and a new rack, I left with the promise that the next time I saw him would be to get him out of jail.

The remainder of the day and most of Tuesday I knocked on every door of every friend or acquaintance to literally beg for assistance in getting bail money. On March 18th my stepmother put up most of the bail because, as she told me then, Roy was not guilty of murder. She knew that dad had a history of violence towards his first family, even though he was gentle and kind with his two new children. Roy was released into my custody.

Unfortunately though, and I do not know to this day why, but she pulled his bail on June 23rd. For reasons only known to her, she changed her mind about Roy's innocence. Roy had many friends who came to help keep him out on bail. On June 24th Mildred Gatty and Ted and Virginia Lazzlo put up their personal homes and property to meet the bail requirements and Roy was set free again.

I had recently reenlisted while flying on a combat mission over Viet Nam and received a tax free re-enlistment bonus of $7,500. It would be needed to pay for or at least part of the lawyer fees.

After a couple of day's rest and medical care for his numerous wounds Roy described the events that resulted in the death of our father.

"What the hell happened, Roy?" I asked.

I already knew the answer since all of our lives Dad threatened to kill us one day. In essence Dad had planned most of his life to die by the hands of one of his sons. But I wanted to know exactly what occurred that fateful day on March 16, 1975.

Roy with Wim Jr and Christian in New Brighton, PA

CHAPTER SEVENTEEN
A Day in Infamy
Murder and Redemption

A bad feeling hung over my head during all of that day in Hawaii where I was stationed; like a black storm cloud hovering over me wherever I went. I even mentioned it to my current girlfriend earlier that day at the movie theater in downtown Honolulu. "Something is wrong at home!" I said. "I don't know what but whatever it is, it's not good!" My sixth sense had never failed me and it was kicking my ass that day and I could not get a handle on it.

Many stories have been told about that infamous day in Pennsylvania. Most of them are factually incorrect, blatantly untrue, if not out and out lies, by those who hoped to benefit from their telling. Many of them can be found online and even a so-called book containing the true facts was published. In order to not give credence to this book I am not going to provide the name in this chapter or within any part of this book. Serve it to say that it is a mixture of half-truths, downright attempts to create a legend in the telling of the stories and to make a profit at the expense of my brother Roy.

Most of the published online crap states that Roy is the oldest brother in the family and that he often fought to protect me and my youngest brother Jimmy from bullies. Anyone who really knew us would tell you that we could hold our own in any fight.

Roy and Jim loved a good fight. Not me. Unless a fight was unavoidable, I followed the basic premise Dad always taught us. If the options are to fight or walk away, then walk away and always face your opponent. Never turn your back to them when doing so. Not Roy or anyone else ever had to fight to defend me or on my behalf.

It was another bad time for Dad in his troubled life. He was going through his second divorce and in financial trouble. He was a financially responsible man who did everything he could to provide for his family regardless how hard times became.

The final day of lifelong threats to kill us all had finally arrived! Dad was leaving this earth for Hell and he was going to take us with him. He first went to Jane's house and knocked on the door. Jane, like the rest of us, had a strong sixth sense and immediately determined that something bad would happen if she let him in the door. She told her children not to answer and refused to open the door. Dad ultimately left.

Dad then drove to Roy's house in Monaca, PA. It was about 6 pm that fateful night. He did not knock and just let himself in the door. Roy's Doberman went nuts and barked furiously at Dad and threatening to attack him. Roy grabbed the dog by the collar and put him in the same room where his precious daughter Rochelle was sleeping. The dog would not stop barking as it viciously clawed and chewed the door trying it get out. It was not the first pet that hated Dad. Every pet we ever had feared and hated him as told in other chapters in this book.

"Are you done with my income taxes?"Dad asked.

"Yes! You owe Uncle Sam some money, but you can review and sign the tax forms now if you want to."

Dad started to review the tax forms and suddenly stopped. He grumbled some unintelligible words and stated "I hate this country! I'm losing everything, my house, my car, the Karate school and Peggy and the kids! It is over!" He crumpled the tax forms into a ball and threw them against the wall, then turned around and started to leave.

Over the many years that I served in the Air Force and traveling all over the world to many countries I collected items to help me remember a specific place. In Viet Nam I purchased a sword from a Montagnard tribesman and gave it to Roy as a souvenir or something to use at the Karate School. While in Japan I purchased a set of three Samurai swords for the same reason. Roy cherished all of these Asian weapons and kept them in his home for everyone to see.

As he was ready to open the door to leave, Dad spied the Vietnamese sword and reached for it. He walked towards Roy while unsheathing it and started to rant and rave that it was time to die. Roy met him half way to the door and grabbed the sheath in one hand and Dad's right elbow to keep him from completely unsheathing the weapon. During that process the sword was bent but still useable to strike a fatal blow to Roy's body.

Dad missed and lost control of the bent and unbalanced weapon which fell to the floor.

Dad rushed Roy and both tumbled to the floor in a fist pounding and kicking mass. They wrestled and fought in this deadly match until Roy was able to get away. Dad threw a couple of kicks to Roy's body with one round house kick making hard contact to is abdomen. Roy countered with a kick to Dad's head temporarily knocking him to the floor where he hit his head on the floor heating grate. The blow to the head opened a large gash that exposed Dad's brain. Some brain matter was oozing from the horrible gash. This blow to the head would stop any further hostile action from anyone in a fight. Not Dad! A demon had taken over his body and there was not going to be a slight brain leakage that would stop him. He reverted to animal instincts that served him well during his POW days.

Dad grabbed the Samurai sword from its display rack on the mantle. He swung it wildly at Roy trying to decapitate him. Upon seeing Dad winding up to make a final and fatal slash to his head Roy reached just slightly behind him and grabbed one of the supporting beams of his étagère and pulled it across his chest. The samurai sword struck the étagère bending he sword in half. The étagère slammed to the floor scattering and breaking all its glass and collectable contents.

Rochell was crying and the dog was barking furiously reminding Roy that he had to protect his baby. Trying desperately to get away from Dad's wrath and trying to get him to stop Roy made the deadly mistake of briefly turning his head towards the baby's bedroom door and losing sight of Dad. This allowed Dad to grab Roy from behind with his left arm while reaching around with is free hand to grab Roy's lower jaw with four fingers of his hand in his mouth. The premise as Dad taught us in our training is that if you can get your hand in your opponent's mouth they cannot bite while you try to rip their out tongue or to tear and separate the lower jaw from the head. This is where Roy suffered the cut marks along his tongue and down is throat. During his medical exam after the ambulance arrived the medics found finger nail marks deep in Roy's throat and along his tongue. The prosecuting attorney at Roy's murder trial claimed that they were all self-inflicted wounds.

The fighting went back and forth for over twenty minutes with both men achieving direct and potentially deadly blows to each other. Dad always carried a pen knife that he used for everything and it was always sharp enough to allow him to shave with. At some point he removed it from his pocket and opened the blade. As he always taught us he held the blade firmly between his thumb and his bent forefinger with only about an eighth of an inch of the blade exposed. This way the knife could be used to make shallow and long cuts to just slash your adversary beneath the skin. With enough of these cuts the receiving opponent will ultimately bleed to death.

Dad proceeded to slash and cut at Roy's torso each time they wrestled. Since Roy was not wearing a shirt it made his body a perfect target for the slash wounds. The cuts were everywhere and oozed blood freely. While at the jail Roy and I counted 56 slash wounds on his entire back, arms and chest. During that inspection I discovered why the bleeding was not fatal. Dad had made the mistake, knowingly or unknowingly, of exposing less than the required eighth inch of blade in his slashing attempts.

Roy broke away and delivered a near fatal kick to Dad's head causing him to fall again. He rose up on all fours and growled like a Tiger before attacking again. Roy reached for a set of Nun chucks and quickly struck Dad with two successive blows to the head knocking him down. The forceful momentum caused Roy to fall to the floor next to Dad. Dad briefly recovered, rolled over and slammed his pen knife into Roy's right thigh imbedding it into the bone. Roy reacted immediately causing him to sit up. He slung the Nun Chucks across the back of Dad's neck, rolled over on top of him pinning him to the floor. One of the Nun chuck sticks was lying across Dad's throat and under Roy's upper body. Roy's intent as he explained it to me was just to subdue Dad and to stop him from fighting.

The fighting caused the adrenalin to flow uncontrollably as it coursed through Roy's body. His own heavy breathing caused him to believe Dad was still breathing heavily as he was trying to get up to continue to fight. The heaving from his heavy breathing caused him to believe that Dad was still alive but the fight was over and Dad was dead! The Doberman stopped barking immediately almost as if he knew that Roy and Rochell were safe again.

Roy lay that way for quite a while before calling his fiancé Tatha. After telling her what happened and to call the police Roy called me in Hawaii to tell me that "Dad is dead and I killed him!'

It is important to note here that if I had been in Pennsylvania that day I would not be writing this today. I value my life as any normal human being does but I can say without any doubt that if Dad had come into my home to kill me I would not have fought back. I had resigned to myself many years before that if that day ever came then I would die.

Dad always knew that Roy would fight him one day. That is why he taught Roy lessons in the Oriental Martial Arts that he never taught anyone else including me his eldest son. He taught Roy everything contrary to his lifelong philosophy that teachers should teach their students well and as much as possible but "Never teach them to be able to beat you!" With Roy he knowingly broke that rule because in his heart, and I will carry this belief to my grave, he did not really want to end the lives of his children and Roy would be his only saving grace.

Mom cleaned Roy's house after the police cleared the crime scene. She dutifully and carefully removed the blood that stained everything in the room. Mom carefully collected the remnants of Dad's brain matter and put them into a small container. She never told me what happened to those remains. To the very end, and regardless what Dad had done to her and the family during his life, she remembered the man she fell in love with at the Air Force dance in Indonesia after the war.

The Murder Trial

We had to find a defense attorney quickly. The incident had attracted public attention all over the country and especially in Pennsylvania. I had even received a call from my uncle Hank in Perth Australia where he heard about it on the television news. They called it the "fight to the death between father and son." My uncle Hank in Australia called me the next day to ask what happened, but also told me that it was not unexpected. It was on the national news in his country too.

During Roy's trial for murdering Dad a rumor was started that if Roy was found "not guilty" there would be a riot and he would not leave the Beaver County Court House alive. The opposing camps, Roy's friends and students and Dad's friends and students were ready to fight to defend their own hero and leader. Beaver police, state police and other police agencies were prepared for the worse.

The two assistant district attorneys were Frank S. Kelker and Charles M. Marshall. They both approached the trial as a political opportunity, if they could win this very public trial. Our defense team was led by two extremely talented and highly competent attorneys, George "Tooky" E. James and Rex Downie. When Atty. James spoke at trial he had the inherent talent to get everyone's undivided attention. The trial would have made a great movie. Mr. James was extremely passionate and animated in Roy's defense.

The trial judge, H. Beryl Klein, disallowed all of the spousal and child abuse defense options for reasons known only to him. Not allowing these elements made all of us fearful of the ultimate juror decision.

One of the prosecution witnesses was a police deputy who defended Dad by saying that if he wanted to kill anyone including his family then he should have been allowed to. Many of his statements under oath were misleading. His sister was called as a defense witness and she debunked every one of her brother's statements.

Roy asked to testify on his own behalf. To clarify some of the false rumors that surrounded the trial and to explain the actual fight that resulted in Dad's death. The trial lasted for 5 days and concluded on Friday afternoon. The jury returned with a verdict of "Innocent" after deliberating for a few hours on Monday. It was unusual for the jury foreman to use the term "innocent" instead of "Not Guilty." Upon hearing the verdict Mom fainted and fell to the floor. The entire jury wept and the people attending as spectators cheered loudly. The judge dismissed the jury and released Roy immediately.

I spoke briefly with three of the jury members about their verdict and why most of them wept when the verdict was rendered. Without exception, they advised me that the history of abuse to the family members helped to prove without a doubt that the death was due to self-defense.

The day after Roy was released we went to the Karate school where graffiti covered the entry door calling him a murderer. Roy's office chair back faced the window on the second floor. As he pulled the chair from under his desk he noticed something wrong with the head rest. He turned the chair around exposing a tear in the leather and what appeared to be a hole. We looked further and were able to pull a spent bullet from the headrest. In the window was a similar size hole in the glass. Someone was sending him a message.

Soon after the trial was over Roy started a Karate magazine and made me his international correspondent. Since I traveled all over the world he wanted me to take that opportunity to write articles for Karate and self-defense schools from worldwide locations. My first and last article was entitled "The Masters of Old Were Wary".

The magazine titled "Kung Fu International" and my first published article never saw the light in public. The night before its release, 25,000 copies and the Karate school owned by my step mother were burned to the ground. Suspicion always pointed to one of Dad's specific students who bragged about the burning, but law enforcement never followed up.

Suspicion always pointed to one of Dad's specific students who bragged about the burning, but law enforcement never followed up. My suspicions always pointed to the radical police deputy who testified against Roy. Several of the witnesses who testified against Roy, publicly stated that they believed Roy burned down the school and the stockpile of new magazines. To this very day, these students believe Roy was guilty of murder, and have even convinced some of their offspring of that fact. Blogs on Karate-related web sites are loaded with bogus comments and stories about the death, trial and aftermath. Readers should be very wary of these falsehoods. I have included the actual transcript pages form the trial at the end of this book as a reference for the actual events at the death scene. In reading them, there will be no question that Roy acted in self-defense.

Our Karate Badge and the Code by Which Dad Lived
Beaver County School of Self-Defense School Logo

CHAPTER EIGHTEEN
Catching "King" Bass

The trial is over and Roy is free again to live his life and give to others as he was always meant to do. The spring and summer of 1975 had passed and Roy asked me to come home to Pennsylvania to go fishing with him. We both loved the peace and tranquility that fishing offered us throughout our lives after leaving home to join the military.

Some of our teenage years were horrible and a source of great pain between us. For many years we fought over what today we consider to be trivial things. However, in those years we did not know any better as we tried to find our identity and a place in life where we belonged. Since mom and dad were constantly at war with each other and using us as pawns, we were left to our own devises to figure it out. It took the Viet Nam war to bring us together again.

The burning down of his Karate school along with the 25,000 copies of his new magazine and the late night attempt at his life by a coward with a rifle had taken a terrible toll on Roy's psyche. He needed a break and wanted me to be with him again. Someone he could trust not to hurt or take advantage of his deeply troubled life. After all, killing a man - especially your father - is not something that one gets over very easily. Killing men in combat was not a problem that caused him to lose sleep for he had done so many times in the Marine Corps. But sleep and peace of mind had eluded him since the day of the Dad's death. Roy desperately reached out for help and I was ready to do so once again.

The leaves rustled on the branches above our heads as the early fall breezes nuzzled each and every one. The heavy smoky aroma of the sun-warmed moss beneath our bare feet engulfed our entire being. The willowy softness served to reach deeply within our troubled bodies and soles to soothe us once again. The rumbling, tumbling rocks echo their protest as the rushing, babbling brook shoves them downstream ahead of itself. With rod and reel in hand, Roy leans casually back against the rough-hewn bark of an aged Oak tree and immediately demonstrated his skill for catching fish.

It should be a time of for relaxation and reflection; however, it's a time for competition between us as well, competition between brothers and one of nature's greatest fresh water fighting fish. Our quarry is the king of the ever elusive bass.

As I attempt to re-bait my hook, the long, slick and shiny night crawler stretches and contracts increasingly within by clumsy grasp. Once more King Bass has stolen the tempting and juicy bait from its barbed prison. After a concerted, needlessly and frustratingly tiring effort, I succeed in impaling the luckless worm on my new shining hook. Roy laughed openly at my clumsy attempt to keep up with him.

For several years we have returned to this same secluded hide-away in order to pursue and capture this fighting prize. Again and again the King had come within my grasp, only to evade final capture. The King must also realize that it's a battle for survival and that cunning must be the game plan which he will use and continue to win over the odds against him. And cunning he most certainly is! Many of the King's long-time comrades have succumbed to temptation and paid for their weakness by becoming a hearty meal for their captors. Only the mighty and elusive King has eluded us.

My cast is straight and true as the baited hook glides lightly through the air and glides lazily to a watery splashdown within inches of my predetermined target. The King lies patiently waiting at the base of an old, rotted submerged tree trunk. Slowly the hook settles to the bottom where it lies lazily on the silt and mud. The frantic unsuccessful squirming of the worm attracts the attention of King Bass. The unseeing eyes search out their target with the unfailing aid of all of the great one's prehistoric senses. The King nudges and prods at the bait in a vain attempt to dislodge the worm from the sharp spines of its prison. Failing at this several times, the King snaps at the loose and flailing tail of the worm and runs with it until the tense line prevents him from running any further. The light nylon line becomes even more taught and a large portion of the worm is viciously ripped loose from its body into the King's massive jaws.

This meager morsel does not satisfy the raging hunger within the bowels of the massive prize. Hunger overrides his predatory caution and, in a final desperate lunge, he engulfs the entire baited hook within his great mouth. He runs fast and deep and in the process snags himself as the sharp curved and spiny hook painfully impales itself into King's aged jaw. At long last he is mine!

"You got him!" Roy yelled. "Don't fight him! Keep the rod tip up but don't fight him. Let him wear himself out."

"Always the teacher," I thought to myself and grinned from ear to ear.

But, no, King Bass has a different slant of view on the situation. He runs and runs and runs with the line as my reel screams in protest. The light rod bends in agonizing contortions in a valiant effort to hold its own against the furious fight of the King. The screaming reel comes to a torturous halt—King Bass can run no further! Cautiously I rewind what seems to be miles and miles of outstretched nylon while constantly maintaining light tension on the thin light line. I know that a moment's slight distraction and a loosening of the line will result in a lost battle between the King and me as he will simply spit out the barbed menace.

King is a fighter to the end, and he means to fight this fight for his life. He runs once again in every direction. In a tremendous burst of speed he leaps into the air with a savage spinning and twisting arc. His keen instincts drive him on in his relentless effort to escape. I must be extremely cautious not to allow him to dive for the assorted rocks, weeds and tree stumps submerged below. Failure to control his valiant attempts at reaching freedom will mean a lost fish. There he can easily entwine the fragile line in and around any object in order to break free from his menacing and painful hook.

King is tiring now as the energy dissipates from his tremendous body. Most of the nylon line is rewound around the cold, merciless and wet steel reel. We can see him clearly now in his still unceasing effort to escape the death-hold of the hook. I keenly sense he is mine now as I lower my net into the cold frothing foam, directly in the great one's path.

All of his energy spent during the battle of survival, he lies listlessly now within the confines of the net. Carefully I free him from his entanglement in order that we may survey my mighty prize. With all the care and gentleness within me I remove the stinging barb from the King's massive jaws. The cold, black, glassy eyes seem to cry out for mercy and release. Deep within my satisfied mind I revel in this moment of glory.

I am the victor! Or am I? Slowly with wetted hands I lower him into the rushing waters allowing them to wash through his gaping jaws and over his gills before releasing him back into the rushing waters. Revitalized energy quickly returns to the old tired and massive body and King Bass once again swims away into his watery domain.

Roy and I sat on the bank of this beautiful creek and talked about what just happened. Roy's face reflected a sense of peace I had not seen in his face for months.

Roy wistfully said:"Life is so short and we never know what is in store for us or why things happen. We just have to let go and let it take us where we are meant to be after all is said and done. I need to get on with my life and let go of these horrible memories."

"I will always be here for you Roy," I assured him.

CHAPTER NINTEEN
Duty and Difficult Transitions

Hickman AFB

The trial was over and it was time to return to my Air Force career if I still had one. My first contact was with my counselor whom I debriefed about all that happened in PA. She advised me that she had been tracking the trial through her friend in PA and continued to debrief my commander and the First Sergeant. She also told me that the mental health department's commanding officer had cleared me to return back to work. He also recommended that my discharge actions be terminated and that I should receive my promotion.

My commander asked me to report to his office where he promoted me to Technical Sergeant with full back pay dating back to the first day it became effective. He advised me that the individual who admitted having the affair with Debbie was discharged under less than honorable conditions.

The remaining three years at Hickam went by quickly. I went absolutely crazy and dated every woman that I could find. Unfortunately it did not matter whether they were single or married. I just wanted revenge and my moral values were set aside for the remaining time at Hickam AFB. Debbie's friends were my specific targets and I made every effort to get them to tell her about the relationships.

It was the day before departing Hickam for my new assignment to Edwards AFB, when I received a call from my supervisor, who asked me to help load some aircraft because the duty loadmaster was sick. Since I was processing out I had no obligation to help, but as always I responded by going out to the flight line. It turned out to be a bad decision.

We were shipping Marines from Kaneohe NAS to the Big Island through Hickam AFB. On the second outbound load on a C-141, I briefed the 5 ton Marine Corps truck driver how to back his vehicle up the aircraft ramp. His safety instructions, since it was a diesel vehicle, included "Do Not Ride the Clutch!" Riding the clutch causes the vehicle to jerk and actually jump as it progresses up the ramp. This causes the untrained driver to often lose control of the vehicle. The driver acknowledged all of my instructions.

I took my position to the front left of the vehicle and in line of sight with the driver and proceeded to guide him in backing up the ramp. As he reached the half-way point in backing up the ramp, the driver started to ride the clutch. The vehicle started to stutter and bounce up and down. The driver panicked and pushed the clutch to the floor but did not use the brake. The fully loaded 5 ton truck barreled down the ramp and struck me. The impact threw me spinning through the air about 15 to 20 feet. I impacted the tarmac hard and started to get up to get out of the way of the uncontrolled truck. It was too late, as the front left tire rolled across my left foot crushing my steel toed boot. The driver stopped the truck on my foot. I screamed "Stop, don't move!" He ignored my order and put the vehicle in reverse and backed over my foot. I can still feel the steel in my boot digging into my toes. I feared that my toes had been cut off.

Three Marines, who also happened to be my friends, dragged the driver out of the truck and beat the crap out of him. Another loadmaster witnessed the accident and called for a vehicle to take me to the hospital. I was evaluated by a doctor and x-rayed for broken bones. They cut my boot off my foot and found only minor bruising to my toes but the steel toe was almost completely collapsed around them. X-rays showed injury to my backbone but no break.

For reasons unknown to anyone, the physician on duty entered the accident in my medical records but did not state the critical facts, such as the accident occurred on base by a Marine Corps vehicle while conducting a military deployment exercise. The failure of the doctor to properly record the accident and the facts, resulted in the VA denying medical benefits for my broken back and peripheral back and foot injuries, resulting from the accident. The VA acknowledged the accident in my medical records, but claimed that the accident was a result of an automobile accident that occurred off base.

Edwards AFB & the Arrival of Wim Kenneth Wetzel

One year before leaving Hickam for my new assignment to Edwards AFB, CA, Debbie started to call me often. She apologized for what she did to me and told me that she had changed. She asked if we could give our marriage a second chance. I believe in the institution of marriage and that once someone says "I do!" that the commitment will last a lifetime. After numerous calls we agreed to set the past aside and try to save our union. Debbie found the money to buy a ticket returning to Hawaii. She had made her mistakes and I had my revenge. It was time to give the marriage a second shot.

We tried, but she could not get pregnant. Her doctor advised her to stand on her head after sex. Her tubes were twisted in some odd way disabling her ability to conceive. "What the hell," we said. "Let's give it a try." We did and not long after we received the good news that she was pregnant.

Seven and a half months later our son Wim Kenneth Wetzel was born seven weeks premature. Debbie had been in labor for 38 hours, and I never left her side. I was in the delivery room when our son was born. He was so tiny and greatly at risk for not surviving. Debbie tried breastfeeding but was unable to succeed. Wim stayed in a special container under oxygen treatments for over a month while the nursing staff helped him to get strong enough to be released.

Wim was born with a very significant cleft right foot. It was almost 90 degrees left of normal. The doctor told us it could be fixed through the use of special shoes worn over a couple of years.

When we were finally able to go home with our son, life seemed good and, for awhile we were happy. Unfortunately, Debbie developed extreme post-partum complications, and avoided taking care of Wim whenever possible. When I came home from work each day she handed him off to me, saying "Here, take care of your kid!" I was happy to take care of Wim and spent every moment I had with him. Breastfeeding was the only requisite skill that I did not have. Wim would only sleep if we were in the rocking chair but even then, he constantly woke up. I do not recall a single night when Debbie took care of him when I was not traveling for my Air Force job. She also refused to put the special baby shoes on his feet to correct the cleft foot. She was in complete denial that anything could possibly be wrong with our son.

Four months after his birth we reported to Edwards AFB where I was assigned to the Flight Test Center Aircrew Standardization office. Debbie was hired at NASA as a Communications Specialist. Her role was a public spokesperson for their events.

Things were rocky during our first 9 months at Edwards. Debbie hated being in the High Desert, listening to the sonic booms and all the test flights. She was fired by NASA for throwing a heavy stapler at her boss' head during an argument. Her temper was out of control and extremely volatile. She went home to Illinois with our son for a couple of months but finally returned. Then one day I came home for lunch only to find her loading the baby in his seat into the car. The back of the station wagon and the seats were filled with baggage. I didn't have a chance to ask where she was going. She just said I am leaving you for good and am taking Wim with me. I asked her why and she said "I met another man who is better than you. Goodbye!"

I was in shock unable to move or respond before she pealed out of the driveway leaving me in a cloud of dust. I went into the house and destroyed every piece of furniture in sight. After calming down, I called my boss Lt. Col. George Prewitt and told him what happened. He was sympathetic to my situation and simply told me that he would be there to support me regardless of what I needed to do.

After numerous telephonic attempts to reconcile and to save the marriage Debbie advised me she wanted a divorce. I told her that I wanted custody of Wim and that I would file for divorce using her infidelity as the justification. She did not care and told me to do it and she would not contest anything except giving up custody. She even asked not to receive alimony or child support because her new man could take care of them.

I finally gave up and filed for an uncontested divorce at the Kern County courthouse. The divorce decree was approved including no child support or alimony. Before the reader(s) jump to conclusions and criticize my avoidance of child support, let me just state that I voluntarily paid child support without a court order. I made out a monthly child support allotment through the Air Force Pay section. She never missed a child support allotment check.

About three months after leaving me I drove to Illinois to see my son. Debbie was living in a cheap dilapidated trailer. Her "better man" had left her for another woman and Debbie was working in a bar as a waitress/bar tender. She took Wim to work every day and fed him hamburgers, hot dogs and potato chips or French fries. He drank coca cola instead of milk.

Debbie gave me the keys to her trailer and asked me to take Wim home and put him to bed. When I walked into the trailer I was shocked to find that the refrigerator was empty except for a bottle of Jim Beam that was almost empty too. There was no food in any of the kitchen cabinets.

I picked Wim up and drove to the local supermarket and bought food, milk and other essential items. I stocked the refrigerator and waited for Debbie to come home. Our discussion was hostile to say the least and she kicked me out. She threatened to call the police if I did not leave. Not knowing what else to do and feeling powerless I drove non-stop back to Edwards AFB. I was totally lost and at the end of my rope.

I spoke with Colonel Prewitt and told him what happened. I asked him for advice on what I should do. He simply suggested that I might pray for guidance and invited me to go to church with his family. He prayed with me and I went to church to put my pain and suffering in his hands. Prayers and church attendance became the norm for me and I found some peace.

One Monday morning at about 2 am Debbie called me. Her call was short and to the point. "Come and get your kid. I can't take care of him anymore." I responded by saying that I would come to get him at the St. Louis Airport only if she gave me complete and unconditional child custody." She agreed without hesitation.

I immediately called Colonel Prewitt and awakened him from a dead sleep. I just told him that I had to fly to Illinois to pick up my son and that I would explain when I got back. He told me not to worry and to do whatever was necessary to care for my son.

I drove to LA International and caught the first available round trip flight to St. Louis and back. Luck and God were with me since a direct flight was leaving within an hour. I called Debbie with the flight information and she responded by telling me that her mother would be waiting at the gate to hand over our son, and would also provide a court notarized document giving me full custody.

I arrived at St. Louis, met my mother-in-law who handed me my son and the notarized document, then turned around and walked away, never uttering a single word to me.

My return flight was scheduled to leave later that day with a scheduled arrival at LA at midnight. Upon arrival at LA I got into my car and drove us back to the base and slept next to him in the office. Where else did I have to go with an 18 month old son who still was not potty trained?

God bless Colonel Prewitt and his entire family. Mrs. Jane Prewitt, Lisa, Lori and Phillip all reached out to help me through this very difficult time. After explaining to him what had occurred Colonel Prewitt told me not to worry and that he and the Standardization office team would help in every way possible. I advised him that I lived in the barracks and had no other options. He picked up the phone and called the squadron commander and asked for special permission for me to take Wim to the barracks until other accommodations could be arranged. The commander talked

Lt. Col. and Mrs. George Prewitt

with First Sergeant who agreed to let us stay in the barracks and better yet permitted me to take him to the dining hall for meals until we could arrange for another place to live.

We moved into my barracks room and almost immediately the other guys in the dorm volunteered to help baby sit when needed. The single fathers who lost child custody were especially helpful. For three months Wim and I lived in the enlisted barracks and ate in the dining hall. The dining hall maintenance staff even set up a corner table with drop cloths under Wim's chair. We were blessed by the wealth of kindness shown towards us. I tried to find a place to live but Debbie had ruined my credit and emptied my limited savings again.

At the end of the three month time frame the First Sergeant asked me to accelerate my move out of the barracks. A couple of the younger Airmen had submitted complaints about living in a child care center. I committed to him that we would move out soon.

We were visiting friends who lived in the base mobile home park and noticed that their next door neighbor had a For Sale sign in front. I walked over to inquire about the price and asked to see the place. They were asking for $4000.00 dollars and if I came up with $1200.00 as a down payment they would carry the balance. The place was clean and maintained well so we shook hands on the deal pending the delivery of the down payment.

I had met and made friends with a fellow Loadmaster, Alberto Capone. Al Capone was single and also living in the barracks. Embarrassed with hat in hand I told Al about my predicament. He asked how much I needed for the down payment. He wrote a check for $1200 and handed it to me and said; "Consider this as a gift. I don't want or need you to pay me

Al Capone

back. Just take care of your son!" I retorted that I considered it as a loan and that I would pay him back with interest. He said again, "It is a gift!

We closed the sale and moved into our new home within the week. Neighbors helped to baby sit when needed. The Child Care Center manager made special provisions for his care if no one else was available. The Prewitt family was always there to support me. We were blessed.

Our lives were starting to get better and life was good. Colonel Prewitt asked to meet with me in private. He asked me if I had ever considered going to college. I told him that I had thought about it but my present situation prevented me from going at night and weekends. He made me an offer that I could not ignore or reject. If I enrolled in Cerro Coso Community College he would let me take classes during the work day and do my homework in the office. The only thing he needed in exchange was for me to continue providing the weekly standardization status report for the wing commander briefings. I had developed a new and highly accurate trend analysis report which satisfied all of the Flight Test Center tracking needs. The wing commander had shown a great deal of satisfaction with the results each week. The report along with other accomplishments I made during my tour resulted in being selected as the Flight Test Center NCO of the Year.

I enrolled in classes that day. My first class was an English Writing Course taught by Dr. Rita Fuhr. Her first assignment directed the students to write one specific writing assignment per week for the duration of the semester. We received a list of subject areas that she expected us to write about. Each paper was required to be at least 500 – 1000 words long. Over the first week and before the second class I completed all of the 13 required papers and turned them in.

Six classes passed and I had not received any grades on any of the papers. Curious about my grades I questioned Doctor Fuhr about why I had not received any responses. She responded by telling me that she had read and graded every paper except one that I had title "A Plan for Dying!" It was a very long and very specific paper about the self-defense killing of my father by Roy. Dr. Fuhr expanded on her response that she had read the paper several times and was so taken emotionally by the content that she could not grade it. I asked her to grade it so that I would know whether my writing was satisfactory. She promised to complete all of the grading soon. When I did receive the paper it was graded with an A++ and a personal note. The note specifically stated that if I ever decided to write a book about my family that she wanted to offer to edit it for publishing. That note and her interest in my family's story sowed the seeds for my ultimate attempt to write this book. It has taken me 40 years to complete it.

I eventually left Edwards AFB with 3 Associates degrees and was well on my way to ultimately achieving my Bachelors, Masters and Doctoral degrees. These achievements could not have been possible without the encouragement and support of Colonel Prewitt and his family. I am and will be eternally grateful to them. For the remainder of my career and the following three civilian jobs I held after retiring I reached out to help several hundred people pursue and obtain college credits and degrees. It was a way to pay back for what was given to me by a great man and war hero.

After being awarded NCO of the Year I also achieved the Air Force Flight Test Center Suggestion Program of the Year award. Colonel Prewitt called a meeting to hand me the award plaques and told me that one benefit for achieving NCO of the Year was for me to select to ride in any aircraft on the base. Captain Lloyd Adams was our T-38 Test Pilot and Colonel Prewitt was the F-4 Pilot. I told Colonel Prewitt that I wanted to fly in both of them. He did not hesitate and gave me the OK.

I was already a civilian Commercial Pilot working in my FAA Flight and Instrument Instructor certification and was excited to ride in these two powerful fighters. I did not hesitate to ask for the opportunity to actually pilot the jets. Captain Adams and Colonel Prewitt agreed to let me fly the aircraft. I had a ball flying the jets. We flew supersonic in both aircraft and was amazed as I watched the fuel gauges drop rapidly at supersonic speeds. Both of the pilots let me do acrobatic maneuvers and Col Prewitt let me conduct a couple of simulated bomb runs. The coup-de-gras was when I flew the F4 the entire length of the desert runway that was used by the Space Shuttle. With a bit more than a little help I landed the F4 for the final landing.

Colonel Prewitt offered to help complete my training to obtain my flight instructor certifications through the Edwards AFB flying club and of course I accepted. That was another life changing experience that could not have been successful without this generous and phenomenal man and leader of men. Until I was permanently grounded in 1994 by the FAA because of heart issues I instructed for over 1500 hours. Every student that I personally trained and recommended for their FAA private and commercial pilot certification flights passed their flight test on their first attempt. Several of my students, male and female, now fly for commercial airlines and still stay in touch with me. Other students were Air Force Navigators who were applying for pilot positions.

"What are you going to do to give back to others as a way to say thank you for your opportunities?" I thought awhile about how to answer Colonel Prewitt's pointed question.

"Well! I was a Boy Scout and Explorer during my youth and always wanted to start a Scout unit."

Since there was not a Scout organization at Edwards AFB I volunteered to apply for a co-ed Aviation Explorer Post from the Boy Scouts of America. The application was approved and the base sponsored all of the activities. We were even sponsored for the first Aviation Fly-In ever held at the base. Teenagers joined the Post and their parents supported all of our activities. The base Flight Surgeon owned a cabin at Mammoth Ski Resort and offered us the use of the place for a weekend. The base motor pool provided me with a 58 passenger Air Force bus and gas for the trip. Since I already had a military license for bus driving I was given the keys. This bus trip would be used for good reasons unlike the bus trip I made in Viet Nam.

The Explorer Post thrived during my tour at Edwards. Wim accompanied us everywhere we traveled and he became the official mascot for the Post. He had a ball and the kids helped me care for him on numerous occasions.

Altus AFB, Oklahoma Tour I & the C-141A/B Loadmaster School

I received my promotion orders to Master Sergeant along with PCS orders to Altus AFB, OK. It was painful for me to leave my Edwards AFB family but orders are orders and I had to move. I sold the mobile home for $5,200.00 and wrote a check to Al for $1,500.00. Al ripped up the check and repeated that it had been a gift. I thanked him profusely and told him that I would never forget him and his kind heart. Al continues to be one of my dearest friends today.

Wim and I drove to Altus AFB and were caught in a tornado right after entering the Oklahoma state line. The hail was about the size of golf balls and my car was badly damaged. The rear of the car actually lifted off the ground and scared the Hell out of us.

We arrived at Altus and met with a local real estate agent. After the sale of the mobile home, I had about $4000.00 in cash for a down payment on our new home. The house price was $48,000 with reasonable interest and low monthly payments. The base housing office and thrift shop provided me with the minimum furniture necessary to move in. We settled in and started a new phase in our Air Force life.

It was a pleasant surprise to find out that MSgt John Burkhardt was my new boss and the Superintendent of the school. My new role was to be his assistant and ultimate replacement when and if he ever moved on to another position. I worked for John in aerial delivery earlier in my career. In my opinion John is an easy going pretty laid back but a highly effective and professional non-commissioned officer and leader. I learned a great deal from him in the past and looked forward to continue learning from him in my new role.

The primary purpose of this school is to train new Loadmasters to become certified in the C-141 Starlifter. The candidates could be brand new Basic Loadmaster School graduates or qualified and certified Loadmasters transitioning from other aircraft such as the C-130.

The instructor staff consisted of highly qualified and experienced Loadmasters who had many years and hundreds or even thousands of hours of flight experience. We had over 30 instructors on the staff. My first task was to attend every phase of training in the course before becoming certified to train in each block of instruction. Since I had many years of classroom and flight instruction hours under my belt it did not take long for me to become certified to train every block. Regardless of the past experience I learned early on that every student must be approached on an individual basis and they just cannot be put under a single category. I had overlooked that when delivering the first scheduled class.

After introducing myself to the class and learning information about every student attending, my opening comment was, "Feel free to ask questions at any time about any subject that you are taught. If you are uncertain about any item in the course it is important that you stop and ask questions. Just remember that there is no such thing as a dumb or stupid question."

After about 15 minutes into the lesson a student raised his hand and asked, "Why do we have to complete this course when we have already completed the Basic Loadmaster Course at Sheppard AFB?" he asked, adding, "I think it is just a waste of time."

Without thinking or missing a beat, I responded jokingly: "That is the dumbest question I have ever heard!" You could have heard a pin drop. Almost everyone gasped and looked at me in shock. The student asking the question actually left the classroom.

I believed my response would liven up the classroom and add some levity to the lesson. Unfortunately, the students did not receive it as such and they all went into a defensive mode for the insulted student. Since no training progress could occur until the situation was resolved the class was put on a 15 minute break. I could not find the student who left so I went directly to John's office to report the problem. The student had beaten me to the draw and was sitting in John's office staring at the floor. John did not need to say a thing to me and just shrugged his shoulders with a questioning look on his face.

I pulled up a chair next to the student and apologized to him for my response. "It was just meant to be a joke to loosen up the class. I regret not thinking that it could put you in a precarious position with the other students by referring to you as being dumb."

John asked if the student was satisfied with the apology and upon getting a positive response he dismissed us. Upon resuming the lesson, I again apologized to the student in front of the class. Everyone laughed when another student responded: "Yeah I agree with you. That was the dumbest question I ever heard!"

The Altus AFB assignment was never boring. We were either teaching classes or flying airdrop and air refueling missions every day. Everyone looked forward to the actual overseas cargo and passenger flights in support of the Military Airlift Command's (MAC) worldwide mission. The Air Refueling missions, especially the night missions, were boring and tedious. They were typically 4 hours in length in the middle of the night with repetitive connecting and disconnecting with the KC-135 refueling tanker aircraft. The C-141 had the ability to actually transfer fuel back to the tanker. In preparation of the hookups to the tanker the boom operator often asked "Are we sucking or blowing tonight?"

When women started piloting and crewing the cargo and tanker aircraft in the various crew positions political correctness became the watch words. Any reference or alluding to sex had to be changed so as not to be offensive. "Cockpit" became the "crew compartment" and "sucking or blowing" became something else. I'm sure you get the idea so I won't spend any more time on the subject.

Soon after I became fully certified to teach the entire curriculum John received his PCS orders. As his assistant it was natural for me to transition to the Superintend position. John had taught me a great deal and I was ready for anything, or at least I thought so.

Two days after John departed for greener pastures one of my instructors came to the office and told me we had a problem with a student that needed immediate attention. The student was fresh out of Basic Loadmaster School and was barely 19 years old. He reported to class in his uniform adorned with 21 ribbons and medals. One of which was the Korean War service ribbon.

I requested to have the student report to me immediately. It was a sight to behold. He looked like a 15 year old and had a shit-eating grin on his face when he reported. I told him to close the door when I noticed that most of the instructors had followed him to my office just to see and hear what was going to happen.

"Airman, where did you get all of those medals when the only one you should have is the Basic Training graduation ribbon and possibly the Marksmanship ribbon?"

"Off base at Sheppard in one of the pawn shops. I thought they looked cool and would look great on my uniform. When I went home on leave before coming here my girlfriend was really impressed."

"Well Airman, I've been in the Air Force for many more years than you and I've never been less impressed I am than now. Where did you get the idea that you could just go buy some medals and ribbons to adorn your uniform? Never mind answering! Get your ass out of my office, go to the barracks and change your uniform shirt and bring that rack of ribbons back to me, then report to class. If I ever see or hear that you pull another stupid stunt like this I will personally hoist you up the base flagpole by your balls for the whole world to see how proud you are. You are dismissed!"

He could not leave my office fast enough. The instructors suppressed their laughter as he walked past them, but burst out laughing hilariously after he left the building.

It was time for my annual qualification check ride. Since I had been qualified on the C-141 for twelve years I was confident that the check ride would be successful. It wasn't and I was disqualified or Q3d. My flight examiner was a Tech Sergeant who attended Basic Loadmaster School with me in 1969. He was out to make a name for himself and working hard to become the Loadmaster on the MAC commander flight crew. While in Basic Loadmaster School he married the school Superintendent's daughter. This guy used every possible edge to move ahead in the Air Force because intellectually he could not progress on his own.

Busting or Q3ing me would get everyone's attention. During the check ride he shadowed me at every turn. My every task and action was documented during the pre-flight and the flight mission. The hostility in the air was palpable and I knew in my gut that all was not well.

During the evaluation debriefing I learned that he failed me. He requested that I sign the evaluation form which is the normal process. I flatly refused and challenged every one of his write-ups as being bogus. I requested a meeting with him and the chief of loadmaster standardization. That did not go well either and I was forced to sign the evaluation. My pride in my job and the Loadmaster profession took a devastating hit. As the Superintendent of the Loadmaster school it meant that I had failed my team of instructors and our students. I felt ashamed and was ready to resign as the Superintendent.

The Flight Engineer during this fateful mission was MSgt Barney Peters. Barney came to my office to discuss his observations of the check ride. He made it clear that from his perspective that the evaluator was extremely disrespectful and unprofessional in his approach to conducting my evaluation. He intended to debrief the Chief of Aircrew Standardization about his observations but cautioned me that the Evaluation team would defend their evaluator.

Barney than asked me a question that really put the issue in its proper perspective. "Did the Q3 affect your paycheck or your rank in any way?"

My response of course was "No!" He responded by telling me "There was nothing you could have done to prevent this because from what I observed – you were going to be Q3d regardless how well you performed the evaluation. His boss will back his decision so just move on."

I was re-evaluated by the Loadmaster Chief of Standardization and passed with flying colors. The Q2 remained in my otherwise unblemished flight records. The initial evaluator was selected as one of the loadmasters on the MAC Commander's flight crew.

CHAPTER TWENTY
Wim-Zee

It was June 5, 1980 at about 7 pm when I met Zee at the Altus AFB NCO Club. Until that day I had been taking care of my son Wim, who we called WK, 24 hours a day, 7 days a week for over 3 years after. As mentioned earlier, Debbie abandoned WK and left me to take care of him. On June 1st Debbie asked me to let him spend some time with her alone in Illinois. She had appeared, at least on the

Wim, Zee and WK 1980

surface, to have straightened out her life and remarried. I saw no reason not to honor her request and put him on a plane to fly to St. Louis. I would regret that decision for the next 24 years of WK's troubled life.

I decided to get out of the house and to go to the Altus Air Force Base NCO club. I sat at the bar and ordered a beer and started a conversation with the bartender. A few minutes later I felt someone tapping on my shoulder. It was Zee in her hostess outfit and she said to me "Hi – I've not met you before. Are you a newcomer to the base?" I could barely speak as I mumbled, "Yes, I reported to the base from Edwards AFB in March." I was shocked that such a beautiful woman would take the time to talk to me. This had never happened before in my life. I introduced myself and she responded with, "My name is Zee!"

She continued to serve drinks and would come back and speak to me whenever she waited for her drink orders to be completed. I will have to say that it was love at first sight, at least on my part. She had the most beautiful eyes and was such an attractive woman that I could not stop looking at her whenever she came near. This went on for about three hours when I decided to go home. Zee had been gone for about 15 minutes so I could not tell her goodbye. Instead, I asked the bartender to tell Zee that I had to leave and would see her again the following evening.

I went home to go to bed but could not sleep. All I could see with my eyes closed were her beautiful warm eyes. I kept myself extremely busy during the next day at work just so that the time would go by faster. I asked my friend and boss, MSgt John Burkhardt if he knew anything about Zee. He told me that he had known Zee as a waitress at the NCO club for several years. He also knew that several others had tried to date her, but Zee, with very few exceptions, refused all advances. He also told me that Zee had three teenage sons, Mike, Wade and Jeff, that she raised by herself. He knew that she was a dedicated mother who loved her sons and that she worked two jobs to support them. John rarely saw Zee dating anyone and that he doubted that she would have any interest in me. John's comments really piqued my interest and I resolved then and there to prove him wrong.

That night I returned to the NCO club at about the same time as the previous night. I sat on the same barstool and waited for the opportunity to strike up a conversation with Zee. During those days I was still a very shy and withdrawn private person who rarely ever was outgoing enough to strike up a conversation with a stranger, but in the case of Zee, I could not help myself. She saw me at the bar and asked me if I was the person who told the bartender "Please tell Zee good night for me and that I will see her again." I affirmed it was me.

There seemed to be a natural connection between us as we talked proudly about her sons and my son and our devotion to the boys. She told me that all three sons had left home to start their lives on their own and that she was now sharing her home with her sister. I told her about my son Wim and how I became his primary guardian when his mother abandoned him. Zee was skeptical about any mother who would do such a thing to her children. That skepticism hung over us like an ugly black storm cloud for the first 15 years of our marriage until my ex-wife proved to Zee that everything I ever told her about Debbie was true.

Zee and I began to date and spent all of our non-working hours together. On Saturday morning, two weeks after we met each other, I heard a knocking at the front door of my house. I opened the door to see Zee standing there with two large palm plants. She told me that they were housewarming plants for my new home. I immediately knew that this thoughtful, warmhearted, giving and generous soul would be my life partner and ultimately my wife.

We could not be together enough. Our passion for one another was almost uncontrollable. Zee would call me or I would call her at work to ask one another to leave early and to meet at her home or mine. My boss John knew whenever I disappeared from my office where I had gone and never questioned me. He instinctively knew how much Zee and I loved one another and he was smart enough to know not to get between us.

As a Loadmaster I had to fly often on missions overseas or throughout the USA. I would call Zee upon my arrival at Altus AFB to let her know I was back and on my way home. Zee would meet with a passionate kiss that invariably led to greater adventures.

Zee and her sister Patti invited me to spend the Fourth of July with them and their parents on the family farm. It was there that I met Ted and Madge Perryman. Madge and I warmed up to each other almost immediately, but Ted was not as acceptant of me. All during dinner and several hours afterward Ted sat across from me with his arms folded, refusing to look at me directly. Madge, sensing the tension between us, suggested that Ted take me on a tour of the farm while checking out the livestock. He seemed to be hesitant in inviting me to do so but ultimately succumbed to Madge's coaxing.

To say that the first 15 minutes of the tour were tense would be an understatement. I finally broke the ice by asking a lot of questions about farming, raising cattle in general and why he liked farming so much. He was straightforward with his short answers, but I sensed that the ice was broken and that there was no turning back from him. I raised the subject of Zee and our relationship. I told Ted that I knew about Zee's first and second husbands, and that I understood why he would be so skeptical of a stranger entering their lives. I made it very clear to him that I would never hurt Zee and that I was falling deeply in love with her. It appeared that he was convinced about my sincerity and started talking freely and openly about his relationship with his children and grandchildren. There was no turning back for either of us as we developed a close relationship with each other over the next 32 years. When we returned to the house there was a general sense of disbelief by Madge and Patti of how quickly Ted and I had warmed up to each other.

Zee and I dated for several months and early in September we decided to move in together into my house. On Saturday morning September 20, 1980 I woke to the sound of loud banging on my front door. I put on my robe and opened the door to find an angry Ted standing there. I said, "Hi Ted, come on in!" He refused, demanding to know, "Is my daughter here?" I told him she was that I would awaken her ,and again asked him to come on in. He again refused, saying, "I will wait for her here."

I awakened Zee and told her that her dad was on the front porch wanting to see her, that he refused to come in, and seemed very angry and agitated. Zee donned her robe, went to the front door and invited Ted to come in. Again he refused. "Pack your bags, you're coming home with me," he commanded. "I refuse to let my daughter live in sin with any man!"

Ted was a Deacon in the Baptist Church and he could and would not condone his unmarried daughter "living in sin with a man." Zee made it very clear that she was not going to pack her bags to leave me and go home with him. Ted told her that if she did not pack her bags and leave with him right then, he would disown her and never see her again. Zee bluntly responded and said, "You sure are going to miss me!" She then slammed the door closed in his face. Ted stood dumb founded outside the door for a few minutes expecting Zee to come out with her bags. He ultimately realized she was not going to do that and angrily drove off in his pickup truck.

A few minutes later the phone rang and it was Madge warning Zee that her Dad was on his way to the house. Zee explained to her that he had already left and what had happened. Madge tearfully told her that things would be okay. She was right.

Ted invited Zee and I to spend Thanksgiving with them as he slowly started to realize that our relationship was a sincere one. He appeared to be resolved with the fact that there was nothing he could do to stop it. He felt that he was obligated to convince us not to live in sin and the we should marry. I agreed and proposed to Zee on a couple of occasions, but she was not ready yet to commit to another marriage since she had already been divorced twice. Zee was 6 years older than me and that fact concerned her a lot. She knew early on that one day I might have to be her caregiver and did not want to put that burden on me. Respecting her wishes I did not raise the subject again.

Zee asked me one day in a playful manner "Would you still want to be with me when I am 70 and you are 64 and my boobs are hanging below my waist with my nipples peeking out from under my blouse?" My answer was a direct "Yes!"

Early in February of 1981 Zee brought up the subject of marriage herself. We talked about it at length and agreed that we would and could have a marriage that would last. I asked her once again to marry me and she accepted. We decided to get married on Valentine's Day, but she insisted we not tell anyone about it beforehand because she did not want to make it a big deal.

I received permission from the squadron commander to get married and we made an appointment with the base chaplain to go through the process for preparing for marriage. Counseling was a requirement on the base those days. The chaplain decided that we were both serious and committed to this lifelong union and arranged for us to be married on Saturday, Valentine's Day at 10 AM.

Zee and I both believed in the sanctity of marriage and that no one should enter one only to walk away when things got tough. Neither of us ever walked away. It was "till death do us part" and Zee had uncannily predicted that moment in her whimsical questioning of my commitment to her. She passed away a few months short of her 70th birthday and my 64th.

Early the morning of our wedding Zee and I spoke once again about inviting her parents to attend. Zee ultimately agreed and called her mother at 9 AM to tell her about the wedding at 10 AM and asked her if she and Ted would honor us by being there. Madge did not hesitate to tell us yes and that they would be there on time. Just before speaking our vows Zee asked me if I was absolutely sure that I wanted to go through with our marriage and that she would understand if I said no. The chaplain appeared shocked when she asked, but I assured him that we were ready. The ceremony was short and sweet and my son was the ring bearer. He and Zee had become very close and they loved each other dearly. After the ceremony we all drove to the NCO club for breakfast.

I chose Valentine's Day to be married because it was a special day of the year and I was not very good at, remembering birthdays and other important dates. In fact, my poor memory for dates got me in trouble just a few months into our marriage. Zee's birthday of June 18th is just one day later than my ex-wife Debbie's birthday of June 17th. Take a guess on which date I gave Zee her first birthday card that first year of our marriage. Zee never let me forget that error. I thought she only mentioned it in jest. Boy! was I mistaken! I lived to regret that honest mistake over and over again for the remainder of our 32 year marriage.

At about noon the day we were married, I received a phone call from my squadron commander Lt. Colonel Milacek asking me to report to him immediately. I tried to explain that I was just married and on my honeymoon. He congratulated me and reiterated the need for me to report to him right away.

Immediately after reporting to Milacek, he advised me that he had relieved the First Sergeant of his duties. He now needed a new First Sergeant and since no one else was available or qualified to perform the job, he chose me for that role. He handed me a beeper and told me that I was on 24-hour duty as his new First Sergeant. He shook my hand and congratulated me saying, "You now have two wives and I'm confident that you will serve them well and with equally deep devotion. Enjoy your honeymoon First Sergeant."

We approached our new lives together with a deep devotion and passion to one another. Zee asked me to go back to school to complete my Bachelor degree and gave me the OK to keep flying and to teach students to get their pilots' licenses. In fact it was her idea for us to purchase a training plane to help generate some revenue. Most of my meager Air Force salary was still being used to pay off debts that my ex-wife incurred when she maxed out our credit cards and cleaned out our bank accounts. Zee made significant tips at the NCO Club and they were used to enhance our income. The revenue generated from the flight instructor charges and the training aircraft went a long way towards making our financial lives more stable and rewarding.

Zee encouraged me to work with Ted to learn about farming and cattle. A couple of my college classes were related to agriculture and cattle ranching. Ted taught me how to grow wheat and to take care of and raise cattle. Working with Ted I learned a tremendous amount about farming. His wheat crop had declined significantly after Zee's sons left home and he was averaging 21 bushels per acre. After the first year of training under Ted we were able to double and increase the wheat yield to 42 bushels per acre.

When we sold Zee's mobile home we were approached by the trailer park owner about leasing or purchasing the park. We did lease to purchase it. The park was designed to hold 50 trailers but only 15 families lived there and the park was in disrepair seriously needing care. Like everything else she did Zee put every free minute when she was not working at the NCO Club into turning the park around. Within six months we filled the park and the rental revenue significantly enhanced our bank accounts and I was able to clear all of my debts.

In the summer of 1983 I obtained my Bachelor Degree from Southern Illinois University with a grade point average of 3.8. The year prior to obtaining my degree I had been preparing to apply for an Air Force officer commissioning program. The Air Force required officer candidates to be commissioned by the age of 35. I was going to be 36 and would need a waiver to be accepted for the program. I knew the Chairman of the Senate Armed Forces Committee and asked him to write me a letter of recommendation to attend the program and to waive the 35 year age limitation. He did so. I contacted the Governor of Oklahoma, the states two Senators, my local Congressional Representative, 4 General officers and innumerable other senior Air Force officers and requested their endorsements and age waiver requests. They all wrote the letters of endorsement and I was loaded for bear. There was no doubt in my mind that my waiver and endorsement package was unstoppable support to be accepted for officer candidate school.

With my degree and endorsement package in hand I asked for and was scheduled to meet the current Wing Commander for his final approval for my application. The regulation at the time required his final approval. After reviewing my package he looked at me and stated; "MSgt Wetzel I am disapproving your request!" Without even giving me a chance to respond he selected the disapproval box on the form and signed it.

I was flabbergasted and shocked beyond belief and blurted out: "Sir – what the Hell? Why are you disapproving the request with all of the supporting gubernatorial, congressional and Air Force senior officer endorsements supporting my goal to become an officer?

His response: "We have plenty of Second Lieutenants with no leadership and management experience. We don't have enough good senior NCOs with your experience. Furthermore I have no doubt that you will be a Chief sooner than later now that you have a promotion line number for Senior Master Sergeant. That is all and you are dismissed!" The Colonel would not discuss my request any further and I left his office terribly disillusioned and dejected. I knew in my heart that it was not to be and any further attempt to bypass his disapproval would only end in further disappointments.

For the remaining three years of our tour at Altus AFB we were extremely busy but very happy. I was fully engaged in my Air Force flying duties and as Superintendent of the C-141B Loadmaster School, going to college full time at night and weekends, farming for Ted, conducting flight training after work and helping Zee with maintaining the trailer park. We were too busy to ever get into any disagreements or fights.

CHAPTER TWENTY-ONE
The Good, The Bad, and The Ugly

The Good

While I worked toward my degree, Zee carried the weight of running the household, insisting that my degree would help me to advance in my Air Force career. She was confident that I would achieve the highest enlisted rank of Chief Master Sergeant sooner than later. Her predictions were right on the money.

When I arrived at Altus in 1980 it was as a Master Sergeant and with Zee's support and encouragement, was promoted to Senior Master Sergeant in the minimum time of two years. I volunteered for my next assignment to the Military Airlift Command Headquarters and was accepted. The position was designed for a Chief Master Sergeant and I was the first to ever fill it as a Senior Master Sergeant.

The position had been vacant for a year and they could not find anyone interested in the assignment at headquarters. The vacancy was for Chief of Mobility Operations and the Air Force could not find any volunteers to fill it. My application was accepted and we moved to Scott AFB, IL. I did well enough in the position and it provided me the privilege and the opportunity to be promoted to Chief Master Sergeant in minimum time in grade just two years later. My promotion line number was released at the 17 year point of my career and I was able to sew on my stripes just short of 18 years. The average time for making Chief in those days was over twenty years. There is a lot to be said to the truth that every successful man is so because of the support of a good woman.

During my first tour at Altus at Zee's insistence and encouragement, I obtained my Bachelors and Masters Degrees with an overall GPA of 3.82. Not bad for someone with severe dyslexia and who was told he would never get far in life. I was promoted to Senior Master Sergeant and received a call from the Air Force Personnel Center. A Chief Master Sergeant position was available at Scott AFB the Military Airlift

Command's Headquarters. Numerous attempts to fill the position with a CMSGT had failed and they needed to fill it. "Would you be interested?" they asked. My response was immediate with a "Yes – when do you want me to report?"

The Bad

About a month after receiving my promotion "line number" to Chief Master Sergeant I was ordered to report to the squadron commander at Scott AFB in Illinois, who at that time was a female Colonel. She was extremely angry when she called me to report to her. Upon reporting she read a letter she had received from Debbie. The letter stated that I had not ever paid her child support and alimony payments. Consequently she told the commander on a telephone call to her that I owed Debbie several thousand dollars. I explained to the Commander that I always paid monthly child support payments through the Air Force Finance Office allotment program and that I had records to prove it. I also explained that the divorce decree clearly stated that there were no requirements for child support or alimony payments.

Regardless of my comments the commander told me she did not believe me and that Debbie had no reason to lie to her. As a consequence of her opinion of my failure to meet my parental obligations she was "red lining" my promotion line number to Chief and that I was going to be processed for discharge from the Air Force.

I was devastated and shocked beyond comprehension. I told the "man hating Bitch" that I would return with proof of my child care payments and a copy of the divorce decree. I left her office and went home to get all of the documents. Before returning to the Commander's office I saw my boss who also was a full Colonel and told him what had happened. I gave him all of my documents of proof. He was stunned at the disrespect I had been shown and told me to calm down and go home. He advised me that the situation would be taken care of by him and that I would be promoted on schedule.

I do not know exactly what happened next except that the female Commander disappeared a couple of days later and was replaced by a new one. My promotion date came and my boss awarded me the Chief stripes in a Command ceremony and Zee proudly sewed them onto my uniform.

The Ugly

As in any marriage, Zee and I had our good days and our bad, but in our marriage the bad days were directly related to the interference of my ex-wife Debbie. Debbie would call all hours of the day and night to talk with WK. During these calls WK would become extremely agitated and upset. We would spend hours after each phone call calming him down and letting him know that we loved him. There was a role reversal between Debbie and WK. WK believe that he should take care of his mother instead of his mother taking care of him. Consequently, he felt guilty during and after every phone call from his mother. She convinced him that she needed him to be with her in a sick and twisted way that made him feel guilty for not being with his mother. Over time, these telephone calls became more intrusive, heart rending and painful for all of us.

At one point early in our marriage we decided to get professional counseling to learn how to deal with this increasingly difficult situation. The counselor asked me directly "If you had the option to choose between your wife and your son, who would you choose?" Initially I could not believe that any counselor would ask this question, considering the difficulty of the situation being handled by Zee and me. It took me a couple of minutes to think of an answer and when I did I said "I would have to choose my son." I knew immediately that this was the wrong answer from Zee's immediate incredulous response, but I was in a no-win situation, regardless of my answer.

Zee's disappointment and anger were immediate as she got up and left. My answer would haunt our marriage and hang over us like a black cloud for many years until the day came where Debbie proved that she was the terrible mother I had always claimed her to be.

Ultimately I made the decision with great pain and trepidation to send WK to live with his mother. He was six years old and I had raised him by myself for five years. My heart was broken and our marriage suffered its first major crisis. But Zee and I decided that our marriage was strong enough to overcome these types of painful situations. We did not hear from Debbie and WK again for three years.

I was at work one day when I received a phone call from a police detective in Santa Maria, California. He asked "are you the father of Wim

Wetzel a nine-year-old boy?" I confirmed that I was and asked what was wrong. He told me that his mother was arrested in Santa Maria as a fugitive from Illinois because of check kiting. The detective asked me." What do you want me to do with your son? Do you want to come and get him or do you want me to put him on the plane to Oklahoma?" My answer was," I will arrange for his airline ticket and you can put him on the next plane!" He confirmed that he would do so.

Zee and I waited anxiously at the Oklahoma City airport for my son's arrival. The flight attendant escorted him from the plane and handed him over to us. She told us that he had been crying nonstop from California to Oklahoma and that nothing anyone could do to calm him down was successful. WK stopped crying as soon as Zee hugged him and told him how much we loved him. Unfortunately Zee still did not or would not recognize or accept the type of mother Debbie was. She just wanted to take WK home and to make them feel comfortable there.

WK shared several horror stories with us about things that happened while he was living with Debbie. He described how Debbie had arranged to unlock a bathroom window at the local Sears store where she worked. At night after the store closed, she would lift WK up so he could open the window and climb in. He would then go into the store and collect specific types of clothing and other valuable items and hand them to Debbie through the open window. They were both caught stealing from Sears, and WK was permanently barred from ever entering the Sears store again. Debbie received a light sentence followed by a short probation.

WK also described in very specific details how Debbie would have him deliver drugs to her clients and to collect the money they paid them. Debbie would roll the drugs into a paper napkin and give him specific instructions on where to deliver the drugs. The drug clients then would give him the money and he would give it to Debbie. Apparently she believed, and I am only speculating on this, that if caught by the police, they would not arrest an eight or nine-year-old child for drug trafficking. Unfortunately, they were never caught using this procedure in Debbie's drug dealing enterprise.

WK was now thirteen years old. The phone calls at all hours of the day and night started all over again after Debbie was released from jail for the check kiting prosecution. The vicious cycle of child parent versus parent child responsibilities started all over again making our life as a family a nightmarish hell. After a year of relatively stable and calm behavior by WK he once again started to behave badly at school and at home. One day I received a phone call at work from a friend who owns a small gas station in Blair, Oklahoma. He asked me if I had written a check for $15 in cash. He further explained that the signature was in my name, but it looked fraudulent. He asked me to come by and look at the check to confirm that it was written by me. I knew immediately that the check was written by WK. I picked up the check and confronted WK with it. Even with the evidence in hand he denied to Zee and me that he had written it and it was not his handwriting. It finally dawned on Zee, after all these years, that what I had been telling her about WK's mother had all been true.

We took WK to a psychologist who recommended that we put him in a home for troubled youth located in San Marcos, Texas. He warned us that WK would be there for a minimum of six months that we should not expect to see him on a regular basis. WK's anger toward me was explicit and totally uncontrollable. He begged Zee to not put him in this home. Zee told him that we did not have a choice and that he would have to go there to get help.

We were told when we delivered him to the home that we could not call him or see him for at least six weeks. They also advised us that he could not call or see us during this time. To say that WK was hostile or angry towards me would be an understatement. I was devastated and the pain I felt within my heart and soul was unbearable. This is where Zee's love came through as she hugged me and told me that I was doing the right thing. Six months later WK was released from the facility and we picked them up to take him home. For a few months after returning home things seemed to be stable and there was relative peace in my family.

When WK was 15, the phone calls from Debbie started all over again. She was remarried and told us that she wanted to have WK visit her in Illinois for a couple of weeks. Initially we told her no. but after many phone calls from her directly to WK we realized that there was nothing we could do to stop him from seeing his mother. Rather than give him a round-trip airline ticket I purchased a one-way ticket to the Illinois. I sensed deep within my gut that I would not see him again and I was not going to waste any more time and effort to try to change him or the relationship between WK and his mother.

We did not hear from him again for four months. He finally called me and told me that he wanted to come home and live with us again. I asked him why and he told me that his mother was too strict and he was not allowed to do anything. She had taught him well and as a consummate liar he continued to tell us how much he missed us and wanted to be with us. With Zee on the other line listening to the call I said that he could come back to live with us under three conditions:

1. You have to stop lying to and stealing from us.

2. You will do your best at school to get better grades and Ds are not acceptable as a passing grade. It does not matter to us whether you always get A's and B's just as long as you give it your best effort.

3. You will contribute to this household by doing chores and helping Zee and me.

I asked him directly "Can you follow these three basic rules of behavior?" Without a second of hesitation, WK said "No Dad, I don't think I can follow those rules." My response was swift and as direct as his answer was to me." Then, son, you are no longer welcome in my house." I hung up the phone and broke down and cried uncontrollably for a long time. Zee comforted me, hugging me and telling me how much she loved me and that I did the right thing.

The next time I saw my son was ten years later in his casket after being electrocuted by a 7000 volts power line while doing roofing work. I blame myself for the death of my son because I had not done anything or everything necessary to turn his life around. It is my belief that my effort at "tough love" ultimately caused his death and I will take that belief to my grave. The huge hole in my heart will always be there. I survived to this day only because of the compassion and love I received from Zee.

Wim had two beautiful children Kali and Tyler. His fiancé Amber delivered their daughter, Carlie, two months after his death.

CHAPTER TWENTY-TWO
Aircrew Life Support and Survival Training

Altus AFB Assignment II

I applied for, and was given, a humanitarian reassignment back to Altus AFB in the summer of 1987 to help take care of Zee's mother Madge and her father Ted. Madge's health was declining significantly and Ted was unable to take care of her in the way he needed to. Very soon after our return to Altus AFB, Madge was put into a nursing home. Zee spent a lot of time with Madge and helping Ted cope with the potential loss of his wife of over 50 years. My return to Altus AFB was necessary because none of Zee's siblings cared enough to take care of their parents. The responsibility fell upon Zee, even though her brothers and sister lived closer to them.

I reported to the base and was asked to meet with the base commander. He advised me that there were no vacancies for another Chief Master Sergeant on the base and asked me what I wanted to do. Since every possible position for a Chief was already filled he did not know what to do with me. My initial assignment was to the Wing Aircrew Training and Standardization office as the Superintendent but there was not much for me to do in that position since another Chief was already assigned there. The wing commander asked if I was interested in any other jobs on the base other than in an aircrew management position. My answer was short and sweet when I told him I would certainly consider it. He gave me a list of six organizations on the base and told me very frankly that they were the worst units at Altus AFB and asked me to pick one. I was shocked and devastated. Since it was a Friday I asked him to give me the weekend to go over the list, do some investigation on my own and to come back on Monday with my decision. He agreed and I went home for the rest of the day.

It appeared that my reward for taking care of my parents-in-law was being assigned to the worst job on base. I walked into the house in a very foul mood and Zee noticed immediately. I told her "I quit! We are retiring and leaving the Air Force for civilian life." When she asked why, I told her what had occurred at the wing commander's office and showed her the list. I also commented that they were the worst run organizations on the base and that I was not qualified for any of the jobs they represented or supported. Zee in her always positive way said "Pick the worst job on the list and get back to work. We are not retiring from the Air Force."

Over the weekend I called everyone I knew on the base to investigate why the six units were on this list. In every case it was because of poor leadership or management but everyone agreed that the worst unit on the base without exception was the Aircrew Life Support and Survival Training Branch. It had earned its reputation as the worst of the worst. Without another thought I reported to the commander and told him that I would take the Life Support and Training branch on a couple of conditions. My conditions were simple and to the point and the Wing Commander agreed to all of them. They were:

1. Give me full control of the organization without interference in my decision and personnel assignment decisions as the Wing Life Support and Survival Training Officer. This was a key element since no Noncommissioned Officer had ever been assigned this position or title.

2. I intended to have a monthly personnel full dress open-rank inspection conducted by a different full Colonel assigned to the base. I requested that the Wing Commander be the first Colonel to conduct the first inspection one week after I assumed the position. Then I requested that he assign a different Colonel from the base be directed to conduct each personnel inspection each month until further notice.

3. After taking over the unit I wanted the ability to communicate with him directly about any issue without having to go through another subordinate commander.

To state that the Life Support and Survival Training shop was in disarray and a badly run organization would be a gross understatement. This single shop of 39 enlisted personnel was responsible for supporting aircraft and survival training equipment for three different Air Force major organizations – MAC, SAC and ATC

Several of the airmen and women had filed for bankruptcy. With the exception of 12 members all had disciplinary actions pending and/or records on file. One airman was in the stockade for a 60 day period. Keep in mind that these were the people who were responsible for maintaining, servicing and installing aircrew survival equipment such as oxygen masks, parachutes, aircrew helmets, life preservers, life rafts and other critical supplies. The unit had failed every major command inspection for a couple of years.

The one and only person who gave me hope was TSgt Michael Black. Mike was the NCO in Charge (NCOIC) and fighting just to survive and to keep the unit from collapsing under its own weight. Mike was a star. As a previous Air Force Recruiter and the Air Force Recruiter of the Year he knew that there was potential in the organization but he had no power to effect any changes.

Every Life Support organization is run by a commissioned officer. Typically a young officer Lieutenant or Captain was assigned to the position to fill a square for future promotion opportunities. It was rare for a Life Support Officer to be in the position for very long which meant that little attention was paid to the care and feeding of the subordinates. They depended on the senior NCO to take care of the personnel issues. That is exactly what happened in this unit. The Altus AFB life support organization was unique in that it supported several different Air Force major commands and a variety of aircraft such as the KC-135 (SAC) (AMC), C-5 and C-141A/B (AMC), T-37 (ATC) and other aircraft.

I met with Mike and introduced myself. He asked me very bluntly, "What makes you qualified to run this unit Chief Wetzel?" My response was simple and just as blunt, "I know how to lead and train people how to be the best they can be Mike! It does not matter to me what technical skills they possess because it basically comes down to pride in their work. Either they have it, don't have it, and can be trained and motivated to have it, or they don't and don't give a shit to ever have it. You and I are going to get rid of the latter shit heads starting now."

I directed Mike to order every person assigned to us to report the following morning at 07:00 in full dress blues without exception. Mike responded by telling me that they can't work in dress blues. "Tell them to bring their normal work clothes but to report in their dress blues and spit-shined shoes regardless. No exceptions!"

That night and the following morning I gathered all of the personnel information available to me. The personnel disciplinary file was full and significant with numerous warning letters and other documentation.

At 06:55 Mike and I were at attention in our dress blues waiting in the open bay work area. The entire crew with a few exceptions wandered in aimlessly and quite slovenly in appearance. Mike ordered them to fall in and come to attention. They appeared confused and dumb founded but Mike reminded them of their basic training and helped them to fall in properly. Once they were in proper formation and standing at attention, I introduced myself. "I am Chief Master Sergeant Wim Wetzel and I am the bastard in charge of this bastard organization!"

As a new supervisor taking over a shop, leaders in the Air Force are taught to typically NOT make major changes when taking over a new unit. This unit required major changes. I continued by telling them that they had a reputation for being one of the worst units, if not the worst, on the base and that was going to change.

Prior to the gathering, I had Mike bring an empty garbage can and some lighter fluid. On a separate table next to me I had stacked all of their office personnel and disciplinary folders and one blank sheet of paper. I picked up the paper, pointed to the stack of files, and asked Mike to pick them up. "These are all of your disciplinary files and the paper I hold represents a clean record for every one of you present. Mike please drop all of the folders in the trash can, pour the lighter fluid on them, and burn the files."

Mike lit the flame and we all watched the files burn. I continued to tell them that medics from the hospital are standing by to conduct urinalysis tests near the men's and ladies bathrooms. "You will all line up near the appropriate restroom and stand at attention until your turn comes up for the test. Mike and I will go first since there are no exceptions. I will review the test results and meet with anyone who fails it. If you fail the test, you will be given ten days to get clean and rid of the drugs from your life. In eleven days we will all, including me, be given another drug test and if anyone fails, they will be processed for discharge from my Air Force. The Base Security Police will come to your on-base home or barracks room with the drug dogs tomorrow morning to search for illegal drugs. They will take the appropriate actions if drugs are found because that will be out of my control."

"Starting tomorrow morning, and until further notice, you will report to work an hour early every day for calisthenics. Unless you can provide a doctor's excuse we will all participate. Bring workout clothes with you each morning. Next Monday morning you will all participate in a full dress open ranks inspection being conducted by the Wing Commander. On the first Monday of every month until further notice you will participate in open ranks inspections conducted by a randomly selected or volunteer full Colonel assigned to the base. After this morning's drug tests you will fall into formation again for your first refresher lesson on how to conduct an open ranks inspection taught by TSgt Black. Fall Out and get in line for your urinalysis!"

Test results proved two participants had drugs in their systems. No one tested positive after the follow-up tests. No drugs were found in the on-base homes or in the barracks. Giving them a day to clean up any illicit drugs may have helped in getting these residents clean. There was little pushback by anyone in the organization since everyone appeared to accept that the unit was in crisis.

Mike took me around the facilities for an inspection. I was appalled at what I discovered. Rat and mice feces and termite evidence was everywhere including in the oxygen masks and other survival gear. Mike had reported the problem to every one of the Life Support Officers and anyone else that could fix the problem.

The main Life Support building, building 194, had been marked for destruction several years prior but there was no indication that there was any intent to destroy or renovate the buildings. The Survival Training and Aircrew Chemical Defense branch was about a quarter mile away in building 129, and this facility was in just as a deplorable state as was the main Life Support branch. I committed to Mike and the other NCOs to fix this problem quickly.

Mike told me that the missing Airman was in the base stockade and had been there for thirty of the 60 days of his confinement. During his first 30 days his wife had a baby boy. She had not been allowed to see him or let him see his new son. I committed to fix that problem. Upon visiting the confined Airman I asked if anyone had been to the stockade to visit. "Only Mike has visited me regularly Chief." I asked if the First Sergeant, the commander, Chaplain or Life Support Officer had visited. The answer was "No."

I met with the stockade NCOIC and discussed my concerns about the failure of anyone to come by to visit the prisoner. He was not concerned and basically said that it was not his problem. I told him to prepare to release the prisoner into my custody before the end of the day and that I would have his release papers when I returned. He just grinned and dismissed my instructions.

I called the Wing Commander and asked for an emergency meeting that could not be put off. He asked me to meet him for lunch to discuss the emergency. During lunch I explained the Airman's situation and expressed my dissatisfaction that the First Sergeant had not bothered to visit the Airman. I further explained that he had a newborn son and that his wife and son had not been allowed to visit during his previous 30 day incarceration. The Wing Commander was not happy with the information and stated: "What is it that you want me to do Chief?"

"I have already told the NCOIC of the stockade to release the Airman to me today. You can order his release into my custody by setting aside the remainder of his sentence by written order approved by the Judge Advocate General (JAG). The justification is basically due to his chain of command' failure to conduct due diligence in their responsibilities to care for their subordinates and their families. He has suffered enough and paid his dues and has served his penalty with good behavior."

"I'll have the order typed up for you to deliver this afternoon."

"Not necessary Sir. The JAG gave me the letter for you to sign. He agreed that a release is appropriate." I handed him the letter, he signed it and said:"You are a piece of work Chief!" I thanked him and let him pay for my lunch and left.

The stockade NCOIC had ignored my request to prepare the airman for release because he knew I would fail in my attempt. He even alluded to the release order as being phony until I gave him the comander's telephone number. The airman was released into my custody and I drove him home to meet his new son.

Six months later we nominated him for the Air Force Leadership School where he graduated with the highest honor; the John Levitow Award. John Levitow was a Medal of Honor recipient in Viet Nam for saving his entire flight crew's lives.

After once again meeting with the Wing Commander and the entire command staff I was able to find a little used facility, building 444, that used to be the 57TH MAS and Flight Simulator Building, that could be converted to the new Life Support facility. I was in competition for getting the building with several senior officers in Maintenance. My argument for getting the building won the battle but I was advised that any modifications would be unfunded. Any changes that needed to be made were my responsibility. One thing that any officer worth his salt will know that any good NCO given the go ahead can scrounge anything needed to accomplish his mission. I gave Mike Carte Blanc to get it done. He did it in glorious fashion and in record time.

Every one of the Life Support crew participated in the refurbishing of the hangar. Not only did Life Support get to move into a new facility, but for the first time in many years, all functions of Life Support were located in the same facility under the same roof, to include the Aircrew Chemical Defense and Survival Training sections. To further streamline operations, the base Fabrication Branch moved into the other third of this facility, and this was the branch responsible for major repairs to much of the life support equipment, such as parachutes, life rafts and life preservers.

Zee participated in the rebuilding of the organization as well. When I told her about the bad financial conditions the married families faced she went to work to help the wives. She asked Mike's wife Donna to gather the spouses for a meeting. They all attended and Zee was direct in her intent to help and train the spouses in financial management. One wife stated "Mrs. Wetzel I don't understand what the problem is. I have all these checks in my check book and they are all being rejected." Zee asked how much money she and her husband had in the bank. The response would have been funny if it was not sad and pathetic. "As long as I have checks in my checkbook then we have money in the bank." Zee had her work cut out for her but she was successful in helping turn every one of the families' financial conditions around.

For the remainder of my tour at Altus the Life Support shop passed every Operational Readiness (ORI) and Operational Readiness Evaluation (ORE) with Outstanding or Excellent ratings. Mike was promoted to Master Sergeant and selected as Aircrew Life Support NCO of the Year.

Roy with Christian and Kaylan

CHAPTER TWENTY-THREE
A Bright and Rapidly Burning Star
Roy Eduard Wetzel, 1948 – 1995

Roy's life ended tragically and far too soon due to complications of mechanical heart valve replacement surgery in the summer of 1995. Roy was only 47 years old and in the prime of his life. Life in general had turned around for him as he began to reap the benefits and joy of living that had so long eluded him.

The Karate School was doing well and his students routinely won first place and grand champion trophies at Karate tournaments held across the country. Some of his best students moved from Beaver Valley and started schools of their own across the country.

In July of 1994 Zee and I invited Roy to come to Texas to spend time with us at our lake property in Granbury, TX. We had a beautiful double lot on one of the rivers leading into Lake Granbury. Until Zee started to get seriously ill in 1998 we had decided to retire there. We wanted to share the place with Roy and take him fishing. Second only to fishing, teaching fishing was his passion.

We picked Roy up at the DFW airport and I immediately noticed that he was not well. He would not talk about his health but I knew in my heart that Roy was not long for this earth. Roy expressed his disappointment in not finding or seeing Cowboys and Indians in Texas. He seriously expected to see them everywhere. As an alternative we took him to Fort Worth's stockyards to Billy Bob's Bar and Restaurant, and toured the yards. We even had a picture taken of Roy sitting astride a Long Horn Bull. He had the biggest smile on his face I had ever seen.

After setting him up in the guest room we went fishing off our boat dock. Roy immediately caught a seven foot water moccasin and ultimately dragged him onto the dock. I could not climb a nearby tree fast enough as he wrestled the damn hooked snake to keep it away from him. He ultimately gave up and threw the rod still connected to the snake into the water and joined me in the tree.

Zee was laughing hysterically from the porch of our house. It was the same snake that constantly stole her bait when she was fishing off the dock. The snake climbed up the river bank and slid into a huge opening in a tree further away from us. I grabbed my shotgun and blew its head off before dragging it to the ground. Zee measured it at 7 foot 3 inches.

A week went by in no time at all. We had a ball fishing and boating all over Lake Granbury and just enjoying our passion for fishing. When Roy left Granbury we both had a feeling that we might not see one another again. We hugged several times before he boarded the airplane to return to Pittsburg.

A week after returning to home Roy met with his heart doctor. His Agent Orange related heart problems were getting worse and the cardiologist was watching him closely. The cardiologist was also one of his Karate students and a close family friend. While in his office Roy's Aorta blew due to an aneurism; the same type of aortic aneurism that caused me to have open heart surgery years later. He collapsed in the cardiologist's office and literally bled out. I don't know how his life was saved but he was saved, taken to the hospital and had major surgery to repair the aneurism and to replace his damaged valve with a mechanical valve. He got a kick of letting me hear his valve clicking through our phone calls.

The hospital released him with specific post-operative and physical therapy instructions. Roy did not listen. Must be a Wetzel thing. As soon as he was feeling well he began a rigorous exercise routine to get fully back on his feet. One week after release from ICU Roy did some crunch sit ups. The stress on the surgery staples caused them to pop loose and protrude through his abs. I could still see the staple outlines when we visited for Christmas vacation.

Roy was hosting Karate tournaments and really enjoying his successes and life in general. In the summer of 1994 he was hosting a tournament when he started to feel ill. In his words to his Karate instructors "I'm going home. I feel like I'm getting the flu!" One of his instructors took him home to rest. When he did not get better they took him to the ER. The ER admitted him for treatment and ultimately put him on oxygen and life support. X-rays and other tests could not determine the source of what obviously a major staph infection. They could not find it to treat it properly.

My step-sister called me in Texas and told me that Roy was dying and had asked for me. Twenty-five hours after a non-stop drive I entered his isolation room at the hospital in Pittsburg. I saw "fear" in Roy's eyes for the first time in our lives. He could not speak but was able to squeeze my hand. His exposed skin was covered with what can best be described as bumps like a chicken skin or goose bumps. As I held his hand I said; "I'm here Roy and will stay here as long as you need me."

As I write this my tears well up and fall down my cheeks uncontrollably. I can still feel Roy's life leaving him slowly but surely and I am still overwhelmed with sadness 21 years later.

Roy was laboring for breath and I could feel him fighting to live but it was in vain. My last words were: "It's OK Roy! Let it go! I will make sure that the kids will be taken care of. I love you!" He passed from this life moments later as his massive muscular body relaxed in final peace.

The autopsy indicated that the cause of death was the separation of the mechanical valve from the heart due to a massive staph infection that had grown behind the valve. The x-rays did not pick up the infection because the mechanical valve was shielding it from view.

Tatha, Roy's ex-wife and the mother of my niece, Kaylan, and nephew, Christian, was the executor of the estate. She asked me to be co-executor and to help with the funeral arrangements since Roy wanted a full Marine Corps funeral with an Honor Guard. I contacted the local Marine Recruiting office in Beaver Falls for assistance. They were not helpful and recommended that I contact the Marine Corps office in Pittsburgh. I did and again got the runaround. My patience was wearing thin. The Beaver Falls recruiting office finally recommended that I contact a local volunteer group of elderly retirees who conducted funeral services. That was unacceptable to me because Roy was a decorated Viet Nam veteran who had been wounded several times and deserved a better and full military honor guard.

The Pittsburgh office called to tell me that a Marine Honor Guard would be at the church service and accompany the family to the Beaver cemetery for the military funeral. The church service was full with Karate students – past and present and many friends and family. In his honor I wore my full dress uniform and had obtained an American flag. The Marines did not show up and were missing in action. I was furious at them for dishonoring my brother and a combat hero but the funeral had to proceed. I apologized to the family for the absence of the Marines and explained to the attendees that I would contact the Marine Corps to find out what happened. I presented the funeral flag to my nephew.

After the funeral and the internment of Roy's ashes we all returned to Roy's home to reminisce and have lunch. I promised Roy's children that I would resolve the Marine Corps issue, and I sent a scathing no-holds-barred letter to the Commandant of the Marine Corps, our Congressmen and other military and government officials.

I received a direct response from the Commandant letting me know in no-uncertain terms that he was very displeased with the lack of respect shown to Roy's family. He apologized on behalf of the Marine Corps and promised to fix the problem immediately. He was true to his word and directed the Pittsburgh office to send a senior officer to Tatha's home to apologize and to offer to make things right. The local officer responsible for the Marine honor guard visited Tatha and the children to personally apologize for their failure to show up for the funeral. He committed to providing a full Marine Corps honor guard in the event that the family requested a do-over (my words). We did have another funeral and a full contingent of 11 Marines conducted the ceremonies.

CHAPTER TWENTY-FOUR
Retiring from the Air Force
1990

"Chief Wetzel – Report to me immediately!" that was the direct order I received by telephone call from the Vice Wing Commander Colonel. This Colonel's name was similar to "Hitler" and so was his attitude, so Hitler is how enlisted personnel referred to him in private. He was a rather short and unassuming officer barely tall enough to qualify to be an Air Force pilot. He was so short that a platform was built for his office chair behind his desk and out of sight of visitors to his office so he would appear taller. Arrogant and self-serving were words routinely used by enlisted personnel who dealt with him. On at least two occasions he was punched by enlisted Airmen at previous bases where he had been assigned. He was universally disrespected and disliked by the enlisted ranks.

A little background information about professional relationships between Colonels and Chiefs in the Air Force might be helpful here. Some will disagree with me in this opinion, but we will just have to agree to disagree. Typically when Chiefs and Colonels meet to discuss official business, the actual practice of reporting is informal rather than formal. What I mean, is that Chiefs do not routinely march in stand at attention, salute and state "Chief Wetzel Reporting as Ordered!" Then stand at attention until ordered to stand "At Ease Chief!" or given permission to sit.

Prior to this particular meeting I had never been required or requested to report to the Wing Commander or any Colonel or General in a formal manner. I went to Wing Headquarters and the secretary told me to go right in because the Colonel was expecting me. I knocked on the door and he directed me to come in. I walked in and simply asked him what he needed from me.

His response was immediate and direct. "Have you forgotten military decorum Chief? Leave my office and report properly!"

I was caught off-guard and shocked but responded with "Yes Sir!" Stood at attention, did an about face and left the office. I waited a moment and knocked again. The Colonel stated "Report Chief!"

I marched in, stood at attention, saluted and reported "Chief Wetzel reporting as ordered Sir!"

"At ease Chief!" he ordered.

"I prefer to remain at attention Sir!"

"Have it your way Chief."

"Airman (name not used) received a second DWI and you recommended an Article 15 (non-judicial punishment). I want him to receive a court martial since he didn't learn from his first DWI."

I responded "Sir I have already discussed this matter with the Wing Commander since there appears to be extenuating circumstances related to the charge."

"The Wing Commander is at Travis AFB and I am in charge here." He snorted. "You will support my recommendation for a Court Martial. You are dismissed!"

I responded, "With due respect Colonel this offense does not justify a court martial and I cannot in good conscience or by my professional judgment comply with your request. Can this decision be deferred until the Wing Commander's return?"

"No! It will not be deferred," he shouted, "and I will recommend judicial punishment."

"In that case you will have my retirement request papers on your desk by noon tomorrow." I saluted, did an about face, and marched out of the office.

He literally screamed "Chief – get your ass back in here. You are not dismissed!"

I ignored his response and continued to leave. As I walked out of the office the Executive Officer (a Captain) and the two secretaries stood up and gave me a silent standing ovation. The Captain shook my hand and I left.

Immediately outside of the executive office there was a stairway to the second floor where my direct supervisor the Wing Director of Operations (DO) had his office. I climbed the stairs and knocked on his door and entered. At the exact same time the infuriated Colonel entered the same office through the private entrance from the executive suite stairway to the DO's office.

"What's up Chief?" the DO asked just as the Colonel was entering his office.

"Ask the Colonel Sir – he can probably answer your question better than me."

Ole Hitler was fuming and said "I want to press charges against the Chief for insubordination."

The DO told him to calm down and tell him what happened. The Colonel gave his side of the story in an obvious way to make me look like the instigator of the clash.

The DO asked me if what the Colonel stated was correct and I responded "No Sir, but it does not matter at this point. When a senior noncommissioned officer can no longer take care of his troops it is time for him to depart the fix. I am submitting my retirement papers and will be delivering them to your office for approval."

"Don't be hasty, Chief," the DO advised, "and please reconsider. I am sure we can resolve this issue to everyone's satisfaction. Go home and think about it and see me on Monday."

I promised to think about it over the weekend and give him my final decision on Monday but I knew that in my heart that my career was over. Zee and I talked about my decision all weekend and she begged me to stay in the Air Force. I had 24 years behind me and had already been approved for the special extension to 33 years rather than the normal 30. With our combined time as Air Force spouses and her time with her first husband, Zee had served our nation for over 30 years.

As much as I love the Air Force, Zee loved it even more. I had always promised myself that once it was no longer fun or enjoyable to be in a job, whether civilian or military, that I would quit and move on to better things. The bottom line in this case was that it was not fun anymore. Each day had become a chore and I needed a change in my life. It was time to move on and on Monday morning I handed my retirement request over to my boss.

The End of an Era - Transitioning to Civilian Life

CHAPTER TWENTY-FIVE
Life as a Civilian: New Challenges

I called a previous boss, Major Skip Orrell, who was working for Hughes Training, Inc. in Arlington, TX. Skip had previously advised me that when I retired to call him for a job reference. I called him and explained my situation and he told me to come in for an interview. He made arrangements and I was hired without going through any interviewing processes. I had 90 days of leave saved up and used every day. On the second day of my leave I started to work at Hughes. Zee and I lived in our 28 foot motor home at the Grand Prairie, TX Flea Market for three months until we purchased our new home in Arlington.

During the next 8 years in civilian life I worked for Hughes Training, Inc. and Raytheon Training, Inc. Life was pretty good in our new home in Texas. There were a couple of rough spots as there are in any marriage but we prevailed and worked through them.

My immediate boss, Dr. Sue Arnold, was a great boss. Working for her was a great privilege and joy. She gave me the freedom to do my job without interference and always supported my decisions. Sue was offered a great position at Citizens Communications to take over all of their company training programs and she accepted.

Two weeks later Sue called me and asked if I would be interested in working for her again at her new company as the Manager of Training. My initial response was "No! because the new location required a one hour drive through Dallas rush hour traffic each way from Arlington to Plano, TX. Then she said I will double your salary and start you out with 30 days-vacation per year instead of the standard new hire time of 15 days. "How soon can I start?" I asked. She said as soon as you can get away from Raytheon.

The Citizens Communications job provided me with significant opportunities for civilian senior executive management. Sue made sure that I received every opportunity to have a say at the executive decision table. Then we received devastating news that Sue was moving on to another position. My new boss, unfortunately, was the direct opposite of Sue's leadership and management style and being a decent human being. She was the "Bitch" from Hell and disliked and literally hated by every employee in the company. On two separate occasions she slapped employees and actually got away with it.

I could not wait to leave the company and she made it possible by having me fired. When I got the word of my firing the Human Resources Director told me that they would give me another 30 extra days of employment if I would train someone with everything I knew about the training management job. "Sure!" I said. For the next 30 days I stayed too busy looking for another job and did not have time to train anyone.

For the first time in my life on May 1, 2000 I was unemployed and eligible for unemployment benefits. I filed for unemployment and collected my first check two weeks later. I was mortified and felt ashamed cashing it. I received the second check and never cashed it. I still have it in my safe today. Instead, I took a job as a car salesman at Crest Isuzu in Plano, TX. The sales training class lasted 5 days and I graduated at 4 pm on Friday. I sold my first car at 5 pm the same day.

It was hard and hot work six days a week and often as long as 16 hours a day. The dealership policy was to stay open until any active sale was closed. The summer months in Texas often exceed 110 degrees. The sales lot was built with black asphalt thereby increasing the temperature by 20 or more degrees. Work started each day at 8 am but I always showed up at 6:30 or 7:00. During my rookie month, I sold 11.5 cars. The .5 car meant that I needed help to close the sale and had to share ½ the commission. The sale closed at 2:30 in the morning.

My worse commission was $25.00 after working with the customer for three days. The customer for this sale was to a leader of a Mosque in Dallas who was later arrested and convicted for collecting donations for terror organizations.

The dealership General Manager asked me to train other sales personnel on how to properly sell cars. He had been watching me closely and was impressed with my sales style and that I had closed more car sales as a rookie than anyone ever had. My answer was "No thank you. I don't ever want to conduct training again. I've been training since I was 10 years old in my father's Karate school and I want something else to do."

Three months after starting at Crest Isuzu I received a call from Vic Lauerman, the head recruiter at NEC. He asked me what I was doing for work and was shocked when I told him about my job. "Why," he asked, "are you wasting your skills and talent selling cars?"

Vic wanted me to come in for an interview and meet the VP of Human Resources. He received my resume from an anonymous source and it appeared that my training management background and my Masters in Human Resources Development ideally met a vacancy that needed to be filled. I met with him for the first interview, the HR VP for the second and third interview, the President of HR for the fourth interview, the President for the fifth interview and the VP of HR again for the sixth interview. At the conclusion of the sixth interview the VP asked me to come back for one more – the seventh – interview. I declined and told him I was not interested. If he had not accepted all of the proof of my skills, accomplishments and leadership and management background then there was nothing else that I could bring to the table.

Finally I said: "If you hire me today and provide me with the adequate resources to set up the employee development office, my department will have paid for itself, my salary and my assistant's salary in six months. If I am unable to meet this commitment in that time frame I will hand you my resignation."

He accepted my offer and challenge and hired me as the NEC Manager of Employee Development. Less than six months later I exceeded all of the expectations and approached him with the facts and status reports. After reading the data he commended me. I asked for a promotion and pay raise to Director Employee and Organizational Development. He initially balked by telling me that promotion to Director at NEC typically takes several years, not six months. I was not satisfied with the answer and offered to train someone to replace me before leaving the company. My promotion became effective immediately and I held the position for two years before being promoted to Senior Director.

The customer service department was in bad shape, with customers constantly complaining about the terrible service and treatment they were receiving. One employee actually told a customer to get F'd. The customer called the company president, who called the VP of HR and me, and directed me to set up customer advocacy and support training for every employee in the company that dealt, even remotely, with customers. I advised him that the case that prompted his directive was a disciplinary issue, NOT a training issue. The employee needed to be counseled and/or terminated. The president insisted on training everyone and firing the employee.

With the help of my assistant, Kristen Davis, we developed a mandatory customer service certification course and trained all customer-facing employees. Even though the customer service improved overall, the department where the incident occurred continued its poor service practices. I called a friend of mine, Doctor Sherry Buffington of Quantum Leap Systems, who had successfully completed an employee analysis and development program for me at Citizens Communications. Sherry and her daughter, Gina Morgan, did a remarkable job in turning the severely problematic department around. Almost immediately after their intervention within the department, customers contacted my boss to let him know how pleased they were with the turnaround.

In the summer of 2005 I was making the rounds and visiting with General Managers when I ran into Steve Fisher the Engineering General Manager. Over the previous 4 years Steve and I had become close friends. He congratulated me for obtaining my Doctorate in Business Management and asked if he could read my dissertation on building a corporate university. He did not tell me why but I gave it to him.

A week later Steve asked to meet with me about the dissertation. He wanted my permission to use parts of it for an executive presentation and his recommendation to establish a corporate university at NEC with me as its executive. I agreed and he used key elements, data and graphics in his presentation. The executive staff accepted his proposal in its entirety to include offering me the position pending my salary requirements.

My counter proposal was simple and direct. Dad's words rang in my ears: "Don't ask. Don't get!"

I needed to establish an audio/video delivery center and the appropriate funding to support it.

I wanted complete autonomy and no interference in running the organization as I saw fit.

I had to hire a staff of up to 10 employees to develop and convert all of the classroom courses to computer and distance delivery training.

My salary requirement included a 40% increase over my current salary. His responses here was "In that case your salary will be more than mine." My response was: "I'm sorry but that is my request." He agreed.

Steve wanted to know how I could justify the cost for the infrastructure in the audio/video delivery center. I committed to him that the company would receive its return on that investment within six months after it was implemented. My department exceeded the expectations by far and the National Training Center was launched successfully and it generated over $6 million in training revenue annually until I retired from the company in July of 2012.

"Life is not a problem to be solved,
but a reality to be experienced."

Soren Kierkegaard

CHAPTER TWENTY-SIX
Zee's Final Years

On our 18th anniversary in 1998 we were painting the bedrooms in our home with the help of Zee's youngest son Jeff. Zee called out to us and told us she needed to go to the emergency room because she was having a heart attack. We casually and stupidly said "We are almost done painting the bedroom, can it wait for a few minutes?" She said "No! We need to go now and it is too late to call 911."

Jeff and I loaded her into the car and we called 911 on the way to the Arlington, TX hospital. Immediately upon arrival they put her in the emergency room where Zee suffered a massive heart attack and flat lined. The heart surgeon tore open her blouse, lifted up her bra and pounded on her chest twice before inserting a long needle directly into the heart to get it started again. He waited a couple of minutes and gave her another injection. Zee took a deep breath and came back to life. The heart surgeon sensed that Zee was a heavy smoker and when she recovered a few minutes later he tapped her on the forehead and said "Lady you have smoked your last cigarette!" Zee immediately responded with a wry smile that I will never forget "No I haven't!"

Tests indicated that she had degenerative heart disease, COPD, asthma, degenerative arthritis and other medical problems. She recovered fully from the heart attack and we brought her home a couple of days later. From the day of our anniversary that year until February 2011 Zee suffered from many medical problems and was hospitalized numerous times. She flat lined three times during those years but always bounced back to go on living her life the best way that she could. However in the fall of 2008 her health began to deteriorate significantly and rapidly. She and I knew her time was limited but we chose to fight on as long as possible and I committed to her that I would be with her until the last breath. She suggested that I take her to a nursing home, drop her off and to forget about her.

In January of 2012, I was diagnosed with severe heart related problems including an enlarged heart. The heart doctors advised me that I needed surgery to repair or replace three leaking heart valves as soon as possible. I advised them of Zee's condition and that I could not have the surgery because she needed constant 24 hour a day care. The doctors provided me with the necessary medications to continue allowing me to care for her. For the next 13 months I started to have problems with breathing because the leaking heart valves prevented the proper exchange of oxygen to my system. But I had a mission to care for Zee regardless of my health as I had promised her in our vows and many times throughout our marriage.

During the next twelve months, Zee was put into two separate nursing homes after breaking several bones. The first time she broke a bone was when she was trying to pick up a piece of trash she dropped in our kitchen. While bending over to pick up the trash she lost her balance and the terrible fall caused her to break her left ulna, left hip and left pelvis. Zee spent 35 days in the hospital fighting MRSA while her fragile bones were trying to heal.

One day I visited her in the nursing home and as I walked into the room I heard her counseling a physical therapist who was complaining about how difficult his life was. The guy was feeling sorry for himself and Zee advised him how to deal with his situation while telling him that things would get better if his attitude would change. The technician left the room smiling and commenting to me how special Zee was. But I was not surprised because she always thought for the benefit of others before thinking about herself.

Zee was released to go to a long term care nursing home because the hospital determined she needed intensive twenty-four hour care that I could not provide her. She stayed in the nursing home for 5 weeks allowing her bones to heal and to get strong enough to go home. Zee did not like having to depend on others for her care. One day she had to go the bathroom and after making several attempts to get a nurse or aid to help her to go she took it upon herself. Everything went well until she returned to her hospital bed. In the process of trying to get back into her bed she fell and the bed and it threw her about 5 feet against the wall and floor. She broke her right arm and wrist in several places and lay there for quite a long time yelling for help. The finally responded and an ambulance took her to the hospital.

Three weeks later, she was released to return to the nursing home but I refused to let them take her to the same facility. We found another nursing facility closer to home where she remained for the next month before being released to come home in November.

At about the same time I received a call from my doctor and was told that my tests were indicating that my leaking valves were getting worse and that I should prepare to get them repaired soon. My answer was simple and to the point that any surgery would have to wait. Other medical issues were beginning to occur because of my neglect to go to the hospital and my doctors in general. These medical problems included an enlarged prostrate with elevated PSAs, repetitive kidney stone passes, aortic aneurism (5.6) and a broken back with the number 5 lumbar disk broken in two places. Regardless of the severity of my own health issues they would have to wait for attention and surgery as necessary. Zee needed all my attention and the other personal and medical problems were simply distracters to that end.

Between the first of November and then end of January 2011 Zee was hospitalized for one emergency after another for a total of over 40 days. Her health began to decline significantly but her indomitable spirit never waned. She fought to live each and every day with a fighting spirit that amazed our pastor and her doctors. The month of February was a horrible and painful month for Zee and she confided with me that she would be leaving us soon. She was hospitalized several times until February 20th when the primary care doctors at the hospital advised us that there was nothing else they could do for Zee and that she would need to have Hospice care. Zee took in stride and insisted that she be allowed to go home to die there.

Our pastor Alice Coder routinely came to the hospital to visit and pray with us. Zee told Pastor Alice in clear and direct words that she would not be with us much longer and that she wanted to ensure that Pastor Alice would preside at her funeral. When Pastor Alice asked Zee which bible verses she wanted to have mentioned at the memorial service Zee simply said "You have known me long enough to determine that." She did not want the family and friends to be sad but to celebrate her life in a positive way. "Just pick the passages that most clearly define who I am."

Presbyterian Hospice staff members were wonderful throughout this very trying period. The first nurse that was assigned to her care was from

Nigeria and he was a male. He was concerned that Zee would be offended by being taken care of all her bodily needs by a man. Zee immediately put him at ease and told him that there was no part of her body that other nurses and doctors had not seen and that it was OK. He stayed with her for 16 straight hours and not leaving her side to eat or to take care of his own bathroom requirements. He would only go to the bathroom after I assured him that I would not leave her side in his absence.

Other nurses, or better yet Angels, stayed with Zee on twelve hour shifts. On Tuesday February 22nd Zee told her nurse that she wanted to go to the bathroom herself and that she was tired of using the bed pan and depending on the nurses to take her there. Unfortunately it was the only time that I left Zee alone with her nurses because I had to go to my office at NEC.

Zee convinced the hospice nurse to get her a walker and with the nurse's assistance she would walk to the bathroom. The set up the walker and allowed her to take about 10 steps to test her strength. After the 10 or 15 steps Zee admitted that she was too tired and could not go to the bathroom. She lifted up her walker to make a 180 degree turn back to the hospital bed when her back bone snapped causing her to fall screaming to the floor. The nurse called for help and they put her back into bed. For the next 24 hours every move and every touch would cause Zee to scream horribly.

I called the Hospice care doctor and reminded her of her promise to keep Zee pain free. I also told her that her staff had failed to do so and she needed to intercede immediately. The doctor came to the house with several other medical personnel to conduct a complete assessment of Zee's condition. She then told me that the only way that Zee would remain pain free was for them to put her into an induced coma but when they did Zee would have less than two weeks to live. I said "OK – do it now!" For the next two days Zee did not move and on Thursday they re-evaluated her condition and reported back to me that Zee's kidneys were failing and that she would have less than five days to survive.

At exactly 7 pm on Friday Zee came out of her coma and started talking to me in the clearest voice. The Hospice nurse was shocked because she had never seen a patient come out of an induced coma. The first words Zee spoke to me were "I love you. She reminisced about our life together in a clear and direct way as if she was not even ill. She told me that she had seen her mom, dad and WK and that everything was going to be alright. She told me one more time how much she loved me and I told her how much she meant to me and how much I loved her. They were our last words that we shared as Zee slipped back into her coma as quickly as she had come out of it.

Saturday morning the Hospice team re-evaluated her condition and the doctor told me that she had 24 to 48 hours left but to expect less than 24 hours. I called the family members together and told them in no uncertain terms that they needed to come to the house to say good bye to her. Some responded in disbelief and advised me that I had cried "wolf" about her health condition before. I made it clear that my words reflected those of the Hospice doctor. Her sons, grandson, nephew and brothers came to say good bye that day and stayed until late that Saturday night. Zee had positively affected so many people in their lives and she would not have wanted us to be sad or to tell sad stories. Many stories and laughs were shared that day.

I had also called her sister and advised her to come to say goodbye to Zee. She refused to come to say goodbye and said she and her husband were on their way to Choctaw, Oklahoma to go gambling at the casino and they would swing by the next day on their way home. I explained that the doctors stated that Zee could not last through the night, but it did not make a difference and she hung up the phone. It was a thoughtless and cold-blooded response towards a woman who spent her life loving and caring for my sister-in-law.

I was sleeping in my recliner holding Zee's hand when the night nurse awakened me at 2 am on Sunday about 18 hours after the doctor gave us 24 hours. Our Schnauzer "Lindsey" was lying next to Zee with her head resting across her right arm. She instinctively knew something was wrong and was whining softly. The nurse told me that Zee's breathing had become erratic and very shallow. She told me that Zee was breathing her last breaths and that I should get up on the edge of the bed, hold her hand and to talk to her all the way to her last breath. I did so and in the most loving way that I could I shared how much she meant to me, how much I loved her over all of our years together and that it was OK to let go.

After 5 minutes or so Zee started breathing in an uncontrolled way and her eyes stared straight into mine. I will take the way Zee stared at me to my grave. I repeated several times "Honey I love you so much. It's OK to let go!"

Zee took what appeared to be her last breath and I asked the nurse if she was gone. The nurse said "No I don't think so. As hard as she has fought I believe she will try to breathe again." Right after she uttered those words Zee took three deep breaths staring deep into my eyes and then stopped breathing for the last time. Her eyes remained open staring at me with a death stare that will never leave my memory again. I collapsed over her body crying and sobbing uncontrollably for several minutes. I gained my composure and reached up and closed her eyes for the last time.

The Hospice recovery team came by about 10 minutes later and declared her time of death as 2:20 am on February 27, 2011. All of our lives were and are forever affected by this loving woman who cared so much for us and life in general that she fought all the way to the very end to keep us from having to suffer her loss. They prepared her body and wrapped her in a white sheet. They collected and destroyed all of her medic ations by mixing them with coffee grounds. The ambulance had been called earlier without my knowledge and Zee was taken out of the house immediately. The hospice team hugged me and left our home leaving me alone. It was a terrible lonely and empty feeling that cannot be adequately described.

At 2:30 I called all the family members to let them know that Zee was gone. Her sister was nowhere to be found. I was absolutely baffled by here total lack of sensitivity and caring for her only sister. I cannot help but hope that she will face her Day of Judgment alone. I do not have it in me to hate anyone but this is one person who most closely deserves a level of disgust and dislike of any person I have ever known.

The memorial service was held at our church in Plano. Family, friends and colleagues from my company attended. Zee's brother Bill spoke about and celebrated Zee's life and how she impacted people's lives so positively. I had a hard time holding myself together and sobbed uncontrollably for a brief moment. Zee meant so much to so many people that words could not adequately express the positive impact she had on all of us.

A few days after the memorial service we interred Zee's ashes at the Dallas-Fort Worth Veterans Cemetery. It was always Zee's wish to be interred in a military cemetery among all of the soldiers, sailors, marines and airman she served and loved so much. Then the Estate and Will nightmare began and would last for two agonizing years thanks to the executor of our estate – my back stabbing sister-in-Law.

Unknown to me at that time, Zee's sister somehow convinced Zee to destroy our jointly written wills. She advised Zee that I would not treat her three sons fairly regarding our estate. I don't know what happened and can only speculate but both of our wills in our locked safe disappeared. I would only find out about it after Zee's funeral, when my step-sons, sister-in-law and I met in my home. I mentioned that Zee left a Will, making me the Executor. My sister-in-law advised me that I was wrong, that Zee's new Will made her the Executor of the estate.

The two witnesses that signed the new Will were Spanish speaking workers in the nursing home. When I asked my sister-in-law's attorney how he determined whether Zee was in the right state of mind, allowing her to sign the will, he said, "She answered the two questions correctly – What is your name? And what is your date of birth?" My sister-in-law advised me that the Probate Judge was scheduled to meet with her soon. I mentioned that I needed to attend the Probate hearing because I wanted to challenge the Will. She advised me that I would be told when the hearing was scheduled. A few weeks later, I called her and asked when the hearing was scheduled for and she told me at 8 a.m., on a specific date at the Collin County Courthouse.

On the date of the scheduled hearing, I went to the courthouse at 7:45 and asked a Bailiff when and where the hearing was going to be held. He advised me that the hearing was already being held and showed me where to go. As I entered the hearing room, I saw the Probate Judge meeting with my sister-in-law. I introduced myself and mentioned that she advised me that the hearing was scheduled for 8 a.m. and that I was early. The Judge immediately responded by telling me I was late and that he had already ruled in favor of my sister-in-law being the Executor. I retorted by telling the Judge that she had a conflict of interest in the estate and could not be the Executor, and that the Will was written when Zee was under heavy mind altering medication and, therefore, unfit to write a Will.

The Judge stated, "I have ruled in the case and if you want to challenge the ruling, feel free to do so. Get a good lawyer and be prepared to spend a lot of money. Dismissed!"

My sister-in-law, the Executor, went after my 401Ks, my personal life insurance, my annuity, ½ of my home value and household goods, my farm land, 50% of my recent federal income tax returns, received after Zee passed away and several other personal properties. She removed over $20,000 worth of jewelry and other of Zee's personal effects from the home and claimed that it was only worth $1,500 in the probate listing. Zee's wedding ring alone was worth over $6,000 in pure gold. She even claimed that I did not have the right to pay the $7,500 for the funeral with estate money and that I had to repay the estate. The original probate documents listed over $300,000 in estate value to be distributed to the three step-sons.

The probate lasted over two years and I lost all my savings and had to sell several personal items to settle the estate. Lawyer fees exceeded $40,000, just to protect my property rights. I was attacked by the Executor with a viciousness and cruelty that was beyond any understanding or justification. There is no doubt in my mind that there is a special place reserved in Hell for her. Two of the three step-sons never spoke on my behalf to defend me from her attacks. It is also important to note that the two step-sons were retired military and receiving full retired pay and were gainfully employed. They were not financially dependent upon their mother or me. There was no reason for them to pursue an inheritance that did not exist, except to get share of the home. Even then, decent human beings, knowing how I cared for their mother for 4 years, 24 hours a day, seven days a week administering nursing care without any assistance, would have had the decency to fight the Executor on my behalf.

In the end, their greed ruled the day. They ended up with every penny of my savings and I walked away, never to look back. Ironically, on my next birthday, I received a card from my former sister-in-law, telling me how much she loved me.

CHAPTER TWENTY-SEVEN
Paying the Piper

At some point in time, the effects of being too focused on the needs of others, and ignoring our own needs, catches up with us, and when it caught up with me, it came full force.

Open Heart Surgery

Roy and I, and probably Jimmy, had and have aortic aneurisms. Roy died from his after they repaired his ascending aortic valve and aneurism. Both of our aneurisms were determined to be related to Agent Orange chemicals we were subjected to in Viet Nam. Jimmy is recovering from cancer related to the same chemical and his Viet Nam service.

Roy received a mechanical valve but it separated from his heart a year later when a severe staph infection grew so fast causing it to fail.

I have known about my bicuspid leaking valve since 1994 when they discovered it and that my arteries were clogged as much as 90%. It was the single reason why the FAA permanently grounded me. After 17 years they found no blockage because I took my meds regularly and followed my Doc's instructions.

When I was stationed in Hawaii from 1972 – 1976, I was guiding a Marine 5 Ton Truck onto a C-141 and he lost control of his vehicle. Instead of hitting his brakes he hit his clutch causing the fully loaded vehicle to run out of control down the ramp. It happened so quickly and unexpectedly that I could not get out of the way in time. He hit me on my left hip, I spun through the air about 20 feet before hitting the ground where he parked his left front tire on my left foot.

He continued to fail following my instructions NOT to move the vehicle. Instead he backed up over my foot again crushing my steel toed boot even more almost severing my toes. The other marines dragged him out of the vehicle and beat him senseless.

They had to cut the boot of my foot to save my toes and conducted a full X-Ray of my back and hips. The doctor advised me at the time that there were no breaks to any of my bones but that I could expect to have problems with my back someday.

During my VA physical in 1990 I mentioned the pains in my back and the accident. They X-Rayed me again and found me to asymptomatic and denied me VA benefits for that.

Over the last 18 months I have been under the care of a back doctor because of back and leg pains. A full scan found that my number 5 disk has two breaks that were contributing to the current problems and scheduled me for surgery. During my surgery pre-op they found the aortic aneurism and leaking heart valve. The aneurism was at 5.6 cm – initially determined not big enough to justify surgery. They sent me to a heart surgeon who evaluated the aneurism and leaking valve and gave me clearance to proceed with the back surgery. I was in the surgery suite getting ready for the back surgery when the 5 doctors asked to review my records again.

The anesthesiologist refused to proceed and ultimately all of them decided not to proceed until my heart was fixed first. Their position was very clear in that if the aneurism blew while I was on my stomach getting my repair that no one would be able to save my life and I would bleed out.

As are most heart patients, I was given the options for a mechanical, pig or bovine valve. In fact my thoracic surgeon had decided to give me a mechanical valve and scheduled me for emergency surgery because of three factors related to my case.

1. Aneurisms run in my family

2. Bicuspid valves have a history in my family

3. I have two leaking valves.

I agreed to the surgery but asked for a few days to research the valve options but did tell him that the mechanical valve was not an option for me for many reasons but for two primary reasons:

Warfarin/Coumadin and the major life changes that occur under this drug. Since I own a small farm and have an active outdoor lifestyle -

hunting and fishing - the potential, for bleeding out after the smallest blood related accident because of this medication, is extremely high.

Roy died from the mechanical valve.

The day before the surgery I met with Dr. Wallace about my decision to have a bovine valve replacement because the expected life expectancy of this valve is 15 - 20 years versus the 10 - 15 years for a pig valve. He advised me that he was going to repair my valve instead of replacing it altogether. He has several patients who received this repair and all recovered earlier and more significantly Replacement expectance is 15 - 20 years and no blood treatment medication is required. He fully described the procedure and drew it on the white board so I could take a picture and told me to git-er-done!

During the surgery on October 27, 2011 I bled out 1300 cc of blood and they had a hard time controlling the bleeding. The surgery lasted 8 hours and I stayed in the hospital for seven days. Since Zee had passed away in February there was no one to care for me at home, so the doctor kept me in the hospital for as long as the insurance would allow.

Two days after the surgery I was taken to critical care because all of my extremities ballooned up and in the time span of 6 hours, I had gained 13 pounds in weight due to fluid retention. I remained in the critical care unit for 8 hours as an X-Ray showed significant fluids pressing against my lungs. Two large containers of liquids were drained off, and I immediatley felt better.

Eleven days after the surgery was the first day my feet were not swollen and I felt better. I started walking on a my treadmill that day and walked for about a quarter of a mile. Within a week the distance had increased to a mile at about 1.5 miles per hour. My heart rate and blood pressure was a bit radical, but I felt stronger.

My cardiologist scheduled me for rehabilitation that would last for about 12 weeks. By the time I attended my first session, I was walking over two miles at three miles per hour on the treadmill. During the rehab session, the nursing staff hooked me to a monitor and told me to conduct all my exercises at a very slow and minimal rate. It was boring because the rate was extremely slow. I pushed the envelope with every exercise and the monitors continued to warn the staff that my rates were too high.

After 18 rehab sessions I had enough of the slow pace and stopped going to rehab. By this time my walking pace on the treadmill and walking with my buddy Jim Thompson every other day was over three miles at about 4 miles per hour.

360 Degree Radical Back Surgery

On February 28, 2012 I went back to the hospital for a 360 degree radical back surgery. Research on the Internet indicated that this was a very dangerous surgery but, after years of unbearable pain, I was ready for it. Five surgeons with very different and distinct roles conducted the operation.

The surgery lasted two hours longer than planned and the recovery was lengthy. My doctor told me to expect an 18 month recovery and rehab. Stubborn as always I would not wait for natural healing to take place. I did follow the weight lifting restrictions to the letter but every other restriction such as walking and going up stairs were pushed to the limit. My post heart surgery rehab and extended walking on the treadmill strengthened my muscles and ultimately helped to prepare for the back surgery and ultimate recovery.

Final Retirement 2012

Medical leave of absence (MLA) in the civilian world comes with very specific Human Resources (HR) rules and federal and state employment rules. The most significant one is that once an employee goes on MLA he or she is not permitted to be in communications related to the job until return to work. Only communications through HR are permitted. I complied with those rules for the 5 months I was on MLA.

Sometime during the month of April I received a call from NEC that I had to lay off three employees as part of the company's downsizing process. Prior to going on MLA I had already laid off three employees and I was not ready or willing to lay anyone else off. My department – the National Training Center - was already minimally manned and further layoffs would destroy its ability to adequately support the company and its customer's training needs. Additionally and more important, two of my married employees were suffering major medical problems and had teenage children. I just did not have it in my heart to lay anyone off when I had alternatives.

I broke HR rules and called my supervisor and one of the best friends that anyone could have – Steve Fisher. Without hesitation I advised Steve that I was not going to lay anyone off. Steve responded by telling me that I had no choice in the matter and that he also was required to lay off up to 8 employees. The company was losing money and a major down sizing was in order and required by NEC Japan HQ.

I provided Steve an alternative and asked him to tell HR that I was willing to be laid off if the company would keep the employees on the payroll in exchange. Steve said that he would try but had doubts the company would accept my offer. Later that day Steve called and told me that HR had accepted the offer and set a retirement date of June 1, 2012. Then Steve advised me that once HR accepted my offer and to his complete surprise, he offered to retire his General Management job in place of laying off his eight employees. Surprisingly, HR accepted his offer as well. Steve spoke with two other senior executives about our initiatives to save jobs and they both did the same thing. Ultimately 15 or more employees jobs were saved, but several good leaders were lost.

Wim and Vikie on Their Wedding Day, June 20, 2012

CHAPTER TWENTY-EIGHT
New Beginnings

After Zee's passing, I had no interest or thought of dating again. I did not believe it was possible that anyone would be interested in an old man, especially when they discovered all about my medical issues and surgeries. I actually tried to get into the on-line dating scene through Match.com and completed the extensive questionaire by answering every question honestly and directly. When I submitted the questions for a final response an astonishing and unbelievable answer popped up almost instantaneously. I don't recall the exact wording but it was something like, "Sorry - There is no one in our system that matches your profile!"

Wow! Shocked does not adequately reflect my response. The cold and heartless response pretty much ended any desire for me to pursue dating.

Vikie Wetzel and Washington State

Years before her passing, Zee hired a housekeeper, Chris Koleber, to assist in keeping our home in a decent condition. Chris worked for us for several years and had become a close and dear friend who at times would stay with Zee to give me a break from taking care of her.

The round the clock, seven days a week intense schedule of attending to Zee's needs were taking a heavy toll on my mental and physical health, and my sister-in-law and other family members were of little help. With the exception of my youngest step-son and his wife, they all found it too inconvenient to help me with the mother who often worked three jobs to support them when they were kids. After Zee died, I continued to have Chris clean the house for me because, quite frankly, I hate housekeeping duties. I would rather be fishing and hunting.

A week before Christmas Chris and Dennis (her husband) invited me to dinner at their home and I accepted. On Christamas Eve I had a hard time finding their home and had decided to give up and return to my house. But before doing so I walked up to a home that I thought was

Chris' and the home owner answered. He told me he knew the family and directed me to their home a block away.

After being welcomed into the house I was introduced to Vikie Jordan another dinner guest. The thought immediately occurred to me that "This is a setup!" In addition to inviting me for Christmas dinner to ensure that I would not be alone on my first holiday the hidden agenda was to for Vikie and me to meet.

Good move! Vikie and I appeared to share the same interests and values, and my interest her warm, friendly demeanor piqued my interest. Dinner and the sharing of stories and background information the followed made me want see her again, though at the time, there appeared to be no reciprocation of that desire.

The following morning I called and asked Chris if she would contact Vikie and ask her to give me her e-mail address or telephone number. Chris called, and Vikie gave her permission. Later that day I called Vikie and asked her out for dinner. We had not made reservations and since it was still the holiday season all the restaurants were booked up. We finally had dinner at the 5 Guys Hamburger restaurant.

Dating after 32 years of marriage was not something I was ready for and I doubt Vikie was impressed. She hung in there though. We dated for several months and were married on June 20, 2012. It was a small, private wedding in my home. Dennis is a lay preacher and conducted the wedding ceremony with our closest friends present. My best friend Blain Sheppard and his wife Linda attended through Skype.

Vikie and I talked about visiting Vikie's daughter in Couer D'Alene, Idaho so that I could meet her and her sons. Coincidentally Steve Fisher, my boss at NEC, had previously invited me to come to spend time fishing and recovering from my surgeries at his lake cabin at Deer Lake, WA. I had previously accepted his invitation and arranged to visit him for a week. Vikie was already scheduled to fly to Coeur D'Alene to visit her daughter, so we flew to Spokane together. We wnet our separate ways at the Spokane airport, and arranged to meet a week later at my new daughter-in-Law's home.

I was enthralled and hypnotized by the absolutely God-given beauty of the state of Washington and, without a second thought, decided this would be our new home. I called Vik and said "I'm ready to move to this area!"

During our stay in Couer D'Alene, we looked for property near a lake or river in Idaho. The state is so absolutely beautiful that words cannot adequately describe it. We found a six acre property alongside a river and made an offer to the seller. He accepted the offer and we planned to move once the loan was approved. Wells Fargo Bank rejected our home and property loan request with the justification that I had no adequate available funding for the down payment and that I was unemployed. The loan fell through.

Vikie had expressed an interest in going to Alaska for an RV trip; an adventure in which I initially had no interest, but decided reconsidered and decided to go. In June 2013, we departed for the 3-month trip with a two week stop in Couer D'Alene to spend time with Leslie and the boys. We had a lot of time to spare and decided to drive to Washington to look again for our new home.

We ultimately found a beautiful log home with some acreage. Attempts to contact the realtor failed and the home owner was not at home. We left a note on his front door expressing our interest and provided our telephone number and then continued our search. The home owner ultimately called and provided us with his asking price of over half a million dollars. That was a bit over our budget to say the least. We thanked him for the return call and kept looking.

We then received a call from his realtor/broker, Kathy, who apologized for not contating us earlier. We advised her that the owner's asking price was too high and that we were still looking. She queried me on our desired home criteria. I answered, "Cedar built or log home over 2,000 square feet on timbered acreage."

Kathy mentioned that she had 3 possible homes in mind, that may meet our requirements and that she was the owner of one of the properties. After expressing interest in her personal home, we arranged to meet her there. The 2800 square foot cedar built home was situated on the side of a mountain on 40 acres of heavy pine timber overlooking the valley surrounding Springdale, WA. It was absouletly beautiful and the view was breathtaking. The asking price was too high, but we loved the place and I made a counter offer which was somewhat beyond my budget. Kathy called her husband and discussed the counter offer and they both agreed to accept it. Then Kathy mentioned that they also owned the adjacent 80 acres of unspoiled timber and that we could purchase that as well. We made an offer on the acreage, which was also accepted on a separate contract for a seller carried loan. We would purchase and own the 80 acres even if our home loan application for the home and 40 acres were ultimately disapproved.

I had never used my VA loan before and decided that this would be the best opportunity to do so. We applied for the loan and were initially approved. We called a realtor in Plano, TX and put our home on the market and proceeded on our RV trip to Alaska. Over the next two months we waited for final VA loan approval and finally received it, fully funded at 3% interest. What a fantastic deal. We had our home!

We returned to Plano because we had not received an offer on the house. Though it was imperative that the house be sold, the probate on Zee's estate was still in proress. My sister-in-law was holding my gonads in her vicious vice and demanding that I get another appraisal on my home. She threatened to stretch the probate to the full three years allowed by Texas law to wait for the increased value of the property. To get past yet another obstacle, I paid for another appraisal by a an appraiser of her choice. Fortunately the appraiser supported the initail price, and a few days later we received an offer and the house was sold.

We wanted to start anew so we sold almost everything we owned in an estate sale. Our belongings were valued at about $40,000, but after the sale closed, all we received was a check for $4,500. I was done! I wanted to be as far away from my former in-laws as possible. We left Texas and never looked back.

A new home in a beautiful new state, with a wonderful new wife is like paradise found. To this day, I awaken every morning and overlook the valley below and I never get tired of the view.

CHAPTER TWENTY-NINE
Just When I Thought It Was Safe
The Challenges Continue

The Car Accident

It was a routine day on March 6, 2014 with an early rise for Vikie and me. We had decided to trade our car in for a four wheel drive vehicle. Our home on the mountain side required us to have an all-wheel or four wheel drive car especially since our access road was a mile long unimproved road. I also wanted to go to a tool sale in downtown Spokane and convinced her to get up early at 6 am so that we could be at the store by 8. We did not make it for the sale and only by the grace of God did we survive to live another day.

We decided to take her 2013 GMC Terrain instead of my Dodge RAM because the Terrain had been in the garage for almost two months. The bottoms of the tires were a little flat after sitting in one spot for so long. It was a bit unusual to hear and feel the thump-thump of the flat spots as we started down the one mile driveway.

We believed that it would be safe to drive down our one mile long mountain driveway because the temperatures had remained above 40 degrees for three days; long enough for any ice on our unimproved driveway to be melted completely or turned to slush. All was well for the first two hundred feet before our drive began its downhill slope. Once we reached the crest to start the actual downhill phase, we realized that things were going to be challenging. About 75% of the drive is bathed in sunlight most of the day and all of the snow and ice in those areas had melted. But the initial downhill section is always in the shadow of the massive pine trees on our timbered property. Even though the temperatures have been above freezing for a few days, some of the shaded areas remained frozen under a deceivingly thin layer of slush.

Seeing the condition of the road, I advised Vikie not to hit the brakes to prevent the car from skidding, though the vehicle was picking up speed. She did a remarkable job trying to control the rapidly increasing descent, but as we approached the first left turning part of the "S" shaped descent, the car began to skid out of control. Vikie did her best to regain control, but the skid to the right became too unmanageable for even the most experienced driver.

The right front tire hit a soft snow bank and the right rear tire left the road causing the car to skid to the right and into an uncontrolable roll to the right. After the second roll, I incredibly started counting. On the eighth roll, the car landed upside down against three huge pine trees. The final impact sounded like a small bomb exploding as the windshield shattered and all of the airbags blew out.

I remained conscious throughout the entire ride through Hell and kept talking to Vikie, telling her it was going to be OK. At some point she lost consciousness and does not remember everything that happened. When she regained her senses her first comment was "I guess this means I will get a new car, huh?" Ya' gotta' love her! Almost simultaneously we both thanked God for saving us.

As we hung upside down in our seats secured by our seat belts in the rather dark car Vikie said "I smell smoke!" Then somehow she turned off the ignition and we waited for the fire because we could not move. Upon realizing that there was no fire, I reached up and released my seat belt. I can tell you from that experience that you can actually kiss your own ass. Think about that because I don't want to try to explain how that can happen.

My first and only thought was to help Vikie. She too was upside down with her thighs being supported by the bottom of the steering wheel and her seat belt. Blood was pouring from her head onto the car's ceiling and I started to panic a little as I imagined the worst for her condition. Immediately I looked for an escape route but all of the windows were crushed into the ground or the trees. The doors were all pinned either against the ground or the three trees. I found one intact window on the back seat passenger side, and was somehow I was able to crawl to the rear ceiling and to attempt to break the window. I tried to break it with a large hunting knife and several kicks to no avail. Vikie was in pain and I crawled back to get her out of her seat. Because of her height she was hanging upside down quite a distance above the car ceiling (now the floor) and I knew that releasing her seat belt from that height could really hurt her, especially if she had injured her neck or back.

210

I crawled under her body and raised her as high as possible before releasing her seat belt. She fell relatively gently into my arms and we just hugged and cried while thanking the Lord. Guilt overwhelmed me for asking her to go to a stupid tool sale. I cried uncontrollably in my guilt but Vikie brought me back to reality in a calm and soothing voice. It was enough for me to get my act together again. Then, quite miraculously, the rear hatch door opened and the sunlight shone into the car. We both believe that it was Divine intervention and God was giving us the light to follow out to safety.

As we exited the car I looked past the trees that were holding the car in place only to see that beyond the trees there was nothing else to stop our descent. The trees and the phenomenally built GM car saved our lives. If the trees had not stopped us we probably would not have survived the final impact. I took a couple of pictures of the crash site.

Vikie was hurt badly by the exploding steering wheel airbag. Her nose was broken, her right eye was bleeding and damaged badly, three of her top front teeth were missing, her right leg was hurting and blood was dripping from her hair. I took her picture for the record and accident report. Though we were free from the car, our ordeal was not finished yet. We had to climb back up the hill about 100 feet to the road and then walk another quarter of a mile on icy slushy road to the house.

Vikie inspired me again as she fought her way up the hill in two foot deep snow and climbing through heavy brush, all the while in severe pain. There was no way she was going to allow me to go to the house to get help or call an ambulance without her. After slipping and sliding all the way back to the house we took an inventory of our injuries. Mine were minor. I escaped almost unscathed, but Vikie was badly hurt. Still, she refused to go to the hospital.

I called the insurance agent to report the accident and he insisted that we get to a hospital quickly and any way that we could. We knew that any help or ambulance could not come up the steep road so we decided to take the truck. Vikie was reticent. She did not want to get into another vehicle and drive down that icy road again. She insisted on walking down and having me meet her at the entrance. She hesitantly changed her mind after I promised her that I would put chains on the tires and drive as slowly as possible.

We traversed the icy slushy obstacle course safely and headed directly to the Spokane hospital an hour drive away. I intended to drop her off at the emergency room and then park the truck, but Vikie would have none of that. She insisted on going with me to park the truck and go to the ER together. I parked the truck and accompanied her on a very painful walk to the ER.

Providence Holy Family Hospital ER was packed full with patients. Everyone, including the patients and the hospital staff, looked at Vikie with matted blood in her hair and severe bruises on her face limping through the door and almost simultaneously everyone looked at me, apparently trying to deduce whether I was a wife beater. To allay those assumptions I stated loudly enough for everyone to hear, "We just had a major roll-over car accident and we need help!" The admittance nurses jumped out of their seats to take care of Vikie and whisked her away, leaving me standing in the entryway alone.

I sat in the waiting room for about thirty minutes with everyone staring at me as if I was some type of evil being. Finally I approached the nurse and asked why they were not letting me be with my wife. I stated that "I did not beat her. We had a car accident and I have pictures to prove it." I showed the nurse the pictures and she said that I appeared not to be injured and therefore I had to wait until my turn. It was just too much to take and I insisted on being with Vikie. Another nurse came to me and asked to see the pictures and proceeded to do a triage on my condition. She immediately took me to visit with Vikie and then put me in a separate room for an evaluation.

If I told the story of how the accident occurred once, I told it at least 10 times to doctors, nurses, x-ray technicians and pharmacy staff. People were amazed. It seemed they could not get enough information about this seemingly miraculous event.

Finally, at 4 pm we were released to go home. Vikie did not want to go back up the hill but reached deep down inside herself to get the courage to make it home. After reinstalling the tire chains we took a slow and easy drive back up the driveway to our home on the mountain.

I share this experience with to give you a specific example of the miracles that God gives us in times of need.

CHAPTER THIRTY
The Nightmares Continue

Prostate Surgery- PTSD - Agent Orange

This discussion of my experiences in dealing with the Veterans Administration is not meant to be an indictment of the organization and its overall service and value to our nation's veterans. I can only describe how I have been treated by it since retiring in 1990. Several of my military friends also deal with the VA only to be ignored or constantly delayed in receiving their benefits. Disapproval of first time applications appear to be the norm and unless the veteran appeals a decision the VA considers their disapproval final and closes the books. The general consensus by the majority of veterans is that the VA just waits for us to die so that treatments and benefits will not be required.

My fellow veterans are well aware of the Hellish nightmare the VA puts American Veterans through. They know how forgotten we are once we are through serving our country. They know what we endure. It is to give those who are not veterans and who don't know better understanding, that I provide the following is a summary of my claims and communications with the Veterans Administration. I wish I could say that this is unusual, but it isn't. It's a story that repeats again and again thousands of times a day.

Prior to retiring or leaving the military all veterans are requested to apply for VA benefits for injuries and diseases related to their military service. Many veterans choose not to apply for benefits. The reasons are simple; they have heard the horror stories from other military men and women and there is fear of reprisal. Injuries suffered while serving are often not reported to medical authorities or reflected in military records because of fear that doing so will result in retaliation or in being discharged. Military flying personnel fear losing flying status if they report their injuries.

Non-physical injuries, such as post traumatic stress (PTSD) or Traumatic Brain Injury (TBI) almost never get reported because, not only can such reports result in discharge, they lie like a poison in the veteran's records and can follow them for life. Reporting non-debilitating physical injures is bad enough, so you can imagine the resistance in reporting non-physical ones. Things have to be really bad before a veteran will report a non-physical injury such as PTSD. Even when it has been diagnosed, most veterans won't seek treatment for it because of the horror stories other veterans have shared with them.

In my case as a C-130 and C-141 Loadmaster I suffered two major cargo compartment back injuries, horrible migraine headaches due to TBI's and an altitude chamber ride, and hearing loss due to working around aircraft engines running during on and off-load operations. None of these were ever reported to the Flight Surgeon during annual medical evaluations because I knew that temporary or permanent grounding or military discharge could occur.

During my 24 year career as an aircrew trainer I met hundreds and maybe thousands of aircrew and other military personnel. I am willing to bet that most, if not all, of those men and women suffered injuries, some major, due to their jobs. Suffering through the pain and agony of these injuries was and probably continues for active duty personnel today just so that they can continue to serve the nation.

In June of 1990 I was fully evaluated by the VA in the Dallas/Fort Worth, TX area. When I received the report of the overall evaluation the VA rated me at Zero percent. Please note the chart provided below for all items listed on July 1, 1990. The 40% determination was given only after 4 appeals which took over a year to complete. Each of the 4 appeals resulted in an additional 10% but several of the problems continued to be rated at zero percent. To make matters worse I had to go through re-evaluations every year for three years until I filed a complaint with the VA for harassment.

I settled for the 40 percent until August 2012 when I started suffering major pain resulting from a back injury described earlier in this biography. The Air Force doctor at Hickam AFB told me after my treatments that I should expect to suffer back pain later on in my life. He recorded the injury in my medical records but failed to mention that it occurred while working on the Hickam AFB flight line and that I was struck and run over by a Marine Corps 5 Ton Truck. The VA used those missing facts for rejecting my disability. Their disapproval letter clearly states that there is no evidence that I was injured doing my job and that the accident was probably due to an off-base car accident. I appealed the decision immediately in 2012 and submitted witness statements from my supervisor and another loadmaster to prove that the injury was job related. My orthopedic surgeon (back surgery) submitted his documentation and professional opinion that the broken back was an old injury most likely related to the accident at Hickam AFB.

The VA rejected the appeal and I resubmitted new appeals several times and finally asked RepsforVets to file the appeal using their attorneys. The appeals were filed on February 28, 2014. During a call to the VA that same year, I was advised that it would be a year or more before they got to my case.

In November of 2013 the VA rated me at 70% for PTSD. With my previous ratings totaling 40% I had expected to be rated at 100%, but the VA's calculations rated me at a total of 70%.

Starting in January of 2010 I started suffering from high PSA levels and other prostate related problems. Since I was so focused on caring for Zee at the time, I failed to take care of the problem. After she passed away, the PSA results started to climb rapidly until my urologist recommended a prostate biopsy. The results came back as positive for malignant prostate cancer. The professional opinion and diagnosis of the urologist was that the prostate cancer was due to my work with Agent Orange (AO) in Viet Nam. We discussed several options to deal with the cancer, including leaving it alone and waiting to see if it got worse. I said to him "Let's just put one bullet in a gun and then rotate the chamber and play Russian roulette, if we are going to wait." I told him to remove the prostate.

The prostatectomy (total removal of the prostate gland) went well but I started suffering severe pain, an inability to urinate, and had three unitary tract infections (UTIs) over a six-month period that would not heal with medications. The urologist conducted an evaluation using a scope and was unable to get into the bladder because the tube going into it had almost closed post-surgery. He scheduled an immediate out-patient surgery to stretch the opening so that I could pass liquids. During the surgery he discovered a second and more serious reason for the pain I had been suffering. Someone had left a surgery clip in the bladder during the surgery and it had migrated into the bladder. After the surgery and for the following two months, I suffered two more UTIs that still did not heal with medications. I filed for VA benefits due to prostate cancer on March 28, 2014. Four months later I received the VA letter rating me at a total of 100%.

Exactly one year after my prostatectomy I received my VA letter stating that I no longer had prostate cancer due to removal of the prostate and had no sign of malignancy, therefore my overall benefits were going to be reduced to 60%. The letter further acknowledged that my erectile dysfunction and bladder control issues due to the prostate cancer surgery were not considered military related.

The connection between prostate cancer, Agent Orange, peripheral neuropathy and several heart related diseases has been proven. According to its own rules and regulations, any Viet Nam veteran who files for benefits for any of these medical problems is considered "presumptive" to be AO related. Although the VA agreed that several of my problems were Agent Orange related, the disabilities that were clearly there were rated at zero percent for all benefit applications.

The following list is taken directly from my VA disabilities file. Note, that when all of the percentages are added, the total is actually 200%. Due to VA regulations, they use archaic and impossible to understand charts and graphs, to combine and reduce benefit percentage totals.

- PTSD – 70% combat service related to Agent Orange.
- Peripheral Neuropathy – 0% related to Agent Orange but not service connected.
- Allergic Rhinitis 10% - Service Connected
- Tendonitis – Wrist, Elbows and Shoulders – 10% - Service Connected
- Vesicular Dyshydrosis, hands and feet – 10% - Service Connected
- Tinea Pedis – 10% - Service Connected
- Ascending Aortic Aneurysm 0% related to Agent Orange but not service connected.
- Prostate Cancer – 60% - Service Connected due to Agent Orange
- Residual Left Hip Injury with Trochanteric Bursitis – 10% Service Connected (due to the Marine Truck Accident)

- Bursitis, Left Shoulder – 20% - Service Connected

  Subtotal Percentage: 200% - Recalculated by the VA to 90%

This process applies to every veteran regardless of their total disabilities. The hidden purpose is to avoid rating veterans at 100% at all costs. Most disabled veterans fully believe that the VA makes it so hard to obtain benefits and continue to delay final decisions because they are betting that the veteran will die first and they won't have to pay. Unfortunately that appears to be true. Many of my Veteran brothers and sisters died without VA benefits that were very justifiably due to them. One report in 2015 stated that over 300,000 disabled veterans died just waiting for VA health care.

The VA advisory letter advised me that my total rating would be reduced to 90%, cutting my benefits payments by almost 50%. Keep in mind that there is only a 10% reduction in the total from 100% to 90%, but the payments would be reduced by 50%. Unfortunately, this is the type of treatment that every disabled veteran, regardless of the disabilities and pains suffered, has to deal with every day for serving our nation. While hundreds of thousands of disabled veterans continue to wait for benefits they earned in combat, the VA continues to make those of us who have received benefits, prove on a regular and recurring schedule, reprove that they are entitled to benefits already obtained. It is insufferable and cruel treatment of our veterans.

Once again, I filed an appeal and provided other supporting documents from my urologist. His official medical opinion also clearly stated that "there is a reasonable opinion that the existing medical issues will not be resolved during the life of this patient." He recommended that my prostate cancer related disability be rated as permanent.

After personally fighting with the VA over my medical benefits, waiting for over three years for them to address my 2 appeals, two attempts in eighteen months just trying to get copies of my PTSD mental evaluations for one of the appeals and the current process to reduce my benefits by half I conceded failure. I contacted my Congresswoman in Eastern Washington, The Honorable Cathy McMorris Rodgers. I explained my long-fought battle with the VA, my long awaited appeals and the inability to obtain basic information. Congresswoman McMorris Rodgers and her staff member, Louise Fendrich, responded within 48 hours. They contacted the VA for a request for information and a status of my appeals and active benefits requests. Within 72 hours after her request, I received a copy of the PTSD mental evaluation that I filed for twice over an 18 month period. The Congresswoman and her staff requested that I give them at least four weeks for the VA to properly respond. Based on the rapid response I received, relating to the PTSD issue and already waiting over two years for appeals action, I did not have any problem waiting for another 3 or 4 weeks.

On July 20, 2015, I received an update from the VA, notifying me that my total disability rating will be retained at 70%. However, due to the many peripheral and life altering medical problems related to the prostate surgery and PTSD, they were rating me at a 100% permanent and total (P&T) rating. This, in a layperson's definition, means that I will no longer have to go through the constant and recurring re-evaluations again. But the VA can change this decision at any time, even though the letter specifically states that no future evaluations are scheduled.

This timely and quick conclusion would not have been possible without the willing and direct support of Congresswoman Cathy McMorris Rodgers and her staff. To them I extend my eternal gratitude for delivering me from this long fought nightmare.

To every veteran suffering from military related injuries, diseases and illnesses, I encourage you to never give up in pursuing VA benefits which are owed to you. Obtain a veterans' benefits user profile and submit your benefits requests, to their web site at https://www.ebenefits. va.gov/ebenefits/homepage. This site has all the information you need. It is relatively easy to understand and use. I literally visit the site every day, even now, after my final rating decision. Don't be discouraged by disapprovals. Submit appeals as often as necessary. Use the Disabled American Veterans (DAV), or any other reputable veterans support agency and/or contact your Congressional Representative or Senator for support, if necessary. Just don't give up!

Like every U.S. veteran, I did not serve our country to obtain veterans benefits. I served because I felt I owed my country for the tremendous freedoms and opportunities it offered my legal immigrant family and me. But the wars we have fought to defend and protect our country has damaged me and tens of thousands of my brother and sister veterans physically and psychologically, and the VA owes us the proper care and benefits which are supported by law. Therefore, I will continue to fight for my VA benefits and to be a voice for my fellow veterans when and wherever necessary.

God bless this great country and all that she provides its citizens. My family was blessed with the opportunity to immigrate here because of President Eisenhower's initiative to bring displaced people into the country.

Thank you to the American soldiers, airmen, marines and sailors that gave of themselves and their lives to free my parents and relatives from the Japanese internment and prison camps. If given the opportunity to serve again, even at my age, I would do so gladly and proudly.

CONCLUSION
No Man is an Island

"No man is an island," is a famous line from "Meditation XVII," by the English poet, John Donne. It applies to everyone. It applies to my entire life. My entire military career was possible because an Air Force doctor allowed me to pass my induction physical in Pittsburgh, even though I had flat feet. He was right about the terrible foot and leg pains that I would suffer as I walked the many flight-line tarmacs across the globe.

- Because of Penney, I survived Typhoid Fever.

- Evelyn Bryner brought me out of a time of hopelessness and delivered me to a father who tried to make up for his mistakes.

- Major Brown and the First Sergeant in Viet Nam, who recognized that young men can make mistakes but given the opportunity to rebound, will do so.

- Captain Johnson listened to a complete stranger and pulled strings to give me an opportunity to advance in my chosen Air Force career in the Aerial Delivery field.

- Lieutenant Colonel George Prewitt and his family supported me in raising my son, so that my career would survive and prosper.

- Colonel Prewitt's insistence and encouragement led me to give back to my community and obtain my collegiate successes.

- Al Capone gave me the money I needed to make a down payment on a home for my son and me.

- Colonel Milacek selected me to be his First Sergeant on my wedding day to Zee, which prepared me for the senior NCO promotions that were to come.

- Barny Peters taught me to be humble and to turn abject failure around, put it behind me and move on.

- My first wife, Debbie, taught me that one can recover from spousal cruelty, infidelity and financial devastation, and to move on with life. I learned to forgive her for the many things she did to Wim and me.

- Blain and Linda Sheppard were, and are, always there to give me support and unquestioned love and friendship during good times and bad.

- Jim and Nancy Thompson stayed by my side during my recovery from major open heart and back surgery.

- Doctor Sherry Buffington and Gina Morgan helped me discover through CORE who I am and the natural and environmental factors that shaped my personality and life.

- My former boss at NEC for five years, and a wonderful and loyal friend, Steve Fisher, gave me the opportunity to complete my vision for planning, developing and deploying the NEC Corporate University at its National Training Center. He took a chance and lobbied the most senior executives in the company to provide me with the financial, human and facility resources necessary to make our initiative a roaring success. Steve exemplifies the true leader, boss and friend that we should all strive to be. During the last two years of Zee's life she needed 24x7x365 care. No one in her direct family came forward to help and I had no relatives nearby who could help. Steve made it possible for me to work from home most of the time, allowing me to care for Zee. If he had not made this possible, I would have had to quit my job and lose our medical benefits. He remains, and always will be, one of my closest friends and a brother.

- My current and wonderful wife, Vikie, has brought me love, renewed life and compassion as she navigates around my PTSD outbursts and my tendency to be impetuous in my decision-making.

There is not a single accomplishment or recovery from failure during my life that cannot be attributed to someone's help. Every opportunity for advancement and every promotion achieved were because of the basic goodness of the colleagues, family, friends and even people whom I never knew before their support became necessary.

In turn, I have tried my best to return kindnesses and opportunities towards others who needed it. I can look in the mirror and see a good man who tries to live a decent and God-fearing life every day. There is no doubt that there will be times during the remaining days of my life that I will falter and make mistakes but I believe I will also recover.

"Empty Open Hands" is more than just the title of this book. It has meaning far beyond my personal story or biography. It was, and will continue to be, the basis for living my entire life as long as God wills it. This philosophy, or rule for living, taught me that everyone can be successful regardless of the challenges they have faced or may face in the future.

In my heart of hearts, I know without a doubt that I am alive today despite the trials I suffered and the challenges I faced because of the Empty Open Hands philosophy. I lift my empty open hands up every day to allow God to fill them with answers to my challenges.

You can and should do the same to be a survivor and successful in all your endeavors. Remember the sage words from my dear friend Dr. Sherry Buffington: *Life is not a destination. It's a Journey. Make it amazing!*

With the generous help of others, and by reaching up and out with Empty Open Hands, your journey can be happy, fruitful, successful, and memorable!

Two roads diverged in a wood, and I—
I took the one less traveled by,
And that has made all the difference.

Robert Frost

© S. D. Buffington

EPILOGUE
Lessons from a Hero's Journey

By Dr. Sherry Buffington

I wrote this epilogue without the express permission of the author because he would never have allowed me to write it had I asked. That's because, in spite of what he has endured and triumphed over, Wim H. Wetzel does not see himself as a hero. True heroes rarely do. But, if ever there was a hero, he is one.

Even this book is a heroic act. If you read the forward (and I hope you did), you know that Wim is dyslexic and has a very hard time reading, and you know that writing this book was a long and arduous journey for him. He wrote this book for you, the reader, in the hope that you would realize that, no matter how bad things seem, you can survive and even learn to thrive.

Though this book was written as an autobiography, it is a true tale of triumph over trauma and tragedy, and rich in lessons for living an exemplary life even in the face of repeated hardships. In the Forward, Wim writes, "Only a strong person with moral character and a desire to change negative environments to positive ones can effect change in their future and that of their off-spring." Actually, people of strong moral character and the desire to turn negatives into positives do a lot more than that. They affect positive change on every level, from personal to global. The whole world would be a much better place if there were more people with the character and convictions of Wim Wetzel.

I have known Wim for more than twenty years and I have never met a man with greater strength of character than he has. What might not come across in this book is how very kind, gentle and considerate Wim is. I mention this because, with his considerable training, both in the martial arts and the military, and the sometimes horrific lessons he learned at the hands of his father, he could have been a very different, less kind and gentle man. He chose the higher ground.

Wim reveals, "We were taught at a very young age how to kill with one blow to specific parts of a body. Common sense and a desire to never hurt anyone always ruled my decisions in conflicts. Only once in my life did I strike out and hurt someone and that was in Korea. I regretted it then as I do today."

He says, "There were many times when a defensive weapon would have solved a confrontational issue but I chose to reach out with my empty open hand to offer compromises. In every case my opponents were surprised by this approach and returned the gesture."

Only character keeps a man with such power from wielding it to get his way in life. It takes character, conviction and courage to walk away from a fight you know you can win. In the face of any conflict, we can choose to be right or we can choose to be kind. Time and time again, Wim has chosen to be kind.

That a man who has endured so much trauma and tragedy; who still battles post traumatic stress and lives with physical pain every day, could continue to move through life as a kind and gentle soul is the real gift in Wim's life story.

There are millions of men and women who have endured traumatic events and many of them are suffering the effects of post-traumatic stress. If you are among these, or know someone who is, take hope from the fact that you can use the strength you have gained through endurance to get through every challenge and come out the other side even stronger and more capable. In that sense, you have an advantage over those whose character has never been tested by difficult challenges and forged by the fires of trauma and tragedy.

Ultimately, what will get you through whatever difficulties you face in life is not the strategies you might learn in a counselor's office, but the character you develop as you rise above each challenge.

Wim explains, "In my case, I turned all of the negative influences of my father around and learned from them. I learned not to repeat the taught behaviors but reached deep within myself to find and use my natural God-given talents, to reach out to help others and to ultimately help and heal myself. Without knowing why or how, I made the decision to stop the vicious cycle of physical and mental abuse demonstrated daily by Dad. At the early age of thirteen, I committed to never abuse someone else for my own benefit. Dad had also demonstrated some powerful and positive behaviors and rules of the road, and those I chose to adopt and replicate during my life. These include:

1. A man's word is a reflection of his name;

2. Fulfill your commitments, regardless of the challenges that may cause others to just give up;

3. Don't be ready to accept "No!" as the answer without speaking up and trying to have the answer changed to "Yes!"

4. Reach out to help others when achieving successes and finally;

5. If you don't ask – you don't get!"

Wim explains, "Every decision I made and every step I took after leaving home for my Air Force career and throughout the rest of my life was based on these simple but effective rules."

Wim's life is a testament to the power of knowing who you are, what you stand for, and how you will show up in life. It's a testament to how strength of character can keep you true to your vision. It's a beacon that keeps pointing to the fact that character, above all else, builds inner-strength which very little in life, no matter how horrific things seem in the moment, can conquer.

It takes real courage to lay it all out, both the good and the bad; to open one's self to scrutiny the way Wim has done in this book. He did it for your sake; so you can know that there is hope; that in spite of everything, you can find happiness and love and satisfaction; that by making courageous choices you can move beyond trauma and tragedy, and make your journey though life a heroic journey.

In this book, Wim says, "I want to be remembered as a good person." No worries, Wim. You most definitely will be. You will also be remembered by all who have had the privilege of knowing you as the true hero you really are.

Official Stenographer's Transcript of Roy's Murder Trial
Beaver, PA Courthouse
Commonwealth of PA vs. Roy E. Wetzel

Q. Where were you stationed?

A. I was stationed in Cuba, United States, and Vietnam.

Q. Were you in combat in Vietnam?

A. Yes.

Q. Is it true you were injured in the war?

A. Yes.

Q. How many times?

A. Three times that I got Purple Hearts for. A couple other minor injuries.

Q. How many brothers and/or sisters do you have?

A. I have two brothers and two sisters.

Q. Your mother's first name?

A. Gerry

Q. What was your father's name?

A. Willy.

Q. I would like, first of all, to direct your attention to the date of March 16th of this year (sic 1975). Were you in the company of your father, Willy Wetzel, on that day?

A. Yes, I was.

Q. What was the earliest time that day that you and he were in each other's company?

A. My earliest recollection is about 1:00 o'clock.

Q. And, where were you first in each other's company?

A. At the school in Beaver Falls.

Q. For what purpose, if any, had Willy Wetzel come to the Beaver Falls School?

A. I don't know.

Q. Was it customary for him to appear at the school on Sundays?

A. Yes.

Q. How many days a week is the Beaver Falls school operating?

A. It's three days a week we hold classes.

Q. What days are those classes held?

A. Tuesday, Wednesday, and Sunday.

Q. Had Willy Wetzel been coming to the school on any of those weekdays?

A. No.

Q. And, why not? Or is there a reason perhaps why not?

A. He never came during the week. He worked. He had a job at Westinghouse.

Q. Now, what time had you gone to the Beaver Falls School on that particular date of March 16th?

A. I believe it was -- I think I got there at quarter after ten in the morning.

Q. And, what was your reason for being at the school that day?

A. Instruction.

Q. Once your father arrived at the school, did you and he have any conversation with each other?

A. Very little.

Q. Do you recall what little conversation you had was about?

A. I can't recall too much, because I am in the habit, and so is the rest of my family, and anybody knows when he starts talking, you kind of disregard it because it's the same thing over and over and over.

Q. What was the nature of that talk, even if you don't recall the details?

A. He talked about his two children to his second wife. That was the main gist of the conversation that I remember.

Q. Did you make any statements to him in response to his complaints about his two children to his second wife?

A. Yes. Well, to begin with, he had maintained all along they weren't his children to begin with. And he couldn't understand why, since he was separated, that he had to pay support for the kids that weren't even his. And he said he was going to work on the kids to get back at Peggy. I remember saying, "Don't you realize what you are doing to those children?" One of them has been to Mental Health Clinic. He is under nerve medication. He came out flatly and said, "I don't care, just as long as I get back at that bitch. I am going to get her." That's all I can recall stating to him. I said, "Don't you realize what you are doing to those kids?" We went through the same thing.

Q. As best you recall, how long did he remain at the school that particular Sunday?

A. That particular day he stayed till, I believe it was about 4:30.

Q. Was that customary once he came to the school on a Sunday, to stay that long?

A. No. He usually made an appearance, then he left. Sometimes he wouldn't come at all. It was hard to say when he would come and when he wouldn't.

Q. Did he make any efforts that day to supervise or instruct any classes?

A. No.

Q. And, had he been making any efforts on a regular basis say in the last year, to supervise or instruct classes

A. No.

Q. Whenever he left the school that Sunday, were you aware of his leaving?

A. Yes, I saw him leave. I saw him go out the door. I don't know whether he left right then or not. I just saw him go out the office door.

Q. Close to the time he left, did he say anything to you?

A. No, he didn't say goodbye or anything, no.

Q. Well, was there anything unusual that occurred in the normal course of events at the school that day?

A. No, sir, not that I can recall.

Q. What time did you leave the school?

A. I left -- I believe it was about close to 5:00 o'clock

Q. And, where did you go after you left the Beaver Falls school

A. Went to my home.

Q. Once you arrived home, what did you do? How long were you at home?

A. Long enough to come home, take a shower, change my clothes, and I took my fiancé out to Arthur Treacher's and had supper.

Q. Arthur Treacher's?

A. That's up by the Mall.

Q. Did you two have your dinner at Arthur Treacher's?

A. Yes, we did.

Q. Do you have any recollection of approximately what time you returned home after you and your fiancée had your dinner at Arthur Treacher's?

A. It's hard to pinpoint, because I wasn't keeping track of the time.

Q. Approximately?

A. I'd say we got there at 6:00 o'clock, maybe, I don't know. And we ate. I told her, that's my fiancé, I was going to do some work at home, if she wanted to go some place, go ahead and go. She said she'd go down to her mother's house and go out to a movie, I think at Gee Bee's.

Q. And, what work was it you wanted to do at home?

A. I was working on some distribution figures for the magazine.

Q. Were there any tax papers that you worked on that day?

A. That I worked on?

Q. Yes?

A. No.

Q. Now, once you were home, after having dinner with your fiancé, did you remain home the rest of that evening?

A. No, I didn't. I went down and got my little girl.

Q. How old is your daughter?

A. Four years old.

Q. And, where did you have to go to get your daughter?

A. West Bridgewater. That's where my ex-wife lives.

Q. And, for what reason did you go to get your four year old daughter?

A. She had called me and she was crying. She was upset. And I talked to her mother. She said talk to this kid I can't handle her. So, the baby was upset. I told her I would keep her overnight.

Q. Had you been, from time to time on a regular basis, exercising visitation rights with your daughter?

A. Yes, I got her regularly. I would pick her up on Thursday, about noon. I would take her out to breakfast and keep her all that time, keep her overnight, and bring her back late that next day. So, I would keep her about two days a week.

Q. After you arrived back home with your daughter, did you have any phone conversation with anyone?

A. I think right after I put the baby to bed, yes.

Q. And, who was that conversation with?

A. Back up. I think there were two conversations. I had a call from my sister and I had a call from my fiancé

Q. Which call was first?

A. I think my sister's was.

Q. And by your sister, you are referring to Jane Bojanic?

A. Yes.

Q. What was that call about?

MR. MARSHALL: May I ask what the materiality and relevance is of these phone conversation prior to the event?

MR. JAMES: We will attempt to show the materiality, Your honor they have a bearing upon Willy Wetzel.

THE COURT: You may proceed.

MR. JAMES: Thank you.

Q. Would you tell us what the first phone call to you was about?

A. I got a call from my sister saying that my dad talked to her, tried to get her to pay his bills. The following the morning he come to the school with a stack of bills. I gave him money. He said something about his car not working properly. He asked my sister and she had no car that ran. So, he then asked, as far as I can recall, he asked her what my mother's phone number was She asked me if she could give it to him. I said no, under no circumstances, because she had been harassed enough. He'd arrive about 3:00 or 4:00 o'clock in the morning and rap on her door.

Q. Did your sister say anything to you about how Willy was acting or talking on the phone?

A. She told me, she said, be careful, he's acting real strange. She said, "I'm scared."

Q. Now, when did the second call come with relationship to the first? In other words, how far apart?

A. A couple hours. I'd say a couple hours.

Q. And, who made the second call to you?

A. My fiancé.

Q. And, was that call just an ordinary call?

A. Yes, it was an ordinary call. She called me saying she had come home from the show.

MR. MARSHALL: Your Honor, again I object.

THE COURT: The objection is sustained.

MR. JAMES: All right.

Q. Now, after you received the phone calls, were you still working on the papers that you talked about?

A. No, I wasn't actually working. I was kind of fiddling, because at that point I had just got done putting the baby to bed. We were playing games.

Q. Did you, that evening, have a visitor at your apartment? Did someone come to your apartment?

A. Yes, my father came.

Q. Approximately, as best you recall, what time was that?

A. It was after the phone call somewhere. I'd say between quarter after ten, 10:30, somewhere around there. I really don't know. I wasn't keeping track of the time.

Q. How did you become aware of your father's presence at your apartment? How did you know he was there?

A. I was sitting in the dining area and I heard the door rattle. And I knew who it was immediately, because my father, he doesn't knock on doors, he just opens them. And I had gotten to the point where, if I knew he was coming, I would make a point not to be there. And all the rest of my family did the same thing.

Q. Did you have any idea he was coming up that particular evening?

A. No, sir, I didn't.

Q. What did you do once you heard the doorknob rattling?

A. I got up, because I knew who it was. And I turned on the porch light and I held the door and I let him in.

Q. Once he entered the apartment, was there any conversation between you two?

A. Not immediately. He walked in the door. He looked at me and he sat down on the couch in the corner, towards the wall where the drapes are. And he sat down. He started going to sleep. It's a habit of his. He would come to people's house. He would sit there, not say a word, and just kind of konk out to 3:00 or 4:00 o'clock in the morning. You'd wake him up. He would go home.

Q. After he sat there a while, did he say anything to you?

A. When he first sat down, I asked if he would like a cup of coffee, or something, to drink. He said no. He sat back. He was rubbing his face. He said he was tired. He said no, no.

Q. After that happened, what next happened?

A. Well, during the conversation, I can recall him relating the same thing he had done at the school, about his children. And there would be no use in this country, he was going back to Indonesia. 'I said, "You can't go back. If you go back, you will go to prison.

Q. Now, eventually what occurred with regard to your father's Income Tax papers?

A. He asked me if they were done. I said, "Yes, they are done. All you have to do is give me the name He owns stock -- "and I need the name to fill out the back. Other than that, it's done." And I said, "Do you need it?" He said, "Yes, I want it." So, he said "Where is it?" I pointed at the table. He walked up. He sat down at the table.

Q. What did he do once he sat down at the table?

A. Well, he picked the form up and started looking at them. And he said, "I can't read this." He didn't have his glasses. And my glasses were laying on the table there. And he said, "Let me see your glasses." I handed him my glasses, which he put on. He said," I still can't see." He started looking around. He said, "Whose are those?" He was referring to the étagère that is the room divider. He picked up the glasses. I said, "These are Jim's glasses." They are different than mine. They are round. He picked them up and put them on. He said, "This is a little better I can make it out now." He put the glasses down. He just sat there. He paused momentarily. I don't know how long. I said, "Do you want a pen?" He said, "Yes." So, I handed him a pen. And again he paused for a couple seconds. He then started to sign. He signed -- I'm pretty sure he signed his first name. Again he paused. And he started to sign the rest of his name. I think I said at the Preliminary Hearing, I don't know whether he ever finished signing his name or not. I don't know how he did it. He started the signing. He kind of raised his pen across the paper. He signed and went like that (indicating), and he threw the pen against the drapes in the dining room there. He took the Income Tax form, balled them up, and made a statement, you know, "Fuck it. Fuck this country," and he balled it up, threw it on the table and started to get up and walk away. At this point I didn't say anything. I don't even remember. The only thing I said to him, "Do you want a pen?"

Q. Now, when he started to walk away, in what direction was he walking?

A. He walked out towards the front door.

Q. And when he was in the process of walking toward the front door, what did you do?

A. I followed him out. I was going to open the door for him.

Q. Would you tell us in what manner he walked from the kitchen area to the front door?

A. A manner? He walks extremely slow, like hunched over, like he was real exhausted or tired.

Q. Once he reached the front door, what happened?

A. He reached down -- Well, with his left hand, dropped right in front of the door, I'd say six inches to a foot from the front door, he reached with his left hand and put it on the doorknob. He paused. He looked over at the Hawaiian sword, the one that is in the case down there. I had it propped up in the corner. And he looked at it. I didn't think anything of it. He has picked it up before and played with it, told me it was nice. And he picked it up, turned around, and he had his head down. I couldn't see his face.

Q. Now, when he turned around, would his body be facing or be away from you?

A. Facing me. The sword was close enough, he was about a foot from the door, where he was he just reached out and grabbed it and turned around and started looking at it.

Q. You say when he turned around, you couldn't see his face? Why?

A. He was looking at the sword. I think he was. He had his head down.

Q. What next do you recall?

A. Again he started mumbling. He said, "I'm going to lose my house, my car, everything I have got." He said, "This is it." He then lifted up his head and his eyes just literally bulged out of his head. They both bulged. He let out a scream.

Q. What kind of scream?

A. It's like a war cry, a battle cry. It's called a kea

Q. Can you demonstrate that scream for us?

A. Not the way he did it. No way.

Q. What happened after he let out the scream?

A. I said, "Dad, what are you doing?" He started to pull out the sword. When I saw his face, then I knew what he was doing.

Q. What was he doing, in your mind?

A. In my mind he was going to do what he always told us, as long as I can remember.

Q. What was that?

A. He was going to start his thing and finish it. His hate. His thing.

Q. What do you mean by "his thing"?

A. As long as I can remember, all he ever talked about, if anything didn't go right, he was going to take care of everyone in his family and he was going to go, but he wasn't going to go alone.

Q. At that point, when you saw him beginning to remove the sword from its case, what did you do?

A. I reached out and grabbed the end where he had it on the handle, and I grabbed it in the middle of the sheath.

Q. And, how did you grab that, with one or two hands?

A. Two hands. I reached out like that (indicating), so he couldn't pull the sword out. He already had it out I'd say, about six or eight inches.

Q. After you grabbed that sword in the manner you testified to, what happened with the sword, as concern you and Willy?

A. I was trying to keep him from pulling it all the way out. That sword, it is a good weapon. And he struggled against me, and I had him pushed up against the door.

Q. What happened to the sword, or the condition of the sword, as a result of that struggle?

A. Well, during the struggle I saw his leg coming up to kick. He tried to kick me in the groin. I, out of reflex, turned sideways, and he hit me, and the force of the kick, I held onto the sword for dear life, and knew that for a fact. He kicked, and the force of the kick, and my holding onto it, and my body, with it going back, bent the sword almost in half.

Q. This Exhibit K, is that what you are referring to as the sword on that occasion?

A. Yes, sir."

Q. What happened after he tried the karate kick on you and the sword bending? Recall?

A. I used the momentum of the kick. I used his force against him. That is a basic principle of karate.

Q. What is the next thing you How did you use his force against him?

A. It was the force of his kick pushing him forward to me and it bent my body back, and the front of my body forward, and I just -- I let go with the hand I was holding the sheath with… I held onto the other hand, and I hit him with a punch.

Q. Where, on what portion of the body did your punch land?

A. Above one of his eyes. I tried to hit him in the temple.

Q. And, as a result of that punch, what occurred to Willy at that time?

A. Well, I followed up with a combination. I hit him two more times; hit him with a right and left and right.

Q. And, what happened to him as a result of those blows?

A. He fell back against the door, slid down into the corner where the easy chair was, the black easy chair, and where the register is.

Q. After that happened, what did you do next?

A. I just looked at him, because he laid there. I thought he was unconscious. And I turned around and I started walking towards the telephone which was in the dining room on the wall. --

Q. For what purpose?

A. I was going to call somebody. I was going to call the police.

Q. While you were going to the telephone, what happened?

A. I started to walk away. I got about almost out to where the room divider is, where the étagère is, and I heard him crawling. And I saw him on his hands and knees, and he was trying to reach the same sword. And he had his hand on it. And I couldn't reach him in time to stop him from pulling it out. So, I kicked him in the ribs.

Q. After you kicked him, what happened to him?

A. Well, he straightened up on his knees. In other words he was on all fours. When I kicked him in the ribs, I straightened him up. He was almost straight. And I hit him again with one blow.

Q. And, then what happened to him as a result of that blow?

A. Well, actually, he was on his knees, and the force of the blow, it just literally -- It threw him back real hard and he hit again against the wall where the register was.

Q. What were you attempting to do to him by the blows you had thrown up to that point?

A. I was trying to knock him unconscious.

Q. Now, what happened after that sequence of events?

A. Well, he laid here again. I don't know how long he laid there again. I started to get up to go towards the telephone.

Q. What happened then?

A. I got -- This time I got to the phone. I started dialing the number. I couldn't clear my mind enough, you know, what had happened, to come to some kind of conscious conclusion of what number to call. So, I was going to go -- I looked at the telephone. I started dialing. I didn't know who I was calling. So, I went to reach for the telephone book, and I heard him again. He was starting to get on his hands and knees. He screamed, "Son-of-a-bitch, you broke my ribs," and he started to come at me again.

Q. And, what was he doing on this occasion where he started after you again?

A. Well, he got up and he started to stagger. I think he was still woozy from the blows. He started coming at me. And his leg hit the corner of the glass table that is in the living room, and he reached down and grabbed his leg. And he grabbed -- He kind of walked in front of the table and he flipped up the glass and just threw it completely over, flipped it over.

Q. What glass would that be, the glass on top of the table?

A. Right, the glass on top of the table.

Q. All right. Then what next happened?

A. He lost his balance. He reached down and grabbed for support. The base for that is aluminum, chrome-covered. And he picked up the aluminum thing, and I had backed away into the division between the dining room and the living room. And he threw this at me. I ducked out of the way. It hit the corner, the corner of the table hit my leg and my ankle.

Q. Did it injure your ankle at all?

A. Yes, it had a bad bruise there.

Q. What happened after he threw the bottom portion of the coffee table at you?

A. Okay. He started to stagger backwards, and I saw him looking around for something to grab. And he looked over at the television set, and I keep two swords. They are demonstration swords. I collect weapons. And I knew what he was going to do. So, I reached over.

I ran over to the T.V. I tried to grab the sword he had his hands on, but it was too late. I grabbed hold of the sheath, but he already had the sword pulled out of it.

Q. Now, when you say you grabbed a hold of the sheath, are you referring to Defendant's Exhibit M?

A. Yes, supports.

Q. Of what?

A. Of the étagère. That is the room divider. It's the same thing.

Q. And, what is that room divider made of?

A. Steel.

Q. And, what are the shelves made of?

A. Glass.

Q. After the episode of him swinging the second sword at you, what did you do?

A. All I can remember, it sticks out vividly in my mind, I pulled this thing in front of me, I'd say a portion of the way. He swung the sword. The sword bent around that portion. All I did -- He lost his balance. I remember it going through my mind, I thought, "Good God, if he got me, he would have cut my head off with that thing."

Q. Do you remember what he next did?

A. Yes. He tripped over something. I think it might have been the rocking chair, because it sits right in the corner. He lost his balance. I grabbed him. He was wearing a heavy aviator-type coat. I grabbed him by one of his hands. I threw him down in front of me. He tripped and fell into the kitchen area.

Q. Did he stay on the floor of the kitchen any length of time?

A. No. When he fell, ho fell and he kind of twisted around, like a top, and he landed on all fours.

Q. What did he do at that time?

A. Well, at that time, like I said, I was in a total panic. I started to look around for something, because I tried to stop him just by holding him and that didn't do it. I tried to hit him. That didn't stop him. I tried to kick him. That didn't stop him. I have three or four sets of those sticks. I had them in the corner on the baby's high-chair - that play high-chair, and I reached out, and they were there. He started coming at me. He started spitting and screaming.

Q. What was he screaming, if you recall?

A. He was making sounds like a tiger, like a panther.

Q. When he came towards you that time, what did you do?

A. Well, I waited for him to come at me. I hit him with a series of blows with the sticks.

Q. And, on what portion of his body did you strike him with the sticks?

A. In the head.

Q. As a result of those blows, what occurred to your father at that time?

A. (No response.)

Q. Did he remain standing?

A. I'm not sure at that moment. When I hit him, I saw blood come out of his head, because I came with an upswing. And everything I do is in a series of blows. It is not one. I hit him, I think, at least two times in the back of the head with the same series of blows.

Q. As a result of those blows, did your father remain standing at that time, or did he go down?

A. He didn't go down. He went down, but not immediately.

Q. Describe to us how he went down.

A. He staggered. He fell across the kitchen table, and he fell face down on the table. And I don't know how, but he just kind of flew back off the table, almost like he pushed himself off it, or something. It's almost like somebody pushed him off the table. He flew back and came straight down from that level to the ground. I think he landed on the typewriter, because that is where his head was when I saw him.

Q. Did he lay on that typewriter for any length of time?

A. Yes, he did.

Q. And, what did you do while he was in that position?

A. I stood there and looked at him. You know, I remember thinking, "God, please, please don't do this. Please stay down."

Q. How many times up to that point had you had him down, or had he been knocked down?

A. Once with the hand blows, once with the kicks, and once when I threw him across me.

Q. So, this would be the fourth time he was down?

A. Yes.

Q. Now, as you observed him in that position, did he say anything, or make any remarks, or facial gestures?

A. At this point there was a lot of noise going on. The stereo was on, but it was on low. But I have a Great Dane -- Well, at that time I did. He weighs about 130-40 pounds. And the dog -- The dog knew what was going on. He was throwing himself at the door. He was right at the door adjacent to the kitchen, and he was just hurtling himself against the door. And that created a lot of noise, plus the screwing that my father was doing. At this point I heard my little girl start screaming.

Q. What went through your mind, if anything, when your little girl screamed?

A. Only one thing went through my mind. I thought if he gets me, he is going to get her, then he's going to get my brother. That is the one thing now that I recall. He asked me, "What time does Jimmy usually get home?" I said, "He's home usually by 11:00 or 12:00 o'clock. I can't say for sure."

Q. When was it he asked you what time Jimmy would be home?

A. That was at the school. Then he asked me sometime when he was up at the house that night, too.

Q. Now, from the position of your father with his head on the typewriter, did he get up from that position?

A. He started laughing.

Q. What?

A. He started laughing, like jeering, cackling. I don't know how to describe it. He started laughing like a maniac.

Q. What did he do after he began laughing?

A. He started to get up and go towards the kitchen area.

Q. And, where were you at that time?

A. I was standing in the doorway. I was standing right in the doorway between the living room and dining room.

Q. Once he got up and started moving again, what did you do?

A. I stepped in front of him and hit him again with another series of blows with the stick, and the force of the blows knocked him into the living room.

Q. What were you trying to accomplish on the occasion that you hit him with the sticks?

A. I was trying to stop him. I was trying to knock him unconscious.

Q. As a result of the last set of blows that you mentioned what did he do?

A. (No response.)

Q. Did he stand, or did he go down?

A. No, he went down. He did, like a head dive into the living room, because I had forced him into that area. I didn't want him anywhere near the kitchen or the bedrooms.

Q. Now, that would be the fifth time that ho was down?

A. Right.

Q. What occurred from that point once he ended up in the living room area again?

A. Well, at that point I thought he was knocked out, because he was on his face. He was lying on his face. And I went up and I kind of sat down beside him. And I had my hand on his shoulder. I was crying.

I was trying to plead with him. And he just started to roll over. He started to grab me.

Q. Well, once he was in that position on the living room floor, did he remain in that same spot?

A. No. He kind of worked his way around. He stayed basically in the middle of the floor where he was, where the stereo was. At one point he was over in the corner where the chair was and the register was. I can't say he was there at that spot. He was all over the floor, but he was on the floor.

Q. When you got beside him, while he was on the floor, what, if anything, did you do at that point?

A. I was trying to pin his hands down.

Q. Why?

A. I was trying to hold him down. I was hoping he would pass out. I remember thinking, "Oh, God, all this blood, how can he even move."

Q. While you held his hands down, did he pass out?

A. I thought he did, yes. I don't know. I think it was just a thing to get me to relax, which I did. I let him go. And I started to move in front of him. And the next thing I knew, I ran right into a kick.

Q. What kick was it? What portion of his body struck you?

A. His foot. It's a soccer-type kick. It's called a saber kick.

Q. And, where did that saber kick land, so far as your body is concerned?

A. It hit me in the head.

Q. Would you point to the area of your head where that kick landed?

A. It hit right on this side of my head here (indicating). Right across the temple here.

Q. What effect did that kick have on you?

A. Well, momentarily it knocked me out, momentarily. Because I have been knocked out many times. I know what the feeling is. Because you are busy fighting unconsciousness, because I knew if I passed out, that was it.

Q. What is the next thing you recall after being kicked in the head?

A. I remember a few things, but as far as sequences go, I can't remember. Like I said, I was dizzy. My head was pounding. And I couldn't focus my eyes. I don't know, it's hard to say.

Q. Do you know for what length of time, or approximate length of time you had been rendered unconscious by that kick?

A. No, sir, I couldn't tell you.

Q. Well, whenever your memory started back, what is the next thing you recall after being kicked in the head?

A. I remember a few things distantly, but in what order they occurred, I don't know.

Q. Tell us what you remember really distinctly.

A. I remember him having a severe pain in my mouth. He had his whole hand on the inside of my mouth trying to tear out the inside of my mouth, trying to tear the throat out.

Q. What else do you remember?

A. I remember him, he had one hand on my groin. He was trying to rip that off.

Q. Do you recall anything else once you regained your consciousness?

A. I remember the blows to the face. I don't remember whether it was a kick or punch, or what.

Q. And, at what stage did you experience any cuts on your body?

A. Here again I don't know when I got cut. All I know, I was. At this point I was trying to pin him down, and I was all over him and around him. And we were just kind of rolling around on the floor, and all over I felt just like a little -- I don't know how to describe it, just like a reed, or something like a piece of grass going across my body. I didn't know I was getting cut until I saw the knife.

Q. And when you saw the knife, where was it?

A. He was holding it.

Q. And, what did you do when you saw the knife in his hand?

A. I tried to knock it out of his hand.

Q. Did you succeed?

A. Yes.

Q. When you refer to the knife, are you referring to Defendant's Exhibit N?

A. Yes.

Q. After these events that you just testified to occur can you tell us what next happened, as best you recall?

A. After I got the knife away from him?

Q. Yes?

A. Well, I laid across his body. I was trying to hold him down. I couldn't hold him down. I had his arms pinned to the ground, but he was picking me right off the ground. I was laying there. I could see his feet were trapped under the couch, and I looked over, and I was laying on him. I could feel my body coming off his. I could see the couch just jumping up and down. Here again I can remember thinking, how long can he even move, because it's a real heavy couch. Up to that point, did his strength seem to lessen at all to you?

A. No, he seemed to get stronger as time went on. It was just phenomenal.

Q. What did you next do, as you recall these events?

A. Well, at this point I was trying to conserve my energy, or my strength. I remember trying to hit him. I couldn't even get the energy to hit him with any kind of force or power.

Q. What had caused you to lose your strength, as you recall these events?

A. I don't know. I would have to say the kick to the head. I don't know.

Q. What next happened, Roy, as best you remember?

A. Well, I remember laying across him, looking for something. And I looked up. And I looked on the T.V, and I saw the sword, the other sword, a long one. It's about four foot long. I looked up, like that (indicating), and I saw it, and it was going through my mind to reach up and grab the sword and stick it through him.

Q. Did you make any such effort?

A. No.

Q. And, why not?

A. Because I thought, you know, when the police did get there, they are going to see him lying on the floor with a sword sticking through his belly and it was bad enough as it was.

Q. Did you have any intention of killing him?

A. No, sir.

A. Well, the position I was laying in, the set of sticks that I had dropped after he fell into the living room area, it was lust laying two feet away from his head.

Q. What did you do with regard to those sticks?

A. I pulled one under his neck and pulled the other over it and I laid on them.

Q. And, what was your purpose in laying on those sticks? What were you trying to do to him?

A. I was trying to render him unconscious so he couldn't do anything.

Q. Is there a way that unconsciousness can be brought about by using the sticks in that manner?

A. Sure. You know, I thought you could do it by hitting him on the head. That didn't work. I tried to shut off his air supply.

Q. When you had those sticks around his neck, was he moving at all at that time?

A. Yes, sir.

Q. What portions of his body were moving at that particular time?

A. Well, again, I looked down and I saw his feet. His feet were going -- I mean they were, like, peddling a bicycle. The couch jumped up and down. He had one hand pulling my hair. He had pulled out quite a bit of my hair.

Q. Was there any reason why you laid on the sticks, rather than use your hands with the sticks?

A. Well, there is a couple reasons. For one, I didn't have the strength. I didn't have the strength that it took. I mean, to actually use brute strength, I didn't have the strength.

Q. And, what portion of your body was in contact with those sticks as you were laying across your father?

A. Well, I had my hands on them and I had my chest across his face.

Q. Do you recall how long you remained in that position?

A. To me it seemed like an eternity. I don't know. I think it was a few minutes, because the position I was in, I know at least twice that I rolled over, and at one point I remember I looked up, and again I saw the sword, and I had, you know, I was under a lot of stress and a lot of pressure, and I can react under pressure. And there was just, like, a debate going on in my mind what should I do. Again I looked at the sword. I visualized real vividly in my mind this thing sticking in his belly. I thought, "I have got a loaded shotgun I can run in there and get it before he gets up."

Q. At any time, did you have any intention to kill your father?

A. No, sir, it would have been an easy matter.

Q. Now, when you eventually got up from the position that you described with the stick under your chest around your father's neck, what did you next do?

A. I rolled over and I propped myself against the T.V. and the wall right next to the television, about two feet from his head.

Q. And, how long did you sit in that position, if you remember?

A. I remember sitting there and looking at him and thinking, you know, I can relax a little bit. And this thing went all through my head, he got you five or six times before, he is going to do it again.

My head was pounding. My pulse was going -- To me it looked like he was breathing heavily.

Q. Had you realized at that point he was dead?

A. No, sir.

Q. What did you do once you determined that it looked like he was still breathing?

A. I crawled over and I laid my head on his chest and I tried to listen for a heartbeat.

Q. And, then what next did you do?

A. Well, I couldn't tell whether he was alive or if he was dead, because my head was pounding and I was breathing heavy. My adrenalin was going. My head was pounding. I couldn't tell if it was me or him that we breathing.

Q. Did you return to the position where you had been sitting against the wall?

A. No, sir. I looked at him. I thought, "If he's not dead, he's going to get me again." I reached out and pulled the sticks out from under his neck and laid the in my lap.

Q. Why did you do that?

A. Like I said, I thought he was going to get up again. I wanted to be at least ready.

Q. How long did you remain in that position with the sticks being held in your lap?

A. I don't know. I really don't know.

Q. What is the next thing you remember doing after you were holding the sticks in your lap?

A. At some point after that, the realization hit me that he was dead. So, I took the sticks off my lap. I laid them beside the T.V. and my legs. And I got up to make a telephone call. I picked up the phone with the purpose of calling the police. And I had lived in Center Township. It was in the phone book, but I wasn't in a state of mind that I could look up the phone number. I tried. I tried. I must have dialed four or five numbers, and the only one that stuck out in my head was my fiancé, because I call her every day.

Q. What did you tell her when you called?

A. I don't know exactly, but I think I said, "Call the police," you know, "Willy is dead and I am bleeding to death."

Q. And, what did you do after making that phone call?

A. I hung up the phone and I went into the bedroom to see if the baby was okay. And she was asleep. She was sound asleep.

Q. What did you do after you checked on your daughter?

A. I came back in. I remember I walked in and I calmed down the dog, because he was still throwing himself against the door. And he is a huge dog. So, I went and calmed him down. I shut the door and I sat down in this little protrusion between the living -- I mean the dining room, and the kitchen. I sat on the floor and leaned back against it.

Q. Was that the position you were in when your fiancé arrived?

A. Yes, I think so.

Q. Now, you had testified that once you saw the look in your father's eyes, you knew what he was going to do. Can you tell us what type of childhood you had, being raised under Willy Wetzel?

A. What type of childhood?

Q. How did he treat you as a child?

A. Going back how far?

Q. Back to your younger days as a child, when you were disciplined.

A. There's a lot of things I will never say about it, but the first time I can recall being mistreated is I was about five years old, five and a half years old. I will never forget it as long as I live.

Q. What did he do to you?

A. He stripped me down at the waist. He grabbed me by my feet and shoved me down in the toilet that was plugged up. He used me as a human plunger.

Q. As you became older, do you recall any physical abuse he did to you?

A. That was an everyday occurrence. The thing I do remember about him, it is so bizarre, he would, when he would beat one of us, we would all have to watch. And when he was doing the beating, he would laugh. He would just laugh.

Q. And, were those type of beatings regular occurrences, or infrequent?

A. They were regular. I mean, they were like clockwork. What would he beat you children with?

A. Like my brother testified, anything he could get his hands on.

Q. Did you love your father?

A. No, I didn't. I can't say I did.

Q. Did you respect him?

A. Around 12 years old, he used to walk around stripped to the waist flexing in front of the mirror. I made the mistake of laughing at him, you know.

Q. Well, what happened when you laughed?

At this point in the testimony no further records were retained by the Court.

NOTE: The previous transcript was copied verbatim from the court records. Grammatical and spelling errors were not changed or corrected for this book.

The State of Pennsylvania does not retain court transcripts from trials that result in "Not Guilty" verdicts. However, they do retain testimony from the defendants in the trials. The preceding transcript was provide to me by the state as it was recorded for the Commonwealth of Pennsylvania Vs. Roy E Wetzel.

About the Author

Wim Wetzel is a retired 24-year Air Force combat aircrew veteran who served as a C-130 and C-141A/B Loadmaster. During his military career and civilian careers he held numerous highly successful senior leadership and management positions.

Both of his parents were captured by the Japanese in Indonesia and were held in prisoner of war and internment camps for over 4 years. His family legally immigrated to the United States in 1956.

As a 100% disabled Viet Nam veteran, Wim is a staunch advocate and fighter for disabled veterans' benefits and rights.

To contact Wim, go to www.wetzel-empty-open-hand.com. There you will find a contact page, a photo gallery and information on how to become part of Wim's Empty Open Hands community.

CPSIA information can be obtained
at www.ICGtesting.com
Printed in the USA
FSOW01n0604020816
23295FS